MAKING INFORMATION MATTER

MAKING
INFORMATION MATTER

Understanding Surveillance and Making a Difference

Mareile Kaufmann

BRISTOL
UNIVERSITY
PRESS

First published in Great Britain in 2023 by

Bristol University Press
University of Bristol
1-9 Old Park Hill
Bristol
BS2 8BB
UK
t: +44 (0)117 374 6645
e: bup-info@bristol.ac.uk

Details of international sales and distribution partners are available at bristoluniversitypress.co.uk

© Bristol University Press 2023

British Library Cataloguing in Publication Data
A catalogue record for this book is available from the British Library

ISBN 978-1-5292-3357-5 hardcover
ISBN 978-1-5292-3359-9 ePub
ISBN 978-1-5292-3360-5 ePdf

The right of Mareile Kaufmann to be identified as author of this work has been asserted by her in accordance with the Copyright, Designs and Patents Act 1988.

Cover design: Hayes Design and Advertising
Front cover image: Clifford Hayes
Bristol University Press use environmentally responsible print partners.
Printed and bound in Great Britain by CPI Group (UK) Ltd, Croydon, CR0 4YY

FSC
www.fsc.org
MIX
Paper | Supporting
responsible forestry
FSC® C013604

Contents

List of Figures

About the Author

Mareile Kaufmann is Professor at the Institute for Criminology and Sociology of Law, University of Oslo. Her research focuses on digital criminology, in particular data technologies and practices in the context of surveillance and crime control. She works with qualitative research designs that combine theory with innovative angles and strong empirical components. Mareile published broadly on profiling and data analysis, Internet politics, resilience, critique, and method. She edited a number of special issues and is a member of several editorial boards. Her work was awarded prizes and she received funding under diverse excellence schemes.

Acknowledgements

True to the spirit of *Making Information Matter*, I need to thank the many individuals that made sure this book would materialize.

My former and current employers played a big role, because they accepted my proposal of studying surveillance cultures and those who respond to them actively. As a result of that, it was critical to get access to sites and spaces for empirical work. I thank those who approved research ethics applications as well as those who granted me access. It was both a relief and an inspiration to be allowed to venture into some relatively guarded environments. I am thankful for anyone who agreed to explain, converse, provide insight, let me in on secrets, allowed me to learn. These include commercial software providers, developers, police and intelligence officers, hackers, children, their parents and teachers, as well as artists.

I had a lot of discussions with colleagues and co-authors on my way, and some of them introduced me to research traditions that are now at the heart of my approaches, ontologies, and epistemologies. Thank you.

I am grateful for the professional and engaging work of commissioning editor Paul Stevens, as well as the Bristol University Press production team. The reviewers of my manuscript made an excellent contribution to the book and their helpful comments co-shaped this result. I also want to thank anyone who agreed to endorse this book. It is an investment of your time and into the future of the book.

My family, especially Åsmund, and my colleagues were essential to this project: you encouraged, listened, and enabled me to spend time researching and writing.

This book expands on ideas and materials that I have written and published about before. These are listed in the references. All chapters of *Making Information Matter*, however, are original texts.

1

Introduction

Nothing about data is a given. Data, from Latin 'datum', translates into a 'thing given' (Harper [nd], 'data'). We need to reconsider this given-ness of data. If anything, data are given to us by something or someone. Data are given into an emergent situation. They are not fixed, pre-existing entities. This book, however, is not just about data. The vernacular use of data refers to digital or analogue datasets that are generated, collected, assembled, and used for creating facts. I employ the term *information* instead, because it includes data, but refers to more overarching notions of communication and knowledge and their imbrication with processes of shaping and giving form (Harper [nd], 'information'). Giving form is a material process. Indeed, the etymology of matter, going back to the word 'mater' meaning 'origin, source, mother' (Harper [nd], 'matter'), adds to this book's understanding of information. Not only is information given to us by someone or something (mother), but it is material. What is more, giving form and shaping indicate processes of being in-formation.

In short, the term information already summarizes this book's basic argument: Information is not a standalone. It is given to us by humans and things. It actively changes and is changed in processes of making, shaping, and giving form. Information is material and it matters.

That information matters has become increasingly graspable: information materializes as police patrols and incarceration rates, as online spaces in which theories bubble up and entire movements form. Browsing and genetic data become manifest in customer and behavioural profiles. Information shapes our bodies through self-quantification or biometric capture. It forms markets, science, space, aid, killings, art. Whether recorded, recoded, unregistered, or deleted – information co-creates our present and future. We are 'becoming-with' (Haraway, 2015b: 161) information. Here, two aspects are central that I develop further in the discussion on the role of information in society today: Information is not only material, but it exhibits a liveliness that co-shapes our lives. Here, collective processes of *making* move to the fore, which means that we, too, play a role in making information matter. If we take both points seriously, we need new tools and motivations to identify how information materializes, turns lively and matters, and where the openings for our own engagements are. What does it mean to make, and to make together? And what ethos guides our visions of making and mattering? *Making Information Matter*, then, is not just a theoretical and empirical research project. It is also an initiative to reflect about the agencies of information and ourselves in processes of mattering.

The book makes four propositions:

1. an ontological argument about understanding matter, information, and making together,
2. a methodology and method for grasping the liveliness of information and for identifying entry points to study how information makes and is made to matter,
3. four examples of making information matter – association, conversion, secrecy and speculation – to illustrate the method in use and to provide an analysis of dominant and alternative information practices, and
4. an invitation to investigate and calibrate the ethos of making information matter.

The book can be read continuously to appreciate how these four propositions hang together and form an argument. Each chapter also functions as a standalone contribution for those readers who want to focus on theory, method, a specific information practice, or ethics.

To dive into theory 'for starters' is not exactly light fare. Chapter 2 is dense at points, because it provides the framework from which method, the description of information practices, and the reasoning about ethics emerge. Expounding how matter, information, and making relate to each other, however, provides the book's argument with ontological and epistemological depth. The theoretical framework sheds new light on information practices, brings aspects to the fore that we may have been unfamiliar with and highlights their actuality and acuteness. Together, the theory and method of making information matter enable us to ask original and complex questions about the role of information today. The ontological argument draws on literatures that consider any matter as part of collective agencies, emerging relations, and productive processes. These claims about materiality are anchored in different research traditions ranging from Anthropology to Particle Physics. With that as a base, it is possible to argue about the materiality of information, but also to question the given-ness of information, its conceptualization as established, essential, inert, or dead. Instead, the book focuses on the lively and agential materiality of information. This is not only the case with digital data, a specific form of information, but it is true for analogue and any other form of information, too. This is why a vocabulary of eras and ages is abandoned as well: such wording obscures the specificities that characterize the role of information in different contexts. In understanding the liveliness of information, we can also move away from the metaphors of apparatuses, machines, and a Cartesian body/mind split towards organic understandings of materiality. Acknowledging the specificity, variability, and liveliness of information also avoids the reductive labelling of information practices as either watching or hiding, surveillance or resistance. Rather, one can move to new grounds by researching the many lives and life cycles that intersect and make matter. Indeed, when studying life cycles, we also pay attention to ideas, beliefs, imaginaries, fictions that are being inscribed into the materialization of information. That is to say, there is power in how information is thought of. Here, the majority of critical surveillance research focuses on urgent, yet dismal examples of data imaginaries, practices, and obsessions with computation that dominate today's information landscapes. This book would be incomplete if it would not study such information practices, too, but in order to contribute to the discourse with new, encouraging perspectives it also turns towards analyses of how information can be made to matter differently. Most important, it documents how these practices comprise elements of each other.

A theory considering the ever-changing productivity of information also calls for methodologies that can take account of such liveliness. Chapter 3 addresses the question: Which methods can we use to study making, information, and matter? Instead of a rather distanced 'analytic', the chapter invokes the idea of 'grasping', of understanding through contact, conversation, and potentially frictions. Building on the onto-epistem-ologies (Barad, 2003) outlined in the theory chapter, the book develops a methodology of life cycles (see Kaufmann et al, 2020; Kaufmann and Leese, 2021). It underlines that research is a continuous activity and a critical engagement. Considering that mattering, too, is a continuous process, the tool of the life cycle may have reductive tendencies in that it highlights specific 'turns' in the life of information and surveillance practices. At the same time, this methodology may help us concentrating on those important 'rites of passage' (Ingold and Hallam, 2016: 4) in the life of information, where changes pile up and contribute to significant transitions in materiality. Life cycles show how technologies, tools, information, and ourselves take an active role in our common becoming. The methodology allows for critique as it identifies the turns at which different agencies emerge, among which is the (small) margin for our own. Instead of using an analytic vocabulary of systems and parts, evident cause-and-effect, completion and linearity, the terms of life, cycle, spiral, and turns emphasize the organic, chaotic character of being-in-formation.

As mentioned earlier, some of the most central information practices today relate to surveillance and control. Algorithmic capture, profiling, and pattern recognition are clearly central elements of information practices. We find them in public management, such as law enforcement, health policy, welfare schemes, migration, and border control – basically key areas of societal organization that are intertwined with commercial settings and products that follow market logics and business secrecy. That these fields need constant, critical analysis is no longer contested. Manifold studies have already provided influential insight. In putting the method of the life cycle to work, the main part of this book, too, introduces four concise information practices: association, conversion, secrecy, and speculation. They are illustrated with examples drawn from life, that is predictive policing, hacking, children's relationship to secrecy, and art (Chapters 4–7). However, the described characteristics of making information matter can be applied to many contexts. Such engagements are not reduced to specific materials or groups, such as computers or information engineers and other professionals. Quite the contrary: they demonstrate that information matters to everyone and everyone can make information matter. While associative practices tend to characterize professional environments, hackers, children, and artists formulate responses to such practices in more mundane settings. Their examples show that 'possibilities for acting exist at every moment' (Barad, 2003: 827). As rather unusual agents in the landscapes of surveillance, they create "cracks of possibility" (Zach Blas, interview in Chapter 7) in the dominant regimes of capture and control. Conversion, secrecy, and speculation are still based on information, but they *make information matter differently*. Even more, they show us that engaging with surveillance is not only political, but has playful, emotional, sensual, and affective dimensions, too. Combined, these four studies add new perspectives to surveillance discourses. They look at a vast range of information types from analogue to digital information, big and small data, public and private information, as well as data that has been altered and scrubbed. The studies include hand-drawn signs and spoken secret languages, as well as biometric information, which can be made to matter in 3D prints, portraits, and poetry.

All of these – theory, method, and practices of engaging with surveillance – lead us to points at which we ask what the ethics of making information matter are. 'Whose crisis is this?' (Braidotti, 2019: 157). It was thus natural and necessary to answer this question the final chapter (Chapter 8). In the spirit of Rosi Braidotti's work, this book claims that dominant forms of surveillance, such as association, produce crises for everyone and everyone has the responsibility to act. Our engagement matters. However, we also experience crises differently as our access to and embeddedness in surveillance environments is diverse. An ethics of making information matter and of exercising critique, then, needs to take account of this diversity. In the same way in which this book's argument embraces our positionality (often phrased in terms of 'bias') and ethos as fundamental to making matter, it also argues that information itself cannot be stripped of its ethicality and values. If information is material and productive in specific ways, the central concern becomes what information *should* matter? And how do we and information make matter *together*? In our shared activities of imagining, generating, storing, processing, and re-using information there is situated and limited room for critical agency and reflection about the intentions of information practices. Karen Barad reminds us that options for shaping our common becoming are 'open at each turn' (Barad, 2003) and we remain 'resolutely accountable for the role "we" play in the intertwined practices of knowing and becoming' (Barad, 2003: 812, double quotation marks in original). This means that we – you, I, and everyone else in the transversal we – need to grasp information practices in order to imagine alternatives. The final chapter brings us back to the beginning of this introduction. *Making Information Matter* is a theory, a method, an analysis of information practices, but also an invitation to reflect about what matters in new ways.

The calls are loud and clear: Let's get started

Hito Steyerl formulates a passionate call for taking that job of making information matter seriously: 'It could become the art of recoding or rewiring the system' (Steyerl, 2013: online). We need, however, serious and continuous engagement if we do not want our efforts to 'just end up as ornament' (Steyerl, 2013: online). Her call is echoed by many voices that study information and surveillance technologies within a variety of fields. Here, the 'need to attend to the lives and specificities of devices and data themselves' (Ruppert, Law, and Savage, 2013: 31–32) is paramount.

Having in-depth knowledge of the ongoing information practices is a premise to be able to create new visions:

> If data are so central to our lives and our planet, then we need to understand just what they are and what they are doing. … What we need is a strong humanistic approach to analyzing the forms that data take; a hermeneutic approach which enables us to envision new possible futures even as we risk being swamped in the data deluge. (Bowker, 2013: 171)

Mark Andrejevic formulates a clear need for a shift in our infrastructural imaginaries in order to critique and influence who controls both, information and infrastructure (2021). In line with that, Deb Verhoeven calls for interruptible infrastructures: 'How do we imagine … a digital information infrastructure in which agency, impact and power are the key conceptual axes? Who has power? What affordables do we put in there?' (2016: online 37:00). Deborah Lupton asks us to create '(p)ossibilities for the generation of alternative or counter-perspectives and greater opportunities for people to 'feel' their data in ways which make sense in the context of their own lives' (Lupton, 2020: 127).

Creating expertise and identifying alternative imaginaries and possibilities are part of this call to engage, a call this book intends to answer. In order to engage we need to become aware of our own role in matterings, even if that is uncomfortable. Wendy Chun reminds us that making matter works 'only if we occupy the collective chimera we are offered and become characters, not marionettes, in the ongoing drama inadequately called Big Data' (Chun, 2016: 62). Laura Forlano suggests that we need to start considering our 'digital work as practical action' (Forlano, 2019: 12). Simone Browne calls on us to create 'productive disruptions' in informational regimes (2015: 164) and Ruha Benjamin asks us to devise emancipatory approaches to technology, those that go beyond the unequal information technologies we have today (2019). This does not only mean to pay attention to 'science frictions' (Edwards et al, 2011) in the process of making information matter, but it may also mean to generate friction and forward critique when necessary. Constant commitment to this project is needed if we do not want our critical efforts to end up in the 'non-performative' (Ahmed, 2012: 174). Donna Haraway famously challenges us to 'stay with the trouble' and become-with each other through companionship (Haraway, 2008, 2016). Critique through companionship means also to become-with those forms of making information matter we potentially disagree with (Austin, Bellanova, and Kaufmann, 2019). It may mean to make matter differently, which also means to provide companionship to those who need more voice and provide those groups who lack representation in current information landscapes a platform (Harding, 2015). To make information matter is not a value-free engagement – even in scholarly settings.

The book's contribution is here to provide new thinking and empirical tools, inspiring examples, and renewed motivation. The focus on the liveliness of information and the method of following its life cycle, as well as the critical examples of making information matter, can create new entry points for reflected engagements.

2

Understanding *Making Information Matter* Together

Making Information Matter advances three ontological arguments: first, information is not virtual, but material, and it matters. It influences routines, values, politics, and how other matter comes into being. Second, information is in-formation. It changes and becomes lively as it travels across sites and co-creates phenomena. Third, the lively character of information, its materiality and agency is dependent on processes of making. Tools, infrastructures, protocols, ideas, and people are part of making information matter. You are making information matter. In societies where the influence of information is no longer put into question it is crucial to be aware of these dynamics. Only when we navigate the how and why of making information matter can we identify the openings for our own agency.

I spend this chapter explaining the theoretical groundwork for the book's argument. A combination of different sets of theories is needed to develop the ontology of Making Information Matter. Hence, reading this chapter demands more of your investment than reading any of the chapters that follow. You can choose to read chapters as standalone contributions. Familiarizing yourself with the book's analytic base, however, can help you to appreciate the actuality and impact of the argument and provides you with the basis for the methodology, practices and ethics discussed in Chapters 3–8. This chapter argues that making, information, and matter are intertwined and that they can also be used as a set of resources for future studies. Hence, this theorization is also a vantage point or a roadmap for reading the book as a successive text: the parts on method and empirics show how the theory is doable, and the final chapter leads us to the ethos of making matter.

In the spirit of this book's argument, I do not develop this theoretical argument alone. I draw on works from the scholarly fields of Anthropology and Physics, Information Sciences and Art, Political Theory, and Literature Studies, to name a few. What unites these works is that they emerge as an answer to static and essentialist understandings of the world and to any form of representationalism. Instead, they look at matter in-formation. From these contributions, I will deduce and develop an ontological triad of *relations, becoming* and *interiority/agency*. They are key conditions from which an integrated understanding of making, information, and matter can emerge.

It was not obvious whether making, information, or matter should be the starting point for this chapter. Which one comes first? Does one of them express a more basic ontology than the other? Answering this is a philosophical problem. I decided to start backwards (matter – information – making), because theories about matter open a discourse that is reflected in theories about information and making. This signifies a fluent approach to the theoretical argument, where any of these concepts has relevance for any other.

Matter

There is nothing self-evident about matter and materials, but we may feel unease by letting go of associations with matter as bounded. It sits deeply in our scientized culture to think of matter as something the essence of which we can identify and replicate in experiments, because it provides us with a sense of calm and the shortest route to rely on or criticize materials. Thus, what we consider rational and how we think of agency ties in with our conceptions of materiality. That is so because our prevalent scientific culture is marked by an ontology of splits, inherited from Descartes' *cogito ergo sum*. The assumption that the human mind is distinct from its own and other bodies due to a 'cogito' (rationality) provides the basis for a subject that can act on and master objects. It splits the mind from matter as it tends to conceptualize matter as discrete, inert and passive. Matter becomes something that is replicable according to laws and can, hence, be manipulated and controlled by humans. This split further provides the fundament for the pursuit of quantifying and measuring materials, of determining causes and effects, of building the rationality of governing by numbers that we are so familiar with today. It is the powerful basis for dividing the world into nature and artifice, human and non-human, organic and inorganic, animate and inanimate, internal and external, knower and known. This ontology of splits has created ripple effects as it has become manifest in many philosophies and practices of science, as well as in political rationalities. It leaves, however, little room for theoretical diversity and excludes different ways of acknowledging how materiality matters.

Indeed, materiality has long been sidelined by both natural and social sciences. In focus was the self-aware and rational human who is superior to matter and materials. Humans would not only cultivate materials, but they would determine them and establish them as materials. Tim Ingold and Elizabeth Hallam (2016) remind us that humans seek to determine material entities by listing, cataloguing, systematizing, categorizing, and ordering them, which was a major project of enlightenment's collectors. Geoffrey Bowker and Susan Leigh Star's *Sorting Things Out* (2000) affirms that categorizing is still a powerful exercise in contemporary sciences. Separating the natural from the artificial, or growing from making (see Ingold and Hallam, 2016) was in itself an influential act of categorization, because it lifted the ontology of splits to a new level. It furthered a distinction between nature's underlying essences that existed 'independent of the agency of man' (Flower, 1898: 7) and those entities shaped by human handiwork, minds and skills (for a critique see Ingold and Hallam, 2016).

In a different gown, anthropocentrism can also be found in the social sciences and humanities. Theories centring on semantics and the power of discourse, for example, tend to consider materials as empty, inert, mute and abstract. Materials are here considered containers to be filled and given meaning to by humans via semantic layers (for a critique see Star and Ruhleder, 1996; Camus and Vinck, 2019; Ribes, 2019). In a similar vein, anthropomorphist views on material cultures argue for the social constructivism of things and bodies (for a critique see Ingold and Hallam, 2016). Humans are, once again, seen as the superior force that imposes form on material or nature: passive matter receives treatment from humans (Deleuze and Guattari, 2004; Ingold, 2011). Karen Barad summarizes her critique of these views, asking: 'Why are language and culture granted their own agency and historicity while matter is figured as passive and immutable?' (2003: 801). Different disciplines provide concrete answers to this question and new ways to bring matter into focus, especially when they foreground the ontological concepts of relation, becoming and interiority/agency, which we turn to now.

Ontologies of relation

Understanding materiality as relational suggests that humans are but one part of materiality, if at all. Concepts such as apparatus (Barad, 2003), assemblage (Haggerty and Ericson, 2000), ecologies (Star and Ruhleder, 1996; Bennett, 2004), Actor-Networks (Latour, 2005), all argue that matter and materials are not singular objects, but embedded in sets of relations, where they perform and produce change.

This understanding springs from many traditions. Humanities scholar Johanna Drucker suggests that materiality is not grounded in a single feature or factor, but multiple things and interrelated activity, each of these is dependent on their relations (2013). Many scholars in Science and Technology Studies (STS) look at relations and what sits in-between. Infrastructure Studies (see Bowker et al, 2010), Actor Network Theory (see Latour, 2005), and digital STS conceptualize matter as a network of relations, many parts of which are now clickable, searchable, indexed, and visualized, associated and able to circulate in different and new ways (see Forlano, 2019; Ribes and Vertesi, 2019). A case in point are predictive policing systems discussed in Chapter 4: they include among other things patrol officers and paper forms, administrative personnel and databases, programmers and algorithms, interfaces and visualization designs, the relations between which keep changing. Because relations keep changing, materiality produces 'meaning as a performance ... situated, partial, non-repeatable' (Drucker, 2013: para 36). Similarly, David Ribes argues that 'no material can be taken as having a forever closed meaning, property, or affordance; in principle they can be, and often are, revisited, repurposed, or rediscovered' (2019: 50). Hence, he lets his studies be driven by the 'irreducibility principle', which sensitizes him 'to the production of additional materials and the work of generating and sustaining more links of reference' (Ribes, 2019: 52).

Some authors have a relatively lose approach to determine and study 'collections' and their relations (see Camus and Vinck, 2019), including bodies, locality, labour, time, efforts, and many more aspects (see Forlano, 2019). In the study of relations, different foci emerge. For Susan Leigh Star and Karen Ruhleder the relevant 'discontinuities are not between system and person, or technology and organization, but rather between contexts' (1996: 118). This is in line with Geoffrey Bowker's concept of 'infrastructural inversion' (1994), which de-emphasizes both things and people as causal factors of material dynamics, but rather focuses on changes in infrastructural relations as the central phenomenon. In doing so, he inverses historical explanations and upsets traditional views on cause and effect.

Ontologies of becoming

A focus on relations alone does not imply a distance from essentialist views of matter or materials. Relationality can on the one side still be understood as essentially semantic, while it can on the other side slide into hard materialism, whereby the physicality of the network becomes the centre of debate (see Blanchette, 2011; Bawden and Robinson, 2013 for a tendency to argue for hard materialism, in popular science: Blum, 2012). Both discourse and physicality can play a role in the study of how matter matters, but neither of them are the only relevant aspects when conceptualizing materiality. Indeed, some of the mentioned relational approaches understand materiality as performance, as expansive and subject to change. In a similar vein, Tim Ingold ties the relationality of materials to a dynamic of constant becoming: 'as the environment unfolds, so the materials of which it is comprised do not *exist* ... but *occur*' (2011: 30, emphasis in original). Karen Barad uses the corresponding notion of *mattering*. She conceptualizes matter and materials as ongoing 'reconfigurings/entanglements/relationalities/

(re)articulations' (2003: 818). This dynamism is central to materials, which is why she tends to employ the wording of *materialization*. Matter, then, is best described in terms of becoming rather than being: it is 'indeterminate, constantly forming and reforming in unexpected ways' (Coole and Frost, 2010: 10). It is 'always already an ongoing historicity' (Barad, 2003: 821). Or the properties of materials are a 'condensed story' (Ingold, 2011: 32), which keeps mutating and emerging anew. Political theorist Jane Bennett even eschews matter-life binaries as she acknowledges the presence of indeterminate vitality within matter. In her writings, materiality is 'a continuum of becomings, of extensive and intensive forms in various states of congealment and dissolution' (2010a: 63). Johanna Drucker, too, moves 'from a notion of *what is* to that *which is always in flux*, from a *literal* to a *contingent* materiality that is exposed by the performative dimension of use' (Drucker, 2013: para 12, emphasis in original).

Matter and materials are then not like machines, systems, or clockworks that are disassembled into their component parts and controlled. Instead, they are conceptualized as entwined with organisms and life, which makes them unpredictable and uncontrollable (Lash, 2006; Bennett, 2010a; Coole and Frost, 2010; Ingold and Hallam, 2016). Many theoretical concepts that summarize the qualities of materialization are, however, curiously indebted to the machine. As mentioned earlier, we study relations and their effects via apparatuses, assemblages, (eco)systems, and infrastructures. This prevalence of machinic concepts within the social sciences is also to a certain extent the result of the ontology of splits between mind and matter, between subject and object, between those who act and those who are acted upon. Yet, some of the authors who deploy machinic concepts in their theories on materiality also forward arguments that speak to a more organic understanding of materialization and 'ontogenesis' (Ingold and Hallam, 2016). I will mention a few of these arguments and authors now.

Ontologies of interiority/agency

The dynamics of relationality and becoming can also be linked to interiority, which means that specific conceptualizations of materiality abandon the Cartesian split between inside and outside. I am using the term 'complex interiority', borrowed from Luc Boltanski (2011: 26), mainly because it is not as indebted to the machine as terms such as system or apparatus. (As mentioned, the latter can emphasize a position of interiority, too.) Ontologies of complex interiority have consequences for the related understanding of agency. Agency is no longer considered the power to act independently, since everything – humans, matter, instruments – is understood to be interior to an ever-changing meshwork. With that, humans neither take the role as the sole actor nor as a superior force in what would be a hierarchy of agencies. Rather, materials, instruments and humans generate, act, and influence each other. This means that matter and materials, too, are active participants in the process of the world's becoming (Camus and Vinck, 2019). What is more, any type of matter can 'enjoy a certain efficacy that defies human will' (Coole and Frost, 2010: 9). Changes in infrastructure (Bowker, 1994; Star and Ruhleder, 1996; Bowker et al, 2010) or in any material configuration 'can transform successive conditions for interaction among elements such that they end up having massive but unanticipated effects' (Coole and Frost, 2010: 14). An example of such an effect is discussed in Chapter 4: the algorithmic performance on datasets can produce surprising effects, where data emerge as stubborn and unpredictable, influencing the process of prediction.

In combining the notions of interiority and agency, Tim Ingold argues that we are immersed in a meshwork. Everything exists in a 'domain of entanglement' (Ingold, 2011: 71). In this meshwork, life is not an attribute of matter. Instead, life is immanent in the process of becoming with each other. 'Things *are* their relations' (Ingold, 2011: 70, emphasis in original). He describes it as 'a flux in which materials of the most diverse kinds ... undergo continual generation and transformation. The forms of things, far from having been imposed upon an inert substrate, arise and are born along – as indeed we are too – within this current of materials' (Ingold, 2011: 24).

While the space for agency seems to shrink in collective meshworks of becoming, there are still options for human engagement (Ingold, 2011). Our role would be to 'read creativity "forwards"' (Ingold, 2011: 216). This requires a focus on improvisation: 'To improvise is to follow the ways of the world, as they open up' (Ingold, 2011). By improvising, we are part of making and creating: 'improvisational activities are the generative practices out of which new technologies are made' (Suchman, 2000: 139). Being enmeshed with the world – rather than dominating it from the outside – renders agency into 'contingent capacities for reflexivity, creative disclosure, and transformation' (Coole, 2010: 113).

Recognizing the codependence of any lives and vitalities, we, like everything else, exercise an immediate form of influence. This provokes reflections about our role in this world and leads to 'practical, politically engaged social theory, devoted to critical analysis of actual conditions of existence and their inherent inequality' (Coole and Frost, 2010: 25). Indeed, while some theories of materialization tend to disregard or forget humans, a place for human accountability in this collective and contingent setup exists. If we think of '(c)ollective life as a complex relational field that emerges in an intercorporeal, intersubjective "between"' (Coole, 2010: 113), then that has implications for how we as humans inhabit politics. We inhabit politics as that which has to be negotiated from within. Karen Barad, too, emphasizes that in her theory of materialization humans remain 'resolutely accountable for the role "we" play in the intertwined practices of knowing and becoming' (2003: 812, see Chapter 8 on ethics). She suggests the concept of Intra-action. Agency is everywhere: 'All bodies, not merely "human" bodies, come to matter through the world's iterative intra-activity' (Barad, 2003: 823). Agency emerges here through material-discursive practices that continuously reconfigure the field of possibilities for other intra-activities to arise. It is important, here, that 'intra-activity is neither a matter of strict determinism nor unconstrained freedom. The future is radically open at every turn' (Barad, 2003: 326). And this 'opens up a space, indeed a relatively large space, for ... agency' (Barad, 2003: 326). This is the space we study when we want to understand how information matters. Studying these *turns* can help us understanding if and how collective new forms of influence are created and how different agencies affect each other. We will revisit these turns quite concretely in the method chapter, where the life cycle and *the turns it takes* provide us with a tool to identify instances of interaction and agency.

Information

We can think of information, too, as a matter of relations, becoming, and interiority. As Katherine Hayles argues, information is not a universal code that 'underlies the structure of matter' (1999: 11). Information is not the abstracted essence of the material world, but it is material and involved in materializations. Yet, the understanding of matter and information as separate entities characterizes predominant theories about so-called information societies. Luciano Floridi (2010: 12), for example, describes the process of informationalization as one of increasing immateriality: 'We are modifying our everyday experience on the ultimate nature of reality ... from a materialist one, in which physical objects and processes play a key role, to an informational one.' In his account of the 'information revolution' objects and processes are 'de-physicalized ... in the sense that they tend to be seen as support-independent' (Floridi, 2010: 12) and 'typified ... in the sense that an instance of an object ... is as good as its type' (Floridi, 2010: 12). He describes that as information – the essence of things – begins to rise in influence, objects and processes are 'clonable' and 'interchangeable'; they remain 'subject to interaction, even if intangible', where interaction is only indirect (Floridi, 2010: 12). In such an account, information and everything else lose their embeddedness, immediacy and materiality. Katherine Hayles observes that this disembodiedness is also in part the promise of ontologies that consider information to be the essence of things. The seductions of 'disembodied consciousness' (Rosenheim, 1997: 9) and 'pure information objects, unfettered by matter' (Paul, 2009: 19) nurture dreams of abstract, patterned information that 'can be free from the material constraints that govern the mortal world' (Hayles, 1999: 13). This conceptualization of information constructs a world in which matter, flesh, steel, and their 'legal concepts of property, expression, identity, movement, and context do not apply' as John Perry Barlow famously announces in his *Declaration of the Independence of Cyberspace* (Barlow, 1996: online). Ubiquitous computing, mass-production, the rise in the influence of patterns, and beliefs in the ability of information to develop intelligence (singularity) seem to be symptoms of this move towards abstract form. Observing these phenomena with the eyes of an information essentialist, it sure looks like information is 'progressively absorbing' (Floridi, 2010: 16) or replacing other forms of life, abstracting any matter to their type. Seeing these two worlds influencing each other, Floridi goes a step further than virtual realists. He concludes that '(t)he infosphere will not be a virtual environment supported by a genuinely *material* world behind; rather, it will be the world itself that will be increasingly interpreted and understood informationally, as part of the infosphere' (Floridi, 2010: 17, emphasis in original).

There is no reason to contest that the influence of information increases and that this increase changes the world and life itself. Life, however, is not reduced to information, where it becomes non-material and continues to exist as an essence or a type. Katherine Hayles reminds us that information is never free-floating, but 'must always be instantiated in a medium' (Hayles, 1999: 13). Information is material. And from the ontologies of relation, becoming and interiority described earlier follows that information is as lively as everything else. It is matter in-formation. If we borrow from Tim Ingold (2011), we can say that information, too, is swept up in meshworks that are always in flux. This reverberates with theories that consider information as 'made of all relations that partake in its production' (Bowker et al, 2010; Camus and Vinck, 2019: 37). Information influences the other elements in the meshwork.

Materializations of information

If we understand information through relation, becoming and interiority, information can no longer be considered mere semantic content that gives meaning to other objects. Neither is it itself an empty container or a pre-existing object that receives meaning from the outside. Information is matter that matters in its specificity (Kaufmann and Jeandesboz, 2017). Understanding how information matters in context also makes it easier to let go of epochal claims about information societies, ages, eras, and revolutions. Still, we can observe that especially digital information has become an influential element of how lives are lived. Digital information matters as it recasts our relationship to bodies and identities (see Lupton, 2016a, 2020). It changes the whole spectrum from how we understand neural interactions (Human Brain Project) to the exploration of space (Vertesi, 2015). Digital information is part of deciding who receives development aid (see Sandvik, 2020), it influences the organization of neighbourhood help (Singh, 2020), as well as whom we kill in warfare (Schwarz, 2016). It matters in how we make payments and steer economic markets (Fuchs, 2010; Brine and Poovey 2013; Zuboff, 2019). Digital information changes how diplomacy is done (Westcott, 2009) and how art is produced (Saugmann, Möller, and Bellmer, 2020). A map of how digital information matters will necessarily be incomplete, not to speak of all other kinds of information. And yet, instead of understanding information in absolute terms, which either leads to its gradual embrace (a growing infosphere) or dispensation (as summarized in concepts of digital detox and the rejection of devices), we can grasp it as in-formation. Such a position asks us to recognize its specific material properties (Ribes, 2019). It urges us to study how information is generative, how it matters, as well as how it can be made to matter.

The material properties of information have been theorized in different ways. It seems intuitive to consider 2D and 3D printing as an illustration of, for example, digital data as matter (see Lupton, 2016a). Rather than exemplifying the material properties of digital data, however, 3D printing describes a change in the materiality of information. It illustrates a movement 'from one material condition to another' (Drucker, 2009: 147). The example is nonetheless an important one, because it reminds us that it is relevant to study how information moves and matters in different contexts.

There is a tendency in scholarly writings to emphasize the materiality of information in its most basic form. Signals, marks, records, nucleic acids, atoms, ones, and zeros as patterned arrangements of ferromagnetic bits – all of them created their own sets of discussions. In Physics, for example, discussions revolve around the relationship between bits and energy. The heat generated upon a bit's erasure is cited as an argument for the physicality of information (see: Landauer, 1999; Landauer's Principle 1961 and follow-up discussions by Bérut et al, 2012; Chiribella et al, 2012; Bawden and Robinson 2013). Especially in the literature on the materiality of digital information we find important studies on the ways in which storage media or file formats enable and constrain transformations of information (Kirschenbaum, 2007). Jean-Francois Blanchette shows in a number of publications how computing is a material process 'through and through' (2011, 2012; Yoo and Blanchette, 2015).

Yet, the quest for the most basic and stable form of information's materiality may distract from a broader material understanding of information. In fact, attempts at reducing information's materiality may also render themselves irrelevant: 'In calling data ordered atoms, what has occurred is an adoption of a particular form of reductionism, in the case, the reductionism of electrical engineering' (Ribes, 2019: 54). The engineering perspective is of little relevance, for example, to biologists. What is more relevant is the 'emergence, attraction, repulsion, fluctuation and shifting of nodes of charge' in an atom (Ribes, 2019: 54). These processes convey that information does not exhibit any comforting stability, solidity, or coherent essence (see Barad, 2003). Instead, what needs attention are the ways in which information is always re-instantiated as matter, how information moves between different materialities, how it is translated between contexts, how information is made to matter and actively matters in meshworks. The task is here to trace how and through which relations information is produced as eminently material (Camus and Vinck, 2019; Ribes, 2019). Geoffrey Bowker's famous wording that 'information is never raw, but always cooked' (Bowker, 2005: 184; see Gitelman and Jackson, 2013; Ribes, 2019) underlines that it always emerges from specific relations. This also affects the often-formulated problem of informational bias. In understanding information as relational, context-specific and lively, bias becomes a superfluous concept, because it is everywhere, in every dataset. The only way to engage with 'bias' is then to identify and reflect about the specificities of information and how to engage with them (Kaufmann, 2020; Doctorow, 2021). Even if notions such as 'raw' and 'cooked' have done excellent explanatory work, they can introduce a sense of linearity from raw to finished. Similarly, wording such as 'incomplete', 'corrupted', 'disjointed', or 'imprecise' information and information infrastructures (Edwards et al, 2011: 684) transport ambitions of perfection and finality. Information, however, is in-formation. It is neither raw, nor finished. In this process of constant becoming, we can think of information as always at a threshold, passing 'from one form of life to another' (Ingold and Hallam, 2016: 2).

The vitality of information

Information not only comes of life and affects life, but the mentioned ontologies of becoming suggest that information itself expresses liveliness. In expanding on the relationship between information and vitality, I seek to answer a call for 'new images and mindsets' (Bowker et al, 2010: 112) that can help shaping the study of information.

'If you are not data, you don't exist' (Bowker, 2013: 170). Geoffrey Bowker describes how the long-standing practice of informationalizing life reached a new level of intensity. As more information circulates digitally, it has also become more powerful: it is vital in the sense of critical or decisive. This has become true for many societal contexts. Digital information about life is constantly generated and regenerated, purposed, and repurposed (Lupton, 2016a). Not only do these dynamics intensify the status of information as vitally important, but the continued generation of information also speaks to a sense of liveliness and productiveness. Information co-shapes how phenomena come about, how the world is being known and understood.

This vitality, in both meanings of the word, urges us to understand how information enmeshes with lives and livelihoods, life chances, and opportunities (Haraway, 2015a; Lupton, 2016a).

Deborah Lupton makes an argument about the ways in which digital information is enmeshed with human bodies to illustrate that data is lively and influences human lives. She draws on Annemarie Mol's *I Eat an Apple* who describes how an apple becomes part of the eater's body to the extent that it is 'impossible to determine what is human and what is apple' (Lupton, 2016a: 3; original see Mol, 2008: 30). Lupton uses the imagery of ingestion and emission to describe the multiple flows of data and how they connect human lives to the data economy. Like eating an apple, then, 'generating and responding to digital data about oneself are highly contingent acts' (Lupton, 2016b: 4). This example helps us understanding in how many ways information is part of producing life (see Raley, 2013: 213) and death. However, it is important, here, not to reduce the liveliness of information to the idea that information travels across sites where it takes on a social life 'through the play of individuals and through the excitement of participation' (Beer and Burrows, 2013: 67). That information circulates in a digital economy, where humans produce, consume, and prosume information (Ritzer, 2014; Lupton, 2016a) is but one aspect of its liveliness. Information is more profoundly a matter of life.

In line with New Materialist understandings of matter we can think of information as productive, especially if we consider the transformative capacities of information as contingent and emergent (see Coole, 2010) instead of driven by intelligence or purposive reason. The liveliness of information moves away from the idea of mastery, but recognizes that information inhabits a power outside humans that is not passively resistant, but energetic; not purposive, but equipped with the capacity to surprise (Bennett, 2010b). Jane Bennett draws on the neo-vitalist philosophy of biologist Hans Driesch, who identifies *entelechy* as the animating driver of the organic as well as the inorganic, ultimately leading him to understand even the machine as vitalistic. This thinking was also reflected in later forms of vitalism as for example that of Georges Canguilhem who sought to understand 'matter within life, and the science of matter – which is science tout court – within the activity of the living' (*Knowledge of Life* quoted in Elden, 2019). Generally, referencing vitalist tropes and theories has to be done with utmost care, because some of its varieties have become politicized and integrated into fascist thought. They have been referenced to justify hierarchies of the living and the allegedly non-living, or they are associated with ethically loaded 'culture of life'-movements that further traditionalist views on abortion and stem-cell research (for a critique see Braidotti, 2010). Jane Bennett, however, historicizes the emergence of Driesch's entelechy and reads it as the progressive desire to destroy hierarchies and ultimate differences, namely 'the (very) difference between "mechanism" and "Vitalism" … which we have established so carefully' (Bennett, 2010a: 61). Driesch's entelechy or 'creative causality' (Bennett, 2010a: 55), so she argues, can be found across any matter. The possibilities and constraints for the liveliness of digital information, for example, could be thought in terms of its countability and computability, its storability, searchability, transferability, and traceability, but also in terms of its many intersections with humans, its instantiations in tools, devices, and other elements.

Donna Haraway's work can help us to further conceptualize information as lively. When she uses the notion of 'companion species' she refers to the species other than human that are here to live with (Haraway, 2003). They are species, because they are marked by a human/non-human liveliness (Haraway, 2015a: np) and they are part of processes of becoming-with each other. If information is a part of our lives today, we can consider it our companion species (see Hultman and Taguchi, 2010; Lupton, 2016b, 2020; Bellanova, 2017; Kaufmann, 2020). We grow, compose, and compost with information (Haraway, 2015b; Ingold and Hallam, 2016; Bellanova and Gonzales Fuster, 2019). Information, and most likely digital information, stays here to live with. The way in which information is produced and processed matters to us (Bellanova, 2017). It is vital – lively and critical – to any form of mattering. Information is not a matter distinct from life that has now accumulated enough agency to impact human lives, but like everything else it is part of an ontology of relations, interiority, and becoming.

In order to further illustrate these dynamics of becoming together, I will borrow another trope from Donna Haraway: the 'spiral dance' (1991: 181). There is liveliness in all elements that we become-with. Not just information, but instruments, tools and other materials live a life, too (see Ruppert, Law, and Savage, 2013). All these lives intersect in a spiral dance, or, as Coole and Frost would say: they 'are caught in a multitude of interlocking systems and forces' (2010: 9). While some of these dances are spontaneous and uncoordinated, others are highly 'choreographed': 'What might appear to be an undifferentiated hybrid mess is actually a deftly balanced coming together of things that are generally considered parts of different ontological orders (part of nature, part of the self, part of society)' (Thompson, 2005: 8).

Information, then, also dances with us: whether it is that we generate information or whether we share or surrender (Raley, 2013) to information that generates us. At times, information about us becomes so lively that it circulates without us being able to make a difference about it. At other times, it is exactly how we engage with information that can make information matter in specific ways. This small room for our human capacity to engage is what constitutes the ethics of making information matter. We will return to this room for agency in the method chapter, where we look at the *life cycle* of information and its *turns* (see Barad, 2003), that is the points at which there is an opening for engagement. In that context of engagement, we can invoke Donna Haraway's notion of companionship again: companionship neither blindly endorses, nor abandons that which matters, but companions accompany and engage (Austin, Bellanova, and Kaufmann, 2019). As companions we find opportunities for critical renewal as we dance and make matter together. This brings us to the last concept of making.

Making

'Particular possibilities for acting exist at every moment, and these changing possibilities entail a responsibility to intervene in the world's becoming, to contest and rework what matters and what is excluded from mattering' (Barad, 2003: 827).

Making is a material process. It describes not just the ways in which materials are manipulated, but also how they are constituted as materials (Küchler, 2008; Ingold and Hallam, 2016). One could also say that materiality is performed (Drucker, 2013). It is in the making. In line with the arguments developed earlier, making matter defies the 'tendency to assign intrinsic and inherent values to material properties' (Drucker, 2013), but rather moves the focus from what a phenomenon is to how it works, how it came about and continues to materialize. As Johanna Drucker observes, this focus brings us necessarily to 'life cycles' (2013) of materials and materiality, with emergent possibilities and conditions for further materializations. Again, this is why the next chapter will develop a methodology of life cycles and their turns which are decisive for the why and how of materializations.

In line with the ontologies of becoming, making is an ongoing process. Making matter is transformative (see Thompson Klein, 2017), which means that materialization processes are historically embedded at the same time as they are continuous, ongoing. The use of the present participle (mak*ing*) signals that an action is incomplete, not finished. There is no conclusion to making, but only a spiral dance (Haraway, 1991; Ingold and Hallam, 2016: 1; Kaufmann, 2020). Making is thus no totalitarian activity, no sovereign mastering of objects as an ontology of splits would suggest. Rather, making is a go-between (Ingold and Hallam, 2016) or a making-with, becoming-with, composing-with (Haraway, 2015b: 161). Indeed, Tim Ingold and Elizabeth Hallam (2016: 9) write that 'lives of making and growing are never lived in isolation but always in the company of others … And since live is a process … of "growing older together", one person's decline maybe another's growth'. This view reverberates with Donna Haraway's composing, decomposing, and composting (2015b).

Making as an activity of going-between, becoming-with, composting, and companionship replace sovereignty with mutuality: it is not only us humans that are, influence, and make matter, but the same can be said about

19

information, devices, things. Tim Ingold writes that '(t)hings are alive and active ... because the substances which they are comprised of continue to be swept up in circulations of the surrounding media that alternately portend their dissolution or ... ensure their regeneration' (2011: 29).

He even goes as far as declaring all organisms as ' "hives of activity, pulsing with the flows of materials that keeps them alive', where humans, too, are 'born and grow within the current of materials, and participate from within in their further transformation' (Ingold, 2011: 29). Jane Bennett, too, reflects about the ways in which matter takes part in making. Her 'enchanted realism' (Bennett, 2001) expresses that matter enjoys 'a certain efficacy that defies human will' (Coole and Frost, 2010: 9). Self-making and autopoiesis are contributions from complexity theory to conceptualize how systems are collectively making matter through self-renewal. Hans Driesch's mentioned entelechy is also described as an activity of self-directing without a clear telos (see Bennett, 2010a). In applying entelechy to the vitality of matter Jane Bennett writes that 'it answers events innovatively' (2010a: 55). Here, we can recall what Tim Ingold says about human makers, who improvise and 'act forwards' when making matter: 'the builder, the gardener, the cook, the alchemist and the painter are not so much imposing form on matter as bringing together diverse materials and combining or redirecting their flow in the anticipations of what might emerge' (Ingold, 2011: 213).

When we understand making matter as something that is never finished, then making can be likened to growing (Haraway, 2016; Ingold and Hallam, 2016). Organic tropes of growing, composing, and decomposing emphasize the relevance of life, death, and intersecting life cycles in making matter. Growing emphasizes that making matter is a collective practice: there are conditions for growth that are in part dependent on other matter, in part dependent on the nurturing, care, and nourishment of growers (Ingold and Hallam, 2016). In letting grow, form is not imposed from the outside, but emerges from all involved elements including growers who inaugurate new life cycles (Ingold and Hallam, 2016: 5). In understanding making matter in conjunction with life and liveliness we are aware, too, that 'all making, in a sense, entails breaking, just as all growth entails decomposition' (Ingold and Hallam, 2016: 8). Further, we should take into consideration that certain forms of growth can also happen without the constructive notions of nurturing and care. We can even consider exploitation as a practice of making matter, as well as neglection can be a way of making matter insignificant, of no longer letting it matter, of letting it die, which matters, too. Making matter is neither economic productivity, nor is it an affirmative, ethical practice – not even in the positivistic sense of 'making something work'. Rather, each specific practice of making matter or growing needs to be investigated in terms of its contributions and the values of its matterings. As we shall see in the description of different practices later on, one practice of making matter can combine contradictory values and different aspects of vitality (Chapters 4–7), but we can also consider an affirmative ethics of making (Chapter 8).

We are all makers

Frequently, discourses about makers focus on human makers, the material they work with, and the intentions they have when making. Such discourses see the human as the sovereign who machines material and owns the process of making. Annika Richterich and Karin Wenz characterize makers as those who base their actions in 'sharing, learning and self-expression', who aim at 'digital democratization of production and manufacturing' (Richterich and Wenz, 2017: 9). While this description captures what may be the maker movement's type today, it still centres around the role of the human, whether as a professional maker or in the context of 'civic creativity' (Richterich and Wenz, 2017: 10). Debbie Chachra (2017) takes distance from the term makers altogether, because she finds that it builds on a gendered history and does not recognize the work done by makers.

The original notions of critical making and DIY that emerged in the 1960s aimed to dismantle dichotomies of doing vs. thinking, production vs. interpretation, application vs. theory (Burdick, 2012; Thompson Klein, 2017: 27) and focused on new possibilities for making (such as 3D printing in the early 2010s). Such discourses gave making and matter an urgently needed stage and refreshed some of the then-gridlocked theories about them. They still, however, reinstated the hierarchies of humans over subjects and had a tendency to see making as a normative practice (making something well, producing something good). An important bridge towards the idea of making matter forwarded in this book are the literatures that introduce aspects of collectiveness and becoming into the practice of making. To Matt Ratto, making is to

> achieve value through the act of shared construction, joint conversation and reflection. Therefore, while critical making organizes its efforts around the making of material objects, devices themselves are not the ultimate goal. Instead, through the sharing of results and an ongoing critical analysis of materials, designs, constraints, and outcomes, participants in critical making exercises together perform a practice-based engagement with pragmatic and theoretical issues. (Ratto, 2011: 253)

Even though this view introduces and important focus on collectivity, matter is still a 'means to an end' (Ratto, 2011: 253), which is to 'develop and share new understandings' through 'materially productive

21

work' (Ratto, 2011: 258). Other literatures of critical making tie collectivity to materialist epistemologies (see Ramsay and Rockwell's 2012 'Epistemology of building'). They move towards acknowledging the role of non-humans when they observe how material interventions can trouble theoretical work, when they underline the necessity of looking for 'theories in prototypes' (Resch et al, 2017: 158) or writing 'object biographies' (Morgan, 2012) and when they consider making a transformative practice (Resch et al, 2017).

This book pushes notions of making a bit further and emphasizes that we are all in the process of making. How and if information comes to matter is highly dependent on the collective that makes matter together, including materials. The ontologies of relations, becoming and interiority outlined earlier make this argument clear. The difference is that human makers can still negotiate their ways through the meshwork. They can attempt to 'harmonize' variations and 'correct' unfolding tasks (Ingold, 2011: 217). Without wanting to overstate the role of humans in making matter, we can see that some actors can attempt to follow visions to make differently more than others. Thus, within an emerging phenomenon we find different forms of making. Information, for example, is vital to how phenomena come about. At times, information may even be described as self-making and self-growing. However, arguing that information becomes conscious of its own activity and influence may take this argument too far. Information may reflect as in capturing and mirroring a specific meaning, information affects and changes human reflections, it may even adapt to the contexts it is active in, but information does not engage.

Indeed, not every element in the meshwork has the capacity to become aware of and reflect about interiority, which is why practices of making matter span across the spectrum from being a part of, re-acting, and adapting to engaging with a phenomenon. Where exactly the threshold for conscious engagement lies is difficult to say, but at least humans have the capacity to make matter across the entire spectrum. They can make matter by being part of a phenomenon, by adapting to circumstances, by being pragmatic and by engaging with them consciously. Hence, there is legitimacy in asking ourselves what (limited) role we as humans play in making matter.

Our role may start with bringing materials and materializations to the foreground. As argued throughout, materials should not be taken as a given, where they sink 'into an invisible background' (Star and Ruhleder, 1996: 112). In *On being included* Sarah Ahmed (2012) uses the notion of 'non-performativity' to describe the processes of things becoming habitual, letting agendas for inclusion sink into the territory of forgotten, but well-regulated themes, which ultimately neglect inclusion. We can answer such a regress of performativity by taking a closer look at materials and how they work. Materials and infrastructures, as Star and Ruhleder put it, emerge 'in practice, connected to activities' (1996: 112). Hence, bringing materials to the foreground matters.

Another role we can take is to keep a sense of wonder: 'While astonishment has been banished from the protocols of conceptually driven, rational inquiry, in animism it is the sense of wonder that comes from riding the crest of the world's continued birth' (Ingold, 2011: 74). Or, as Latourians would put it: we should let our subjects of study surprise us. We should then not be seduced to turn surprise 'into a scientific protocol of progress, where the world is rendered more and more categorized and predictable, while astonishment lingers' (Ingold, 2011: 74). When we reflect about the ways in which ourselves and others are part of making matter we can let go of our expectations towards a specific materialization. We accept fundamentally and with astonishment that things are in flux. And yet, 'rather than waiting for the unexpected to occur' we can use 'every moment to respond to the flux of the world with care, judgment and sensitivity' (Ingold, 2011: 75).

In her work on located accountabilities, Lucy Suchman argues for taking responsibility for the ways in which we make matter (2002). While 'In some real sense, no one of us is responsible for the outcome of our collective labour', there is no good reason to use this as a 'rationale for abdicating responsibility for the products of technological labour' (Suchman, 2002: 97). Her approach to taking on responsibility is very pragmatic. She suggests to engage, for example, by '(r)ecognizing the various forms of visible and invisible work that make up the production/use of technical systems, locating ourselves within that extended web of connections, and taking responsibility for our participation' (Suchman, 2002: 101). When doing so, it is also important to acknowledge 'the limited power of any actors or artifacts to control technology production/use' (Suchman, 2002: 101). Both of these suggestions tie relationality and interiority to concrete value statements, namely to appreciate partiality and heterogeneity when we engage in processes of making.

Making matter with astonishment, sensitivity, and responsibility is a conscious decision to counteract the politics of inertia and death that we find in other practices of making matter, for example those information practices that seek to capture and fixate human and non-human bodies. Rather, we can choose to make information matter by realizing 'multiple micropolitical modes of daily activism' and by putting 'the "active" back into activism' (Braidotti, 2010: 209–10, quotation marks in original). This, however, is not necessarily an easy choice (Braidotti, 2010). Our role in the process of making is to engage pragmatically or consciously – even if it hurts. To engage is not just to use the means of deconstructive critique that once again risks reducing materials to objects, but by making matter in accordance with the values we seek to foster. Here, we can contribute to, but we cannot master matter. The ethos making information matter is further discussed in Chapter 8.

Summarizing the theoretical basis of Making Information Matter

Information is nothing abstract. It is not free-floating or virtual, but information is always instantiated in a medium (Hayles, 1999). In order to understand information we do not need to embark on a quest for its most basic, essential material form, such as signals, records, or atoms. Rather, we can embrace its relationality and instability. Like any matter, information is not a singular, settled object, but information *is* its relations (Ingold, 2011). The quest is directed at such multiple relations instead, where we can let us guide by the irreducibility principle (Ribes, 2019). How information matters is context-specific.

This relationality implies that matter is performed and reformed. Datasets, for example, can consolidate, remain, be sustained, and become difficult to delete, but that, too, requires continued performance. At the same time, I argue that datasets change whenever they are performed in their relation with databases, analytic projects, art, with the people involved in making, sorting, storing, analysing, and translating. Hence, information does not exist, but occurs (Ingold, 2011). It is in a state of becoming, where the ways in which information matters are not entirely predictable. When it is performed and reformed as matter, information has agency. As it enmeshes with lives and livelihoods, it becomes lively and productive – not in a targeted or cognizant fashion, but in contingent and emergent ways (Coole and Frost, 2010).

Information is vital – lively and critical – to many processes. Especially in the light of growing digitization we can consider information a companion (Bellanova, 2017). We influence each other, we intra-act (Barad, 2003), we make matter together in a spiral dance. Within this dance, us humans will never master information, but we can assist in making it grow (Ingold, 2011). While making is not an affirmative practice per se, several authors emphasize our responsibility to act and to engage (Suchman, 2002; Barad, 2003; Braidotti, 2010; Ingold, 2011). When we let us guide by a sense of wonder and creativity, we may be able to act forwards and to make a difference in current information landscapes.

Chapters 4–6 describe four practices of making information matter: association, convergence, secrecy, and speculation. They all point to the ways in which different elements collaborate in making information matter, following different sets of values. However, especially the practices of convergence, secrecy, and speculation show that the many forms of dataveillance and association prominent in society today can still be met with practices of making information matter differently. What role values play in these processes and how we can make a difference is discussed in Chapter 8.

If part of our role is to bring materials to the foreground and to make matter, then we need methods to understand how information matters. We need a method that helps us to identify the 'turns' (Barad, 2003) or thresholds within information life cycles, where re-orientation in mattering is possible. Laura Forlano calls for approaches that allow us to understand 'digital work as practical action' (2019: 12). The next chapter answers this call by suggesting vocabulary and methodological devices that can help studying information practices and identifying the openings for our own engagement.

3

Studying Materializations:
A Methodology of Life Cycles

How do we get to know this ever-changing world, a world that we are ourselves part of? Our research is much dependent on methods that capture the dynamics of becoming and the ways in which we are implicated in them. One methodological premise of this book is thus that 'knowing must be reconnected with being' (Ingold, 2011: 75). This is what Karen Barad captures in the term *onto-epistem-ology*: 'we know because "we" are *of* the world' (2003: 329, emphasis and quotation marks in original). Or as Maurice Merleau-Ponty would put it: we and the phenomena we study sit in the same folds (2003; Coole, 2010). There is mutuality: by doing research, we are part of making the world and the world makes us. This means that knowing the world is also a process of knowing ourselves and our influence. Accordingly, a good methodological attitude may be to allow for all elements in this complex, lively hive – including ourselves – to astonish us (Ingold, 2011; Chapter 2). While such a sense of wonder is a great vantage point for getting to know the world, we also depend on methods that enable us to grasp materializations. Grasping is the empirical, practical and material process of understanding through contact. A method of grasping takes distance from the more abstract 'analytic' that researchers inherited from the Cartesian split between mind and matter. This split implicates that analytics are based on the logic of the machine, the component parts of which are identified and manipulated by humans. Grasping, instead, goes back to a conceptual family of reaching and touching – something that was later captured in the term seizing. It is to understand fully and distinctly. Grasping is an active process, it is doing. By reaching, touching and seizing the phenomena we research, we also make them. We make parts of them comprehensible as we intra-act with them (see Barad, 2003).

Thus, this chapter not only endorses the much-articulated need for empirical research, the necessity of experiencing and plunging into the world. Grasping phenomena and making them matter also involves criticality. Both us and the phenomena we seek to grasp are critical to materializations. Yet, this criticality is two-fold: what is critically important also deserves critique (Kaufmann et al, 2020). Critique is not the distanced analytic of detecting and accusing (as criticized by Felski, 2012). Precisely because we are all part of the same world, critique is a form of companionship (Austin, Bellanova, and Kaufmann, 2019; see Haraway, 2003) and eventually self-critique. The spirit of companionship guides how we can become-with (Haraway, 2015b) the things we study, how we become-with technologies, tools, information, each other. And this idea of becoming-with brings us back to the liveliness of the things we study. Hence, this chapter develops a methodology of life cycles that can help us grasping materializations. It understands research as a continuous activity. Life cycles show how technologies, information and ourselves take an active role in our common becoming. How are material phenomena brought to life? How do they live their own lives and how do they influence that of others? The methodology allows for both, grasping and critiquing as it identifies the turns at which different agencies emerge, among which is the (small) margin for our own.

A methodology of life cycles

Cycles and recurring phenomena are probably one of the most basic subjects of study in research. While some cycles may be as old as research itself (think of astronomical cycles), the cycle has regained prominence during the past decades as a method and explanatory model. The cycle has become appropriated by mechanics and integrated into machine construction. As such, cycles inspire research and development in anything from engineering to business planning and software release (see Covin and Slevin, 1990; Alting and Jørgensen, 1993; Butterfield, Ngondi, and Kerr, 2016). Especially in the context of digital data, life cycles have become an instrument to provide a detailed plan for data management in research projects. Such life cycles typically lead from collecting data, to processing, preserving, accessing, and re-using it (Van den Eynden, 2014). What most of these cyclical models have in common, however, is that they are written as a manual for humans to plan, implement, and manage a phenomenon. These life cycles take the manipulative role of humans as a given and formulate concrete steering instructions for each phase in the life cycle, while the phenomenon itself – software, the market, data, machines – remains lifeless. Luciano Floridi (2010) discusses the information life cycle. Here, the life cycle is, however, entirely metaphorical, because information itself is understood as de-physicalized and typified (Floridi, 2010). In that information life cycle, information is neither matter, nor does it exhibit life or liveliness, which makes us wonder what the term information life cycle actually implies. Consequently, these life cycles are not what this chapter seeks to forward as a research tool, because they are based on an ontology of splits and conceptualize information as disembodied essence. The cycle, however, also signals life, ageing, and eventually a sense of connectedness to other cycles, to ecologies of life cycles. Early vitalists, such as Georges Canguilhem, have provided an important shift of perspective:

> Most work has used mechanism and its account of 'the structure and function of an already-constructed machine' to explain 'the structure and function of an organism'. Much less common has been the reverse, to understand the construction of the machine on the basis of the organism. (KL 101/76 quoted in Elden, 2019: 44)

In organisms we find a whole set of different cycles: there is 'a vicariousness of functions, a polyvalence of organs' (KL 117/88–9 in Elden, 2019), we see 'self-construction, self-conservation, self-regulation and self-repair' (KL 116/88 in Elden, 2019; see Drucker, 2013), which ultimately gives the organism a 'greater latitude of action' (KL 118/90 in Elden, 2019) than the machine. Using the organism to look at the machine is thus a fruitful way to 'understand the machine, rather than simply explain it. To understand it is to situate it in the context of human history, itself embedded in an understanding of human life' (KL 20/91–2 in Elden, 2019: 48).

Even though Canguilhem ultimately sees a split between organisms and machines, humans and non-humans, his idea of referencing the organism as an explanatory model for machinic phenomena comes close to the notion of grasping materiality mentioned earlier. It is an important step that allows us to rethink the role of *life* in life cycles. By referring to the life cycle as it emerges from organic contexts, it can provide the basis for both, a methodology and method to grasp materialization. Indeed, the life cycle is a concrete tool to understand 'forms and forces at work' (Coole and Frost, 2010: 36), including more enduring structures of phenomena, as well as their 'vulnerability to ruptures and transformation – all the while acknowledging that they have no predestined, necessary, or predictable trajectory' (Drucker, 2013). Johanna Drucker, too, sees the need for such methodical tools. Changing the focus from '*what is* to that *which is always in flux*' (Drucker, 2013, emphasis in original) leads us necessarily 'into the lifecycle of production, use, control, resource consumption, labor, cost, environmental impact and so on – so that an artifact's materiality is read as a snapshot moment within continuous interdependent systems' (2013: online).

The life cycle forwarded here corresponds also with Karen Barad's view on materiality as 'dynamic (re)configurings of the world', 'open-ended practices', as always 'intra-acting with other apparatuses' and as constantly moving boundaries (2003: 816–17). It also speaks to David Ribes' historical approach to materials: 'They May Come, Go, or Change' (Ribes, 2019: 57). All of these contributions already hint at different turns in the life cycle of technologies or information. But not only material phenomena live lives. Methods and methodical tools, too, are part of materializations and as that, they also live a social life: they 'cannot be treated as a "given" … but are themselves subject to multiple mobilizations' (Savage, 2013: 10). In tracing life cycles we render the relations visible that make materializations. We study relations 'that allow certain actions, behavior, readings, events to occur' (Drucker, 2013: online). Life cycles help us identifying moments of encounter (Vertesi, 2019) when different lives meet and influence each other.

The methodology of life cycles developed here is not concerned with recurring orders and perfect circles. Instead, it emphasizes that life cycles can be messy. Cycles can ungrow, begin anew, be disrupted and re-cycle. Within one life cycle we can follow how the spectacular integrates with the mundane (see Ruppert, Law, and Savage, 2013: 33). Life cycles can trace those moments when matter resists falling into the shapes required of a material (Ingold, 2011) or when matter becomes lively and pushes into new directions (Kaufmann, 2020). The 'life' in the life cycle, then, brings a refined understanding of vitality to materialization. Vitality refers on the one hand to the vital importance of those involved in mattering, and on the other hand it relates to the liveliness of ourselves, the tools we use, the materials we study and become-with. The life in life cycles expresses a concern with the embodied existence of the matter we study and its liveliness (see Harding, 2015; Lupton, 2018). Life cycles invite us to take the perspective of the matter we study. They always represent a view from somewhere (Harding, 2015). Thus, the methodology comes close to the idea of 'object biographies' (Halton, 2011), where a life story is told from an object's angle. Using the life cycle can be considered an investment of care, especially when we end up speaking on behalf of something that cannot speak (Monea and Edwards, 2016 on Latour), when we trace that which remains otherwise invisible (Bowker et al, 2010) or in the realm of the unconscious (Thrift, 2005). Finally, the life cycle also finds intersections with our own lives. It invites us to look in all directions when we try to grasp matter, including the influence on and of ourselves.

In sum, a methodology of life cycles mobilizes the study and critique of materializations. It is a method to study making, processes, and interactions. It gives us a framework to follow matter from one material state to another (see Hayles, 1999), as opposed to reducing it to representationalism, hard materiality, or inert matter. Life cycles trace how something comes to matter within its set of relations. It is a method that helps us appreciating specificity, pointing to the 'fine edges' that Latour (1990: 15–16) asks us to pay attention to. We can compare overlapping life cycles to 'tease out differences' and nuances in how materials matter differently (Ruppert, Law, and Savage, 2013: 32) or become irrelevant. This method may not only assist us in identifying that which is critical, but also where critical engagement is needed. Most important, it acknowledges that we never conduct research alone, that any understanding is co-created and co-owned by the lives of those we meet on the way.

Life cycles and their turns

Rather than presenting the life cycles of specific tools (see Kaufmann, 2019), datasets (see Kaufmann et al, 2020; Kaufmann and Leese, 2021), or professions at this stage, this chapter provides a more general outline of *turns* that can recur throughout different life cycles. In order to clarify the relevance of the life cycle, however, the turns are illustrated with generic examples from the life cycle of digital data. While any other matter could have been chosen to exemplify the life cycle, digital data already give some indications about what it may mean to make *information* matter – especially in the context of surveillance practices. The life cycle is not a rigid method. Not only do life cycles encourage alliances with other methodological concepts, but life cycles also move at different speeds. Any of the turns I am going to suggest look different in specific case studies. Turns do not always follow the same sequence, new turns are added, others disappear, and sometimes it is worth investigating just one turn in depth. The primary aim of this chapter, then, is to utilize the life cycle to multiply the foci on materialization and its specificities.

As mentioned before, I borrow the notion of the 'turn' from Karen Barad (2003: 326). The term is not particularly central to her account of posthumanist performativity and she does not use the turn in relation to life cycles. She does, however, deploy it to argue for the moments at which change takes place: 'The future is radically open at every turn' (Barad, 2003). The tool of the life cycle and its turns serves here as a facilitator to research exactly these openings for liveliness, agency, and change. It is a methodical instrument to find intersections with other life cycles, to describe collaborations and to document which turn is actually taken. Indeed, turns are always turns towards a specific materialization and away from its alternatives. To be specific, since materialization is an ongoing process, there are no turns as such. Or as Tim Ingold and Elizabeth Hallam state: 'growth is going on all the time: you do not register it as change, or as a transition from A to B, but as life itself' (2016: 4). However, studying such continuousness empirically is a challenge. This is why we can consider turns as summaries of significant changes, transitions, or thresholds in materializations. Ingold and Hallam also mention 'rites of passage' (2016), which happen in any life. Notions such as the cycle or spiral remind us that any of such turns or rites of passage are really an ongoing process of mattering.

Imaginaries

Considering that materialization is an ongoing process, it is difficult to find a clear entry point to studying materializations. Any first turn would be artificial. One could argue that it would be natural to start a life cycle with generation, with new matter emerging. And yet, our studies always start from some matter that already exists. And this existing matter necessarily influences our ideas and imaginaries about materiality as well as matters that are to be generated (Callon, 2004, 1986). The relevance of this first turn is thus to express this positionality. Even this view from somewhere may not be a clear-cut, straightforward one. Thus, what could be a fruitful entry point to study materializations is to understand the situations and discussions that precede new materializations. We could summarize this turn as *imaginaries* (see Kaufmann et al, 2020). In a sense, it studies what happens before matter is engaged with or new matter comes into being. Imaginaries refer to explicit or implicit preconceptions and expectations about matter. Imaginaries also express strategic ignorances (McGoey, 2012) – the ideas that are deliberately excluded, undercut, or hollowed out when matter is thought of. In projects, imaginaries are most prominent in the phase where a need for a specific solution is discussed, but they can reoccur and change throughout a complete life cycle. Not every person involved in mattering is aware of imaginaries and yet it refers to a crucial turn in the life cycle as it creates possibilities for specific matter to emerge, it defines what matter will be worked with and how. It is here where different imaginaries mix, where translations become necessary and boundary objects appear (see Star and Griesemer, 1989).

Say we want to study the materialization of a new dataset. Such a project starts from somewhere. And this somewhere is quite influential for how the dataset comes about. Lisa Gitelman and Virginia Jackson point to the imaginaries that are crucial for data to appear: 'data need to be imagined as data to exist and function as such, and the imagination of data entails an interpretive base' (2013: 3). The imagination of data determines how it will materialize. Every institution, every discipline, potentially every person involved in a data project has their tradition for imagining data. What are the root assumptions about data? Are data considered calculative material, where the intention of the new dataset would be to integrate them into statistics and associations? Are data considered malleable, where a new dataset would be seen as necessarily ambiguous? What are the strategic ignorances inherent in such conceptualizations? Imaginaries about the format, standardization, and classification of data tend to be subjected to heated debate (Leonelli, 2016). There is – often invisible and unpaid – effort spent on negotiating these aspects before data even materialize. If this effort is not spent at this stage of the project, differences in imaginaries cause knock-on effects at a later stage. Data imaginaries concern their material, social, and ethical dimension. At this turn of a dataset's life cycle intersections with other life cycles already become prominent. There are intersections with the life cycles of pre-existing datasets or data technologies, the life cycles of the people imagining data, the life cycle of data as an abstract term, just to name a few.

To find out how different imaginaries matter, it is fruitful to be present at project planning phases. If no discussion about imaginaries takes place here, it is worth scheduling conversations to ask further questions to those involved. If there is no official planning phase, for example when datasets are not tied to a concrete project, one can still try to identify key persons and materials that were involved in the creation of the dataset and explore which imaginaries they embody. Alternatively, one can trace the conceptual history of the studied material. One can explore existing materials that are likely to influence the generation of the new material. First sketches, outlines, plans and prototypes and the concepts they convey are also great ways to capture imaginaries about specific materials. Approaching imaginaries also implies identifying who has influence on what matters and is (not) going to matter, and why they have that influence. Remember that materials, tools, and infrastructures, too, have built-in imaginaries. Bruno Latour would describe these as inscriptions (1987). That is, materials can be stubborn and potentially exercise more influence in materialization processes than people.

Generation

Not all imaginaries actualize during materializations. When matter comes to life, it takes a turn towards a specific instantiation and away from its countless alternatives. It is here that space for agency appears: all matters involved in mattering shape together what kind of matter emerges. Even if the matter that comes to life is ambiguous, leaving room for several imaginaries to co-exist, generation, too, is a turn at which power plays out. Those involved in materialization have influence over the matter that appears. This influence is sometimes more and sometimes less obvious. It can be connected to intentions, or not. In order to study what happens at this turn, it is crucial to map all the different actors – humans, tools, and other materials – involved in the process and how all of them come together in a specific act of generating material. Do they work together effortlessly or are there frictions? What are the respective imaginaries that all the different actors stand for? Is there already a plan for how to handle and potentially put an ending to matter at this stage? While it can be fascinating to see which non-human actors, such as instruments, technologies, or spatial conditions, influence materializations, it is also here that room for human agency exists. How all of these matters interact is thus not only a matter of ethics (what should materialize? See Chapter 8), but how material is generated influences its further development.

Let us return to the example of a dataset. Digital data do not exist per se. They need to materialize, they need to be generated (Manovich, 2001). Imagining data and generating them are intertwined processes, as data are often generated for a purpose and in line with specific imaginaries (see Kaufmann et al, 2020). Which types of data can capture specific imaginaries best? And what imaginaries are really reflected in a dataset? This generation – the birth of data – requires labour. It is work to generate data. How data are made influences what they will be used for and how they are re-used. Purpose-driven data generation is informed by ideas about what kinds of data are expected to match a purpose. Incidental data generation may introduce purposefulness along with further imaginaries at later steps. In addition, we can also think of a re-generation of data: some data were already generated with a different aim in mind, but are scraped and collected now for a new purpose. Both purposeful and incidental data generation reflect imaginaries about what is true, knowable, acceptable, and complete. The recent activist and scholarly trend of distinguishing between 'good data' (see Mann et al, 2018) and 'bad data' (Galdon Clavell, 2018) is indicative of reflections about the ways in which data imaginaries and data generation speak to each other. In these articles, data are understood to either embrace or disrespect fundamental rights, which implies that datasets can reproduce social in/equalities from the moment of their creation. While discussions about data as 'good' or 'bad' follow specific ethical imaginaries, this book emphasizes that, taken together, moments of imagining and generating data channel the further journey of data. Another aspect of this turn is the question if data imaginaries and their generation already plan for data endings.

The generation of data is also subject to practical restrictions: some data may not be in the right format for tools to process, others are too costly (financially or in terms of harm done when generated) or they may not be directly usable for the foreseen purpose. How data materialize is also dependent on the conditions of existing technologies for data-generation. The generation of digital data can start out with analogue specimens, for example when biological samples are taken (see Ribes, 2019; Skinner and Wienroth, 2019). These specimens then have to be translated into digital data and during this translation again new influences come into play that co-determine what digital data will eventually be generated. Digital data are also generated when administrative forms are filled, in which the tool of the form already structures the data available at a later stage. Here, the data generated is also highly dependent on the human filling the form. Routines – sometimes machinic routines – are then also part of generating data. Increasingly, sensors are used for data generation. The designs and inscriptions of such sensors also influence the data that is eventually captured.

With the creation of any dataset, metadata are generated, too. Edwards et al remind us that such metadata are often produced spontaneously, where '(b)oth the metadata categories and the contents of those categories remain in flux' (2011: 676). In spite of that, metadata influences the further life and use of data. The agencies of all these actors then lead to the specific dataset. This implies, however, that alternative data and datasets are neglected, forgotten, lost, or invisibilized.

The few examples of data generation mentioned earlier already reveal the many intersections with other life cycles during this turn. The life cycles of other technologies and instruments are relevant, the life cycles of those who operate these instruments and write data are part of materializations. Administrative matters, too, such as the life cycles of routines and budgets, influence the dataset under study.

The best way to study this turn is to be present when the actual generation takes place, whether that is in a workshop, a lab, an office, a natural environment, in a smart city grid, a design studio or a software company – just to name a few. It is important to remember that not all processes of materialization happen according to a specific design or plan or as part of a project. For example, rituals and routines can be interesting vantage points to study materializations, too. Thus, the choice of the sites for more spontaneous materializations has to be taken with care. Templates, manuals and instructions for the procedure of generation can be studied and compared to what generation actually looks like in practice. Here, versioning and renewed attempts at generating the desired outcome can give insight into the negotiations between humans, tools, and information in the creation of something new. A different entry point to study generation is to study the design of the support instruments, those that are needed to create a specific outcome. It helps to see them in action, but also to have them evaluated and explained by the people who created and work with them. Conversations with generators – designers, builders, makers – are not only viable alternatives to observing sites and instruments in action, but they often give insight into decisions about the why and how of a specific generation. In conversations, we can ask about design decisions, contestations, frictions, losses, and failed attempts. Indeed, supposedly failed attempts of generating matter could also be an interesting starting point to study the generation of desired materials. Why did it fail? What was considered a failure? Did that lead to a new attempt to generate?

Maturation

Matter is not finished when it is generated, but materialization is an ongoing process. This turn refers to the many ways in which matter matures. Maturation does not refer to a desired process (something ends up being mature), but it describes how matter changes and develops once it is generated. This can include activities related to versioning, which we find in the lives of many technical devices. Maturing can involve processes of 'training' and 'learning' as is the case with algorithms, or beta-testing as is the case with applications and many other products. Matter also matures when it is collected, accumulated, and stored for specific purposes. Maturation happens when matter and materials are curated and cleaned. Any act of maintenance and caretaking, fixing, repairing, tuning, enhancing, hacking, overhauling is maturation. Maturation describes thus a collection of all the different turns that proceed generation.

Maturation includes aspects relating to operation. It describes the way in which materials come to matter within their environments. If we liken *generation* to the birth of matter, and *maturation* to its adolescence and continued training, then *operation* would be its occupation. Operation is not its own turn, but a special form of maturing. Altogether, maturation is influenced by all preceding turns, but may also overturn them. Indeed, many forms of maturation revisit, influence and change imaginaries as well as they regenerate matter.

Let us understand maturation in the context of digital data. Once generated, digital data mature and grow in many ways. Some of these processes are characteristic of most data life cycles, which is why I mention them here. For example, digital data have a tendency to pile up: 'The word data has become what is called a mass noun, so it can take a singular verb. ... Data's odd suspension between the singular and the plural reminds us of what aggregation means' (Gitelman and Jackson, 2013: 8).

Not only are data aggregative, but digital data can also not exist without storage. Storage is a substantial aspect of data maturation. All digital data need to be contained. How data are stored, for how long, where and in which institution, who gets access and not, co-determines the materiality of data and their use. Especially rules and infrastructures for what data can be contained actively shape data (Kaufmann et al, 2020). Some data containers are 'archives' in the narrow sense of the word (Beer and Burrows, 2013). If data are archived for preservation, digital data can get stuck and remain there, which influences their further materialization. Understood more broadly, archives can also include databases of any kind (Thylstrup et al, 2021). While databases are often perceived as something just there, at hand, we need to remember that 'any infrastructure that has been the target topic of activities has probably also been the object of passionate debates'

(Bowker et al, 2010: 99). Indeed, Geoffrey Bowker reminds us of the history of databases: while early versions required users to go deep down into the structure of databases to retrieve one datum, today's databases enable new practices of relating datasets to each other. Thus, data storage, and its own life cycle, is part of mattering. The constitution of storage, its technical specifications, the frameworks for inclusion and exclusion of data, data labelling, standards in formatting (Edwards, 2004), categories, and hierarchies influence the further materialization of digital data.

Digital data also mature when they are curated, selected, or cleaned. Any dataset has to integrate with rules for storage. Some of these rules are broadly defined, others very narrow. Many datasets are not just stored, but actively curated or cleaned in line with the aspired operation. What counts as significant data? According to which type of data analysis are they significant? That is, digital data keep on materializing as they are actively engaged with. Kevin Brine and Mary Poovey (2013) describe the often-unnoticed labour of 'data scrubbing' that renders information commensurate to analyses, for example, by making it amenable to calculations: 'This process of commensuration, which could also be called "cleansing" or "amending," involved removing incorrect or inconvenient elements from the available data, supplying missing information, and formatting it so that it would fit the other data' (2013: 71, quotation marks in original).

Cleaning and scrubbing suggest that something is taken away from the dataset. However, it is equally relevant to consider that datasets are also reviewed, adapted, and revised by completing and adding information. One can consider, for example, the idea of adding synthetic data to datasets that are used to train algorithms in order to balance biases (De Vries, 2020). Another important act expressing the maturation of data are data labelling processes and categorization, especially when datasets are prepared for algorithmic processing (Jaton, 2021). There may be 'data frictions' (Edwards, 2010) when data move between different matters, or from one turn to the next. By doing so, 'data friction consumes energy and produces turbulence and heat – that is, conflicts, disagreements, and inexact, unruly processes' (Edwards et al, 2011: 669). Frictions can even occur within the same institutions, when, for example, team members cannot agree on the parameters for scrubbing, curating, or labelling data or when data analysts curate data differently from those who prepared and own datasets (Kaufmann, 2019; Mannov et al, 2020). Not least, friction can occur because digital data themselves can be lively. At times, data occur in unexpected databases or contexts, where they refuse to disappear. Such liveliness always occurs in the ways specific to the qualities of information.

When in operation, digital data also mature. Digital data always come to matter in the context of specific tasks, for example when they are being processed. To some, the whole life cycle is data processing. What I am referring to here is, for example, the moment data are used to train a tool or are processed by a tool. Here, developers match data to parameters that they are interested in. Sometimes, such operations are the long-planned result of data imaginaries, generation, and maturation. However, more often than not, digital data matter and materialize within all sorts of operations, not always in accordance with original visions. This is the case when datasets are re-used, an aspect the next turn will expand on. Another reason for this can be that different processes of maturation change original visions along the way, or digital data become lively and follow their own, emergent vocations (Kaufmann, 2020).

These are only a few of the processes that characterize the maturation of digital data. There are many more forms of maturation that could be discussed here, such as data representations and visualizations. The mentioned examples are only an invitation to multiply the study of data maturations.

Since this turn relates to many kinds of maturation processes, it is not necessarily constructive to list all possible intersections with other life cycles. The case of digital data, for example, suggests that there are intersections with the life cycles of data storage capacities, data cleaners, and the instruments used for cleaning, the life cycles of labels, standards, metadata, or the instruments that data are subjected to when analysed.

The study of maturation is never complete. It is thus helpful to first map maturation processes before deciding on what may be the key changes to focus on. Key changes are those that matter. Here, it is revealing to take a closer look at those processes that seem a given, where labour is at first invisible. Inquiring about training phases, observing beta-tests, and asking further questions about the why and how of versions can reveal hidden processes of maturation. We can study where and how materials are kept and stored. We can study their storage facilities, public and private, and understand how their construction influences the material under study. We can read frameworks, guides, rules, standards, and hierarchies that play a role in storage or in the versioning of materials. Here, frictions are of particular interest as they reveal which agencies get a chance to realize and influence the further materialization process. We can study how materials are curated, maintained, and repaired: breakdowns are then a starting point to observe troubleshooting. When we encounter the many life cycles that are part of materializations, it is important not to be distracted from the material we originally set out to study. Indeed, we also want to understand the material's own liveliness and how it enables specific materializations.

Death, decay, and re-generation

When one life cycle comes to an end, new intersections, cycles, and spiral dances always begin. Death and decay, then, are not counterposed to life and liveliness, but rather a part of it (see Lash, 2006). Death only becomes an actual endpoint when matter can no longer become-with other matters. Death occurs when matter no longer matters, when it remains set and when 'it stopped being a possibility' (Steyerl, 2013). In many cases, endings can become ethically controversial processes: some may consider the endings of materials as necessary, while others precisely argue the opposite. Practically, however, we will see that such endpoints can not only be hard to identify, but many times actual endings may not occur (Skinner and Wienroth, 2019). Many materials, in fact, undergo a passage from one life to another. In this part, I will mainly focus on moments when materialization slows down. I will observe ends of life cycles and thresholds to new emergences.

It is no surprise that the writings about making and becoming-with that inspired this book also reflect about the relationship between life, liveliness, and death. Maybe it is because it is hard or uncomfortable to grasp a complete cessation of existence, a nontology, or maybe it is because we are currently in a world where we focus on how mattering matters that we find a strong commitment to a 'continued birth' (Merleau-Ponty, 1964; Ingold, 2011) instead of death. Tim Ingold describes it as being 'in a world that is not preordained but incipient, forever on the verge of the actual' (2011: 69). It is an ontology of continually being 'present as witness to that moment, always moving like the crest of a wave at which the world is about to disclose itself for what it is' (Ingold, 2011: 69). This understanding of continued birth also extends to making, where objects are never finished, but finishing rather refers to their phase of use (see Ingold and Hallam, 2016). This is much in line with this turn in the life cycle that we may consider death, decay, and re-generation. It is an integral phase of materialization. Often, this turn is a slowing down, an ending of a specific type of material or a break before new material emerges. All making, Tim Ingold and Elizabeth Hallam write, 'in a sense, entails breaking, just as all growth entails decomposition' (2016: 8). They further describe the centrality of this turn to life at large:

> lives of making and growing are never lived in isolation but always in the company of others ... And since life is a process ... of 'growing older together', one person's decline may be another's growth. Thus as even lives come and go, life itself is carried on. (Ingold and Hallam, 2016: 9)

This vital company and companionship is also captured in Donna Haraway's 'we are all compost' (2015b: 161). She famously describes this fundamental way of becoming-with, of being in the company of others in living and dying as compost. 'If you're in compost, the questions of finitude and mortality are prominent, not in some kind of depressive or tragic way, but those who will return our flesh to the Earth are in the making of compost' (Donna Haraway in Franklin, 2017: 51). In tying composting to humus, the raw material that bios come from and return to, she mainly observes the lives, deaths, and decay of biological matter and materials. As an approach, however, compost applies to any matter, including 'cyborgian politics' (Donna Haraway in Franklin, 2017: 53). More important, composting is an ontological, not a normative statement:

> You can neglect your compost. You can put the wrong things into it, … You can put it in an inappropriate place … Compost is a place of working, a place of making and unmaking. And it can be a place of failure, including, well, culpable failure. Compost can be a place of doing badly. (Donna Haraway in Franklin, 2017: 51)

Compost includes turns of composing, decomposing, recomposing, and compositions (see Frost, 2016). Just like a methodology of life cycles, it emphasizes the making and doing of the many different matters or 'species' (Donna Haraway in Franklin, 2017: 52). It points to the histories and that which the present inherits, including de- and recompositions.

Tim Ingold and Elizabeth Hallam describe death, decay, and re-generation as a threshold (2016; see Lupton, 2018). While some matter ends, many break and disintegrate before they pass into a new cycle. Especially when it comes to digital information the question is less whether technologies or information, data and algorithms die, but at what point a specific life cycle comes to an end and when a new quality of matter emerges. Thus, death and decay can be linked to re-use, imaginaries, and generation. It is for that reason – that all turns hang together – that we speak about cycles and spirals. Together, they signal iterated materializations rather than afterlives, as afterlives would tie matter to a specific task. Throughout these iterations, matter follows new visions and vocations (Kaufmann, 2020). The historicity of preceding life cycles, however, is also always present in the emerging new lives. Indeed, re-imagining brings about 'memories of the future', a term I borrow from the musician René Aubry (2006). In the methodology of life cycles it expresses that there once was a vision tied to a specific matter, which may or may not have materialized, and is now reimagined. Again, it is crucial to understand that neither re-generation, nor continued birth and composting are necessarily normative statements in the sense that death and re-imagination bring about something desired. As we all know, death and loss involve pain. And as the studies of necropolitics (Mbembe, 2003) have shown, they also involve acts and decisions of power over ways of living and dying. In lives and life cycles we witness the (sometimes dramatic) loss of matter, there are unintended and undesired forms of materializations and forms of becoming-with that not everyone appreciates. We also witness the planning for and the difficulty of administering endings. The only time in which death really implies a cessation is when matter no longer matters.

How can we understand this turn in relation to digital data? One could argue that a life cycle of digital data comes to an end with their deletion. Their deletion releases energy (Landauer, 1961), which signals quite a substantial re-materialization, while their deletion also leaves hardware behind. Much legislation, in fact, foresees a deletion of data. From the field of bio-information, however, we know that endings are subject to intense ethical discussions: how can and when should data end? When do we have the problem of orphan data, 'divorced from a guardian and often difficult to trace to their sources' (see Kowal, 2013: 577)? David Skinner and Matthias Wienroth formulate additional problems: Do we know enough about data erasure and can a dataset ever fully disappear? To what extend does a data ending depend 'on the registers within which it is enacted' (2019: 23)? Indeed, deletion is probably not the most common end of the life cycle of digital data. In fact, Jean-Francois Blanchette reminds us that especially digital data are notoriously hard to delete (2011). Sometimes, they have a surprising capacity to survive on specific hardware. Alternative ends of life cycles are transformations of digital data into new file formats (Kirschenbaum, 2007). Most likely is, however, their decay in the form of their disintegration into sub-datasets and their re-integration into new ones. Here, data are reimagined and amalgamate with other data into new data projects. Louise Amoore, for example, mentions data derivatives: 'disaggregated fragments of data, inferred from across the gaps between data and projected onto an array of uncertain futures' (Amoore, 2011: 24). David Beer and Roger Burrows critically trace different modi of data circulations (2013), where digital data matter differently in each setting. Digital data have a tendency to spiral, decompose, and come back. It is through such forms of decay that datasets are basically taken in part out of context and are made to creep. And this is where a specific aspect of the materiality of digital data has become increasingly decisive during the past years. Due to their digital form, their traceability and storability, digital data are no longer subject to function creep, but, as Mark Andrejevic and Kelly Gates (2014) formulate critically: their function is to creep. This is mirrored in what Rob Kitchin also describes as creeping control, where the control over data steadily creeps into new domains (Kitchin, 2021: 2016). Digital data are countable and any data count. Thus, there are no real data residues, because any data matters – not necessarily in an instrumental way, but nonetheless in a generative, constitutive one. The specific materiality of data has given rise to their function as re-usable. Thus, even dormant and forgotten data can be rematerialized in new or intersecting life cycles.

In line with the 'memories of the future' mentioned earlier, it is also clear that simply by re-using datasets for a new purpose, they are not suddenly stripped of the original context in which they were generated (see Kaufmann et al, 2020). In fact, many datasets are generated and collected in precarious situations, which imbues them with their original context. Thus, if data are 'given' – given and inherited from somewhere or someone into a new situation – we can also ask when and under what conditions data are 'taken away' to be reintegrated into new data life cycles. This raises indeed critical questions as to when data can rest and remain in one materialized dataset? When are data allowed to no longer matter, especially because re-use also always matters to related data subjects? Such challenges concerning re-use are also true for doing research with datasets that have not been generated for the purpose of doing research.

We see that even in death, decay, and re-generation intersections with various life cycles exist, most notably that of the new, emergent life cycle. There are the lives and life cycles of those who actively seek to put an end to a specific matter, who break it, as well as those who remake it. These are the lives of those who re-integrate and regenerate, who perform labour, are in labour, and give birth. There are intersections with the life cycles of other materials that play a crucial role in recycling, whether these are microbes or computer programs.

In order to study death, decay, and re-generation, we should be present when life cycles slow down. We observe those moments when something breaks spontaneously or slowly (see Bowker et al, 2010), but also when it is actively put to rest. Decay can also be studied over time – as something that happens in parallel to maturation. Death and decay can happen at offices, but also outside at dumps of any kind. They can also happen at those places where breaking and making is officially experimented with, as for example in labs, workshops, or studios. Endings may happen as a result of a materialization or as per legislation. It is important to be patient when we study the ends of life cycles and the beginnings of new ones as decomposition and re-composition can take time and are not always intended or visible. For some cases, it is fruitful to take present materials as a vantage point and trace their histories, earlier materializations, and life cycles that came to an end and fed into the particular matter under study. Being present when imaginaries for materials are openly discussed is also a possible vantage point to find out whether data actually end or whether derivatives or specific other materials emerge as a possibility for re-use. Studying such discussions is also important when one wants to identify the memories that influence present and future materials.

A spiral dance

As scholars, but also as humans, we have been trained to conclude. Originally, concludere means 'to shut up' and 'enclose' (Harper, nd). Knowing the world, however, is not about finding closure and shutting up. It is an ongoing process. There are many outcomes, but none of them are a final result. This chapter was an invitation to grasp a world in becoming. Here, studying the breaking and making of matter is to study liveliness. The methodology of life cycles raises awareness about the turns matter takes. Any turn is critical to what comes to matter. Any turn witnesses the lively details of materialization, including the lives and life cycles of those who take part in it.

On this backdrop, it is not relevant if we end up calling a tool a *maker*, or whether we say that information *grows* us. The overarching aim of the methodology is to continue and deepen the argument that scholars of materiality have laid out, namely to destabilize the boundaries established between life/matter, organic/inorganic, human/non-human (see Barad 2003; Bennett 2010a). It is together that we make matter. Thus, this is a methodology of life cycles, plural. Life cycles are never isolated. They always intersect. Together they join into a 'spiral dance' (Haraway, 1991: 181). Though Donna Haraway uses this expression to describe the relationship between goddesses and cyborgs, I would like to use the term here to capture the ongoing dance that takes place in materializations. The spiral dance describes a living ecology of intersections. This methodology of life cycles situates itself, then, in a rich tradition of studying relations (Bowker et al, 2010), companionships (Haraway, 2015b), ecologies (Bennett, 2010b), intra-actions (Barad, 2003), in-betweens (Star and Ruhleder, 1996), collectivities (Forlano, 2019), where it combines the study of materializations with vitality. It is not geared towards closures, final resolutions, and conclusions, but it studies overlaps and becoming.

These mutual influences will not go away as our lives keep developing. Matter is going to remain productive within our lives. Thus, we need to understand how we *become-with* it (Haraway, 2015b). Methodologically, life cycles acknowledge the messiness that comes with mutuality, but they suggest a set of entry points to study the mutuality, criticality, and specificity of emergent matter. Life cycles provide focus, but also invite us to reflect, inspire, brainstorm, and expand: which turns and what other life cycles are relevant in the study of a specific matter? And how can we best study such turns and cycles? While immersion and fieldwork, disassembling tools, studying manuals, and observing matter in action are always giving methods, life cycles can help deliberating: for example, what can conversations tell me about a life that manuals cannot – and vice versa?

Studying life cycles also invites us to select and treat our conversation partners with care. When we study specific turns, how can we create more diversity in those we learn from (see Harding, 2015)? Are there lives that are usually forgotten, pushed aside, less invisible, or neglected in the collective process of making matter? Are there lives that deliberately decrease their visibility? Are there lives that we tend not to study, because they are hard-to-reach? We can learn from human individuals and groups, but also non-humans. In my own studies, I tend to combine observation with conversations, because they allow me to ask questions about the why and how, about imaginaries and intersections, which may not always become visible from observation alone.

The methodology of life cycles also considers doing research as a way of making matter. This raises the question as to how we become critical and how we give back? Not only are we part of providing critical knowledge, but the methodology also invites us to give back to those involved in our studies. It is, after all, a privilege to be granted access to sites, to be integrated in processes we study, or to receive the time and answers of the people involved in our studies. Producing research relevant to the groups we study is one way of becoming critical and of giving back. A rich tradition for alternative ways of transferring knowledge, or acknowledging the collaborative dimension of making knowledge, already exists, including making prototypes, performing art, organizing events or dedicated special sections at conferences. Sandra Harding (2015), in addition, points to the platforms that we can give to specific lives, for example by letting them define our research agenda or by letting them be actors in our research, or rather: to create research and insight together. A methodology of life cycles, then, encourages us to engage, as well as to collaborate, include, and give back to research more broadly.

Interlude: Four Practices of Making Information Matter

Making information matter is a 'spiral dance' (Haraway, 1991: 181). It is an ongoing process involving many lives that make, break, and remake what matters in this world. As researchers, we are part of this dance. The central concern is thus no longer *that* information, tools, infrastructures and our own selves matter, but *how*. This is why the next chapters provide analyses of four different practices that are maybe not all equally prevalent in societies today, but equally relevant. All of them are enacted in the larger arena of surveillance, capture, and control, which is where information matters centrally.

The first one, *association*, is a defining information practice in today's societies. Often, but not always, association is practiced in digital, information-heavy environments where algorithms and other forms of analyses are used to identify connections, relationships, and patterns. In most cases, association is used for capture and control and it has potentially become the most prevalent form of governance in densely digitized environments. That is why it is all the more important to render associative practices more accessible by tracing each step, each turn at which information comes to matter. There is awareness about associative practices and how much they influence us. Their formative powers are recognized and discomfort about being subjected to them, or participating in their making is increasingly expressed. Critical voices from mainstream public discourses include those of Eli Pariser (The Filter Bubble, 2011), Yuval Harari (Homo Deus, 2017), Shoshana Zuboff (The Age of Surveillance Capitalism, 2019), and Farhad Manjoo (journalist, *The New York Times*), to name a few. What mainstream discourses do not (yet) do sufficiently is to acknowledge alternative ways of making information matter – whether these are spectacular or everyday activities. This is why I want to give extra space to another three practices of making information matter that create 'cracks of possibility' (Zach Blas, interview) within predominant regimes of capture, control, and association. None of these practices represent an exodus from informationalized societies. They still imagine, generate, process, and re-use information, but they make it matter differently. All of them make that difference from within information-rich, digitized environments. They draw their energy from the possibility of alternatives to associative regimes.

One such practice is *conversion*, the idea of changing the materiality of information deliberately, of finding new functions and roles for information and infrastructures. Amongst other reasons, this is done to circumvent or exploit the ways in which information is usually analysed. Conversion reduces not merely the visibility of information, but seeks to influence how information is made sense of. Such practices break with routines and play with the affordance of information as well as information technologies.

Another practice of engaging critically with veillance is *secrecy*. Practices of secrecy have a reputation of being dubious. They are linked to hiding and to secret surveillance. Secrecy as a societal response is often presented as the refuge for those without access to privacy. Such ideas lead to oversimplified dichotomies of secrecy and transparency, veillance and counterveillance, which tend to reinforce each other. Secrecy needs our renewed attention as a way of making information matter. We need to acknowledge it as a multilayered concept (Birchall, 2011, 2014) and take distance from its seeming ethical negativeness (Simmel, 1906). Secrecy can help exercising new forms of agency. It can make information matter in ways that give voice to the overheard and unleash positive affects.

Speculation is also a practice that can intervene in associative regimes. It makes matter by presenting alternative futures (and presents) to dominant modes of information analysis. While doing so, speculation enjoys the advantage of not having to follow routines and expected objectivities that characterize science and administration. It can deliberately provide playful, abstract, subcultural, minoritarian, but powerful examples of imagining otherwise. Speculation can provoke a radical re-orientation of the values embedded in information practices and technologies.

It will become clear that none of these four practices are absolute. They are complex and the boundaries between them are fluid: association can include elements of speculation, especially when used for predictions. Secrecy can deploy techniques of conversion. Many other examples could be mentioned here. Most practices are ambiguous in the sense that they may combine different types of ethics. This also means that none of them can be linked to either surveillance or counterveillance, capturing or being captured, to power or resistance. They defy easy binaries, but one could say that each practice can provide critique and alternatives when performed within particular environments.

I have chosen to study these practices in environments that can offer insights into how information matters in an authentic manner: association, for example, has become a prevalent practice within law enforcement, especially in the field of predictive policing. To study conversion, I turned to hackers and the ways in which they remake information and information infrastructures. Often they hack associative techniques that dominate the online environments in which they dwell. After having studied fields that mainly focus on making *digital* information matter, I wanted to turn to offline or analogue environments. This is why I took a closer look at children in settings where they are watched by their parents, teachers and other children. A typical way of children to respond to this veillance is secrecy. In the end, I wanted to study practices of speculation that use a multitude of different, maybe surprising materials to make information matter, which is why I turned to artists. The ambition was to provide for different perspectives on making information matter, to inspire reflection and open alternative avenues in mainstream discourses about information. In doing so, I also follow David Ribes' (2019) advice to research the specific material properties of information instead of reducing my studies to one type. Combined, these four studies look at a vast range of information, including analogue and digital police data, big data collected in the context of corporate online activity, as well as information that has been altered and mutilated. The four practices involve information in the form of drawings, prints, secret languages, and poetry, as well as highly metrified information. Naturally, the type of infrastructures and tools used to make information matter also varied including hand-filled forms and complex content management systems, raspberry pis, blackboxes, honeypots, self-written programming languages, secret treasure maps, test tubes, CNC milling machines, and 3D printers – just to name a few.

When I now describe and analyse association, conversion, secrecy, and speculation, I will use the methodology of the life cycle to structure each chapter. The life cycle helps me illustrate the different turns that information takes. Each turn – whether it concerns the imaginaries, generation, processing or re-use of information – is decisive for what ultimately matters. The analysis documents details of materialization and the lives of those who take part in it. Life cycles and their turns are not geared towards closures and conclusions, but multiplicities and becoming; they reveal openings for our own engagement.

4

Association

Association has become a central aspect of surveillance and a key practice of making information matter. It is critical to any kind of profiling that we experience on an everyday basis. To associate is to join, to make a connection 'in an interest, object, employment or purpose' (Harper, nd). One of the most widespread ways of analysing information is indeed to make a connection between different datasets. In her work on data derivatives Louise Amoore speaks of an 'ontology of association' (2011: 27). This means that associating data is not just a knowledge practice, but it describes a specific way in which data materialize and come to exist together. The most common approach of associating different datasets with each other follow a Boolean logic (Kitchin, 2016), named after the mathematician George Boole. We know them as if-then rules, that is: when *if* is true, *then* is executed. By means of if-then instructions disaggregated data are associated 'to derive a lively and alert new form of data derivative – a flag, map or score that will go on to live and act in the world' (Amoore, 2011: 27). The aim of associative practices is to connect different sets of information and to derive patterns from them (Kaufmann, Egbert, and Leese, 2019). What is more, such patterns, again, are likely to be associated with actions that matter to society. Whether a pattern is considered meaningful and actionable depends on many aspects, not least those involved in associating.

Association is a classic analytic practice, which is also used to process analogue information. With the rise of digital information, however, association has shifted in terms of reach and quality. With the advent of big, digital databases association is exercised at a different scale. In the shape of algorithms, association rules powerfully determine consumer behaviour and sales transactions, to name one of the most prevalent forms of profiling in society today (see Agrawal, Imieliński, and Swami, 1993; Agrawal and Srikant, 1994; Srikant and Agrawal, 1995). Already the scientific literature about association rules is extremely widespread, which shows how critical association has become to information practices. By today, association rules and algorithms have grown to shape our life online and offline.

Due to their mathematic form, it is seductive to think of association and algorithms as 'purely formal beings of reason' (Goffey, 2008: 16). Others, however, have discussed association and algorithms as carefully crafted fictions (Gillespie, 2014) with 'social, political and aesthetic dimensions' (Montfort et al, 2012: 3). Whether form or fiction, the practice of association is productive (see Lash, 2007). As a form of making information matter association directs and disciplines attention, 'focusing on specific points and cancelling out all other data, appearing to make it possible to translate *probable* associations ... into *actionable* ... decisions' (Amoore, 2009: 22). Precisely because association is intimately tied to questions about agency, it requires our critical attention.

Studying association can be done with different research attitudes. While Christopher Steiner's critique ultimately suggests getting friendly with 'bots' (2012), Rob Kitchin favours giving critical attention to 'production, deployment and effects' (2016: 9) of rule-based associative methods. A similar stance is reflected in Wendy Chun's call to interrogate the underlying 'assumptions within network science and machine learning' (2021: 22) that give form to information and resulting policy. Eventually, all of these positions imply that 'learning, internalizing, and becoming intimate with' associative practices is a crucial step (Galloway, 2006: 90). Taken together, these methodological standpoints acknowledge the critical relevance of association, which at the same time requires critique. That association matters in society today is indisputable, which is why it is in our own interest to understand and discuss how we are becoming-with association. Or to put it differently: we need to engage with that specific 'companion' called association (see Haraway, 2003; Austin, Bellanova, and Kaufmann, 2019).

In many analyses, the associative rule-set, that is, the algorithm, is the centre of attention (Agrawal, Imieliński, and Swami, 1993; Amoore, 2009; Montfort, 2012; Steiner, 2012; Gillespie, 2014; Kitchin, 2016; Jaton, 2017; Kaufmann, 2019). Association, however, requires not just the study of rules and instructions, but the quality and quantity of information associated is equally important. Practices of association can thus also be studied from the perspective of data and its life cycle (Kaufmann and Leese, 2021), which is what the chapter will focus on.

While it would be possible to study association in many fields, its use for prediction efforts in the security domain has become more and more prevalent. Here, association prompts its own set of challenges. In the early 2000s algorithms made it to the forefront of security practices (Amoore, 2009; Leese, 2014). It was announced that new tools were needed to 'connect the dots' (Chertoff, 2006), for example about terrorist plots (Kaufmann, 2010) and to enable governments to foresee dangerous events in the face of uncertainty (US Joint Inquiry, 2003). Soon, similar tools arrived in the world of policing, where the 'idea is that locating regularities in large and disparate patterns of data can enable associations to be established between apparently suspicious people, places, financial transactions, cargo shipments and so on' (Ericson, 2007; Amoore, 2009: 22).

In the context of my research on predictive policing, which I will introduce in a moment and use to discuss the practice of association, many interviewees mentioned how critically important association has become. Software developer Chris noticed an increasing digitization of police work: "One thing is sure: they're gonna be using computers much more than now." Johannes, head of a predictive policing software development team, too, expects a change in police culture: "Predictive policing will be standard police procedure in 10 years' time. ... It will change policing culture. It will generate new functionalities and new tasks." In fact, police officer Dihyah argued that digital forms of association already *had* an effect on policing. Software developer Frank agrees: "The digital approach allows you to work with much larger quantities of data, which again allows you to recognize patterns in a way that analogue approaches just aren't gonna be capable of doing." Policing expert Erika finds that "(t)here are so many changing patterns in society and I think that data obviously can assist in understanding society better, and that it is a valuable input to the police."

Much has happened in the field of police surveillance and predictive policing. Ever new tools for association and profiling are developed and refined (Bennett Moses and Chan, 2016; Fyfe, Gundhus, and Rønn, 2017). Some of them gained much international attention, like Chicago's Strategic Subject List to predict gun violence. Instead of targeting spaces, this list assessed people, which caused strong public reactions (Asher and Arthur, 2017; Tucek, 2019; Sheehey, 2019; Stagoff-Belfort, 2020). While this particular assessment tool has been discontinued (Chicago Police Department, 2019), many other solutions and companies have become a common name in police work, such as Predpol (nd) and Palantir (nd) in the US and Europe, Azavea (nd) and Precobs in Europe (Institut für musterbasierte Prognosetechnik, nd). Many associative tools are used to assist police forces in identifying hotspot areas and dispatching police officers, following what Wendy Chun critically phrases as a logic of 'optimizing arrests' (2021: 212). Association is not only limited to intervention, where it currently features prominently. Investigative association tools exist, too. Police officer Hans mentions a local solution:

'We use pattern recognition in intelligence systems where you put in intelligence knowledge and mostly make a social network, like who's connected to who? You make maps where you graphically visualize who knows who – to identify the most important criminal. Who's is the boss in the network? How is the network? How does it work, is it hierarchical, is it more integrated? So, there we have some patterns in intelligence databases, to know which criminals are the most important ones.'

Profiling solutions are also developed for judicial decision-making or fact-finding, for example to evaluate data in terms of how risky individuals are and what their likelihood for recidivism or violence is (Berk, Sorensen, and Barnes, 2016; Berk, 2017, 2018). Associative logics are used in forensics, for example to make genomic predictions about the observable traits from the DNA of an unknown owner (Hopman and M'charek, 2020). All of these solutions matter in their respective context of law enforcement and in society at large. They are the result of different intra-actions, different intersecting life cycles.

There are different reasons for the rise of associative tools in policing. The most prevalent reason is the promise of uncovering risks and so-called unknowns. Algorithms are trusted to find and create associations in datasets that – due to the sheer volume of information – humans alone would either spend a long time finding or not be able to find at all. Algorithms, according to these expectations, reduce complexity in datasets and assist with decision-making in densely digitized environments. Associative tools give *form* to police knowledge at the same time as they *formalize* knowledge (see Goffey, 2008). They are expected to create *uniformity* in police analyses, all of which grants them considerable epistemological authority. By 'reducing complexity' and visualizing associations, they are meant to prepare actionable knowledge (see Ericson, 2007; Amoore, 2009). Algorithms, then, much embody the idea of efficient and effective law enforcement (Kaufmann, Egbert, and Leese, 2019), they are implemented as a relief for overworked police institutions (Beck and McCue, 2009). Especially predictive policing solutions are designed to intervene before or when crime takes place rather than to identify the long-term causes of crime. Software developer Frank confirms: "And just to be clear: we're only focused on predicting where and when crime is most likely to occur. We don't predict why or how and who? Those are all things that our particular process doesn't focus on."

Those who consider using predictive tools to target individuals (Van Brakel and De Hert, 2011; Perry et al, 2013; Downs, 2016) see that prediction could be combined with preventive policing. Such a combination yields promises and pitfalls concerning police work, but especially offenders' lives, where the risk of discrimination is high.

As mentioned by Frank, those software solutions that run under the label of predictive policing mainly focus on geography and time. While individuals may not be the target of predictive policing instruments, predictions still focus on neighbourhoods that can also be discriminated against (Chun, 2021). That is the case, for example, when the repeated intervention and data collection of police officers in specific neighbourhoods influences databases and eventually the algorithms trained on these databases. Generally, predictive policing tools draw on different criminological theories that assume rationality in criminal behaviour (Cornish and Clarke, 1986) and consider the environment of a crime (Ray, 1971; Brantingham and Brantingham, 1991). The 'Near Repeat Hypothesis' (Townsley, Homel, and Chaseling, 2003), for example, suggests that offenders will return to the near environment of their first strike in a short time, because they possess information about the environment and can weigh possible risks and benefits (Farrell and Pease, 2014: 3863; Johnson et al, 2007). Other theories consider environmental factors such as the absence of patrols and population density (Perry et al, 2013). Others again assume routines in offending (Cohen and Felson, 1979). All these hypotheses mainly consider space, time, and modus operandi. Software developer Giorgios explains: "If you are considering looking at people at all, then you may want to anticipate where a lot of people would be ... If there is a lot of crime that probably means that there is a lot of people at the location."

In order to make associations within policing, information – even if only in relation to space, time and modus operandi – is increasingly rendered computable. The materiality of information changes as it is translated from analogue to digital data. All parameters that have predictive value in terms of behaviour need to be captured by proxy variables that can be calculated with. While the calculability of digital information is of much help here, there is nonetheless a lot of work that goes into both, the generation, curation, and cleaning of information as well as into the creation of association rules. The life cycles of information intersect here with the life cycles many others, for example those of policing experts, algorithm trainers, police officers, but also the life cycle of the algorithm (Kaufmann, 2019). Thus, I studied the algorithmic association of information with a method that Rob Kitchin describes as 'Interviewing designers or conducting an ethnography of a coding team' (2016: 24). As you will see, I spoke to coding teams, but also all the others that are part of practices of association including those who deploy solutions, because they can give us insight into how data matters to them and how it is made to matter.

In the following, I will describe a generalized version of an information life cycle in the context of predictive policing to illustrate how association operates as a specific practice of making information matter. Crime control is a field that has a long history of exercising surveillance, data analysis, and prediction. Here, the life cycle gives us entry points for understanding how humans, infrastructures and tools matter, too, and where openings for agency emerge (see Chapter 3). The basis for this is a study of seven predictive policing software models with origins in three different continents. I spoke with experts, software designers, and ICT engineers about the specifications of predictive policing software, as well as with police officers about the implementation of these. Quotes and insights from this study are marked with fictional first names.

Imaginaries

Police work is structured around the life of information. Surveillance and control are about generating, receiving and processing information. The police have a history of collecting and processing data for security governance, even if these activities can be messy, too. Before information is even generated or engaged with, it is imagined. Clearly, there is no unified way in which police institutions imagine information. Different imaginaries about information are combined and negotiated in the process of making it matter. Imaginaries influence how and what kind of information eventually materializes. Like any project, prediction begins with expectations about the process and its aims. Ives, a software developer explains: "Before we even look at the data, we have to start working with the stakeholders to find out what it is they want to forecast. They decide that." Ideas about what kind of data may fit such aims best can already be discussed at this stage. These discussions can become quite concrete: is information only that which is generated by police reports, or do other sources provide information for prediction? More so, what are the imaginaries tied to information provided in a specific report and what type of information does a report elicit in the first place? When considering information such as names and postal codes, Ruha Benjamin (2019) points us to the many imaginaries that are linked to them. What is only a spot on a map to some, is to others a symbol for subcultures and specific populations. To some, a name is what ties an official identity to a person. To others it is an indicator for religion, cultural background, or political choice (Benjamin, 2019). While imaginaries about information can be stable in the sense that their collectors have similar expectations towards data, other imaginaries are fluid and individual. How imaginaries meet and need negotiation in the planning of a prediction project, is described by software developer Amanda:

> 'We created an index including socioeconomic status, because there is research that suggests that economically disadvantaged areas are more likely to experience crime than prosperous or affluent areas. ... We looked at residential stability and how long people have been living in those neighbourhoods, because there is research to suggest that the longer people have lived in an area, the more they are invested in an area, the more attachment they have to that place. And they may be more willing to step in or prevent crime or they have more social capacities to prevent crime from happening in the first place.'

Amanda continues to explain that specific indicators are also used to identify migrant populations and minorities:

> 'We looked at linguistic isolation, especially indo-European linguistic isolation. I am not as familiar with that body of research, but I know that immigrant areas – I don't know about the international scale – but at least in the Unites States, but there is actually less crime in places of immigrant concentration. So that is another variable that we put in. And we also included a race variable, because there is a lot of research specifically in the US, again, I'm not sure about the international [domain], about how race is related to crime. There is a whole bunch of research about racial oppression that is driving this relationship. It's not that the minorities are more criminal than the rest of the population, but there are a lot of structural and macro-level policies that unfortunately even still today are driving crime in minority areas.'

In the end, only those variables were chosen that matter to the project in the sense that they 'predict well':

> 'So we compared all these structural variables with our crime variables and we only selected the variables that had a consistent relationship with all type of crimes. … And we did not include the linguistic isolation and the residential stability, because they were going in the wrong directions sometimes for certain types of crime.' (Amanda)

Associations, preconceptions, and prejudices influence what information materializes and matters in a prediction. Or to put it the other way around: even if a prediction procedure is 'only' based on GPS codes, it will not be possible to rid it of the imaginaries that are part of making these GPS codes matter in the predictive system and the related learning processes. One can only ever reflect about these imaginaries, bring them into the open and discuss them. Discussions at this turn in the life cycle of information, however, tend to be dominated by technical and statistical imaginaries instead of a debate about ethical and societal preconceptions.

In addition, this turn is enmeshed with a second, very persistent imaginary about digital information. It is the imaginary that unbiased data exist. A part of this imaginary is supported by the fact that digital data take mathematic form. And mathematics, according to the imaginary, are without bias. The phrase 'Garbage in – garbage out', first mentioned by a group of mathematicians in 1957 (The Hammond Times, 1957), has taken ground as a standard critique in programming and yet, the imaginary of computable information being unbiased is surprisingly stable. In fact, the phrase is regularly used to argue that unbiased data would be preferable. Many of my interviewees were well aware of bias in computable data, but still expect there to be the option to create unbiased data. This would imply that there is such a thing as information rid of all imaginaries. For example, IT professional Bertrand, who is much in favour of creating ethical algorithms, states: "If you have ... high quality unbiased data for machine learning, I wouldn't rule out that you can have a prediction algorithm that can actually outperform a skilled police officer." The idea that one can clear information of preconceptions and imaginaries is strong. It may even be an unsaid assumption within the burgeoning discussion about Fairness, Accountability, Transparency and Ethics (FATE) in machine learning (see Microsoft, nd). Statistical discussions concerning FATE or those about 'good' (Daly, Devitt, and Mann, 2019) and 'bad data' (Galdon Clavell, 2018) that either reflect or disrespect fundamental rights are an important vantage point for engaging with the discriminatory effects of prediction processes. That is to say, bias can be engaged with, but in the spirit of information as matter-in-becoming, engagement is more about choosing which bias should be productive instead of trying to deny it. Discussing biases in the form of preconceptions and imaginaries is a task that stretches from those who collect information to those who process it and act on prediction results.

A third imaginary particularly prominent in associative practices is that information is malleable (Rubinstein, 2013; Davenport, 2014; Gregg, 2014; Bevan, 2015; Kaufmann et al, 2020). The formability of information speaks to the idea that datasets can be shaped until a meaningful form or pattern appears. Formability is not quite the same as being in-formation or re-materializing. Imaginaries of formability or malleability emphasize the actors that subject information to form: the rational actor decides on meaningful form. It implies that forming information is a process relatively free from 'resistance' by datasets. Malleability speaks to the practices of predictions that associate, shape, and re-shape information until actionable forms are identified. Note that malleable forms may cater to the idea of efficiency in predictions, but do not explain causes (see Kaufmann, Egbert, and Leese, 2019). And ironically, producing actionable forms can become very laborious, which puts the ideal of efficiency into perspective. Being in-formation or re-materializing, however, grants information agency, too, as information may materialize in ways that are undesired or not actionable. There is room for friction as information is more actively part of mattering.

Generation

This turn focuses on how data are generated and by whom. Data imaginaries influence the generation of data. These two turns are connected, but not everyone who generates data shares the imaginaries that drive their later use. Epistemological positions and related imaginaries influence, for example, the size of datasets and the amount of data that are generated for the prediction project. Some epistemologies are based on "greedy" (Ives) relationships to information. Here, any data – even if it is the "number of people buying headache medicine" (Chris) – could be of relevance to a prediction. Chris' methodology, for example, advocates the correlation of police data "with various other statistics, like weather being one, traffic data ... Basically you use whatever data you have available. It's very opportunistic. ... The more you know, the better system you can make."

According to this epistemological position, information tends to be always structurally incomplete (see Andrejevic and Gates, 2014: 191). The statement of Ives – that limits are not dictated by the association tool, but by available information – confirms this rationale: "The algorithm will do it. It's just that we haven't enough data about these immediate settings to forecast accurately." IT professional Karl expresses a similar stance: "We don't have all the important data. ... It's noisy, it's not perfectly measured, we would have preferred other data, which we don't have. We do the best what we can with whatever we got."

Others would take a different epistemological stance on the imagination and generation of information. Developer Georgios is confident that "digital data is capturing most things that we would be interested in using. ... I haven't seen a case where there was a type of data that we wanted to use (and) it just does not exist anywhere."

Software developer Frank, again, prefers small datasets. He works with information about "what kind of crime occurred, where it occurred and when it occurred" (Frank). Others, like developer Johannes, are only interested in one specific modus operandi, such as burglaries, and collect information about the stolen goods. Advocates of these stances argue that in the worst case big data approaches could be costly. Developer Georgios deliberates:

'I know that some crime forecasting systems use social media as indicators; we have not used social media in any way and we don't plan to use it for crime forecasting. I think it's most valuable to use it for situational awareness – say a bomb goes off – to know what has happened, to get pictures; then it's super-useful. But I think it's less useful for prediction. It suffers from some problems, meaning that any time you want to analyze social media data you need a language-processing component ... I just don't think it makes a lot of sense to use it when we have already a lot of other data that are ... less private.'

Johannes, head developer of a team for predictive policing software, goes one step further. For him, information is only useful if it relates to knowledge bases that consider causalities:

'A correlation is not a causality! You can always find a correlation, but when you take a close look, it is not a sensible one. … I am not a friend of including just any type of data in software. … Good software builds on knowledge bases. It is based on content, not only pure statistics, mathematics, and algorithms.'

The differences between using big data and select, 'small' datasets not only relates to data imaginaries, but they also involve different practices of generating data. Approaches that work with big data require information that was generated with a different aim in mind, but are scraped, regenerated, and re-used at a later stage. An example of this is the use of weather data: it was generated with the intent to predict weather patterns, but is collected and integrated into associative practices for crime prediction. Other approaches only work with information that is generated for their specific purpose. That is information created only for the sake of predicting crime. This requires a generation of information via dedicated infrastructures, such as sensors, surveys, or other reporting activities.

Any predictive policing approach, however, is dependent on information about crime. What kind of information materializes here is highly dependent on those who generate data. A known influence on the creation of information is that the rate of victims reporting crimes is low (Chan, 2011). There are several other aspects that influence the generation of information (Kaufmann et al, 2020). For example, when it comes to the ways in which police officers themselves generate datasets, a known challenge is their personal judgements related to reporting. Software developer Amanda considers these a 'caveat':

'The computer program is only using crime incidents that resulted in a formal incident report that's been created. It's not using information when an officer stops on the street talking to a lady sitting on her stoop … The individual officers have their own kind of perception of what crime is.'

In addition, police officer Dihyah problematizes that in his district "approximately 20% of the police population are registering 80% of the information in the database". This implies that these 20 per cent have a considerable influence over the kind of information that exists. Not only do these officers decide what is worthy of reporting in the first place, but they also report their own interpretation of the situation. Here, Dihyah deliberates about the way in which data collection by the police has to follow the standards of police law, which are, in his opinion, subjective. Similarly, developer Ives mentions that the information they receive, for example about prison inmates, is fully shaped by the police's, magistrates' and prison guards' incarceration practices and prone to discriminatory practices.

Already at the moment of generation, the life cycle of information not only intersects with that of officers, victims, and reporting standards, but also with that of other infrastructures such as sensors or forms. The analogue technology of the police form pre-structures the generation of information. It mainly affords the generation of information that the form asks of officers. Amanda criticizes that such forms only ever represent the information "that the officers find". She continues describing a different characteristic of the form that influences how information is generated: "The police department is still using paper forms. … Officers handwrite when an incident happens, they fill out the paperwork, they submit the paperwork and then it is recorded into a database." This act of translating information from one material form to another shapes the information that is eventually available for predictions. Policing expert Erika and police officer Hans, too, mention that much information has to be translated into digital formats in order to make it readable and possible to process by a computer. This translation is a common effort of humans, technologies, and other infrastructures, where negotiations about the format of information take place and decisions about what type of information is kept are taken. Thus, decisive re-materializations of information already take place during the stage of generation. The problem of optimizing information to computation is accompanied by a discussion about the loss of information. Software developer Ives mentions that

> 'in practice you may lose some precision because there are limits in how many sources you are prepared to invest in, let's say digitizing a picture. Same thing is true with everything else. You may not be able to reproduce the same precision that is in the information unless you take the effort.'

Amanda shares her concern that the process of translating analogue into digital information is always an incidence for human mistake and that with digitization, social context may also get lost. However, since social context is relevant for the processing of information at a later stage, some police stations have developed procedures to preserve meta-information. Officer Dihyah explains: "So they were obliged to fill in a short story. They had to present in written text what is the story here? What is the suspicion? Why do you think this is suspicious? You have to put it in words. Because we can't really tell that from the data you provided." Such a procedure is a radical opening in the way in which the dataset could include extra information about causes or imaginaries, which could become influential in the further processing of that data. However, the creation of this context information is again highly dependent on the person registering it.

Overall, a description of this turn in the life cycle of information has shown how much the generation of information influences its further development. How information materializes matters to prediction.

Storage

The storage of information ties in with the specific materiality of the instruments and tools used to create it. For example, the hand-written report of a police officer is a material instantiation of information, but it is also a form of storage that co-determines the specific durability, mutability, and accessibility of information. Thus, any material instance of information is also an instance of storage. Different forms of storage are again differently suitable for creating predictions. While hand-written police reports used to rematerialize as needles and pins on maps, most police information today rematerializes in databases. Here, information intersects with new life cycles as for example those of hard disks and data scientists. Note that the materiality of information transforms again when it passes to more structured forms of storage. This materiality determines the prediction process. That is to say, what information ends up in a structured database, how and where exactly it is stored influences predictions.

Storage is both a material and a rule-based process. It involves, for example, hard disks with specific material dimensions and technical specifications, as well as managerial, legal, and procedure-related factors. Machines and people together decide on how data are stored. The different challenges of digitization were already mentioned earlier: will one lose or gain aspects of information by storing it? The digitization of information has considerable consequences. Amanda explains how far-reaching they are: "you can query the data, you can select a crime incident that you like – which you wouldn't be able to do if you just had stacks of paper forms sitting on your desk. It makes analyzing the data much easier and more time-efficient."

Storage is, however, a more extensive procedure than rendering analogue or paper information digital. It is a decision-process about what is rendered digital in the first place and for how long it is allowed to exist in that material form. Storage hierarchies and aspects of inclusion and exclusion become relevant here. Furthermore, storage frequently includes material as well as regulatory restrictions of access. Here, the collaboration between police stations and private developers or platform owners can cause considerable 'friction' (Edwards, 2010). Where and how is data stored? Who will get access and under which conditions? These questions are debated constantly, because storage and access to information reform the practices of governing specific situations, especially in law enforcement. A debate of rising importance is, for example, to what extent information about DNA is collected and whether it should be made available to state institutions (Skinner and Wienroth, 2019; Philipps, 2021). Thus, the life cycle of information not only intersects with those of technical solutions, but also with life cycles of regulatory frameworks for storage and the people implementing them. Police officer Dihyah mentions influential aspects of storage that involve both, tools, regulatory frameworks, and humans: "We have the law on how to store and how to delete data. We have all this data, all this information, but we don't have procedures, we don't have any systems that further help us in deciding which data to keep, which to delete." He continues to explain how much data work is needed.

'This data management is manual. Every time something is registered in the database, someone has to sit and read text. ... Every bit of information has to be read and assessed. ... While quality indicators should be objective, they end up in fact being subjective assessments: How necessary is this? How well can you connect this data with other data, about which criminals, victims? All these assessments about how and why to keep this information are made by people.'

In some policing procedures, information is not just translated into one type of database, but into several databases simultaneously (Kaufmann and Leese, 2021). Almost like a cell, information divides into different materializations that end up living different lives as they materialize in different contexts. With this integration into different databases the same information may live one life that is instant and speedy, and another one that is slow and more durable (Kaufmann and Leese, 2021). In different material form, information can live parallel lives, which need to be respected in the management and endings of data.

Once combined with other information in a database, information still changes. There are several imaginaries that guide the work with databases, how they are maintained and developed further. Police officer Dihyah suggests that one needs regular evaluations of databases: "We need to know what we know. We need to connect all databases so that we get one answer: this is what we know! Then we can ask [about] what we don't know. ... [and] what we need to get ... from those who collect information." Developer Chris, too, sees the need to continued engagement with stored information: "What's in the dataset? Is it complete? Have they given us everything? We need to first understand whether data needs to be cleaned, we need to understand quality of the data. ... There are errors in all databases, you will never find the perfect database."

Again, in both positions we see how different ideals and imaginaries of storage converge: the idea of a unified knowledge base meets the insecurity about whether databases ever can be complete; understandings of information as structurally imperfect are combined with that of ideal and unbiased information.

A structured study of data storage and databases, their technical, procedural, and regulatory framework, the norms, laws, and values emerging here, the procedure of translating information from one format to another, as well as database maintenance designate important turns in the life cycle of information. These steps are critical to questions about why, for whom, for how long and in what material form information is going to exist.

Curation

Not all information available in a database is going to be analysed or considered relevant for predictive purposes. In preparation for various processes of calculation, information is subject to a range of practices that can be collected under the term curation. This turn in the life cycle includes a reassessment, a choosing of information and its ascription to analytic registers. Often, this turn is related to imaginaries, generation, and storage, but it also involves more concrete interactions between information, tools, and people in the preparation of predictions. Practices of selecting, 'cleaning' (Erhard and Do, 2000) or 'scrubbing', which is to render data amenable to calculation (Brine and Poovey, 2013), are joined with acts of assigning information to categories, labels, and standards. All these processes are carried out with the intention to make information matter in relation to the foreseen prediction activity. It is yet another re-materialization, because information is deleted, added, or merged with new information organization systems. Not all research projects pay specific attention to these practices, but these processes can sometimes become the core of the prediction project (Leonelli, 2016). Some even have dedicated entire research projects to developing infrastructures for the organization of information (Goff et al, 2011). By today, this turn has become recognized and problematized, not only because it involves a considerable amount of labour, but also since many of the assumptions that drive these re-materializations of information go unnoticed or are – at worst – obfuscated (Brine and Poovey, 2013).

Curational processes tie in with the different epistemologies of prediction described earlier. For those working with very few prediction parameters and very select data, cleaning processes are elaborate: supposedly relevant information needs to be identified in a dataset, any additional information needs to be deleted and potentially, existing datasets have to be supplemented with particular data that may be hard to come by. Software designer Johannes and his team, for example, include only highly cleaned and specific information in their analyses. For curation he involves policing experts. Developer Chris mentions that datasets also have to be cleaned of what one considers "errors".

All information is assigned to categories, where the definition of these categories and discussions about which information matches these categories best can become a laborious task: "We have very different information and we try to level up and to have very generic categories. ... There is a lot of categorizing that isn't very logical. All over the place. Different labels on the same information and vice versa" (Dihyah).

This goes to show that the actual category also has agency in the process of prediction. Police officer Hans describes that categorizing information is also a question of internal politics and competence: "and at some point, you have this challenge: who decides if this is black or white?" Similar issues also apply to the indexing of text, a challenge that Dihyah mentions, because indexing involves decisions about which texts are rendered visible and invisible.

Other epistemological approaches do not engage much with cleaning. As mentioned earlier, to software developer Georgios any available information can be meaningful, which means that information can also create surprising effects in relation to crime predictions: "Some cases seemed unusual at first ... For example, the phases of the moon. ... There is no literature about why that is that case, but with full moon you may be seeing more outside."

Some developers even actively exclude cleaning processes, because cleaning could ignore information that could become relevant otherwise:

'If you want to clean up the data ... I'm gonna remove some predictive accuracy, I'm gonna make everybody worse off. There is gonna be more injustice in those decisions, but I'm gonna make everybody equally worse off. The question for policy makers is: is that a good trade?' (Ives)

Ives finds that decisions about which dataset to use are too influential to be taken by software developers: "I don't make that decision – that's up to the policy makers."

Even if approaches working with less selective datasets may not actively clean or scrub information, they still involve acts of curation. Curation, here, concerns the collection and combination of different data sets. For example, some information is scraped, taken from public domain databases. That raises the question as to which type of information should be scraped. Giorgios, for example, used twitter data to infer insights about relevant events and crime locations. Police officer Hans mentions that databases are professionally sold to programmers and developers. This information still needs to be curated. Any – big and small – datasets need to be organized in terms of the type of proxy variable or parameter they stand for. Decisions have to be taken as to which information or dataset represents what factor in the prediction process, something that the next part will explain in more depth. Amanda explains:

'(W)hat drives community crime patterns? Things like socio-economic status, residential stability, linguistic isolation and race and ethnicity – they are ... all available through a census. And while those things don't necessarily cause crime directly, they provide you with information about the characteristics of places that might encourage or promote crime events to occur there.'

What becomes apparent from all these ways of making information matter is that information itself has agency. It introduces controversy or debate about what kind of scrubbing may be needed, it may resist cleaning approaches, or it may be difficult to assign to categories. Information may not match with the life cycles of data scientists, political decisions on standards, or categorization and indexing tools. And indeed, this agency of information can become quite powerful. The turns I described so far relate strongly to visions of data analysis. A vision would be a set of key ideas that guide the analytic process. These visions are subject to debate, some may be realized, and others not, which causes discussion. Nonetheless, effort is spent to actively integrate visions into each re-materialization of information. Information and datasets are imagined, generated, and curated in line with the vision of the project. However, information acting up or categories not working may introduce vocations. Vocations would be the spontaneous callings of information into a direction that was potentially not foreseen in the project (Kaufmann, 2020). One example is the case of moon phases that correlate with crime patterns. In the next turns, we shall see that even more and different openings for vocations appear where information becomes lively and suddenly matters differently. When this happens, information can take the project into a new direction.

Processing

To process information is a broad term. Any step in the life cycle of information so far is a form of processing. At this specific turn, however, it refers to the meeting and merging of information with calculative tools for association. The life cycle of information has so far already intersected with the lives of various tools, such as administrative forms, computers, storage systems, data management systems – all of which make information matter in new ways. At this point, information intersects with the lives of analytic instruments.

As mentioned before, information is critical to the making of associative tools. Information is key to any calculative instrument in the sense that algorithms and data are imbricated with each other. Yet, it is important to distinguish between two types of algorithms. Prediction projects mainly work with so-called discriminating algorithms (see Smith and Buechler, 1975) as the algorithm's mode of operation is to make distinctions within information according to instructions. It discriminates between different data according to given instructions that it 'learned' from datasets. This is different from Generative Adversarial Networks (GANs, originally designed by Goodfellow et al, 2014), which are not going through the same kind of training phase. GANs are not based on information in the same way in which discriminating algorithms are, because they do not work with predefined distinctions. GANs are designed to create rather than to discriminate. Their aim is to interpret what they believe to be the essence of information without software trainers intervening in the same way (see Kaufmann et al, 2020). The classic model used for predictions are, however, discriminating algorithms.

The chapter could now switch to describing the complete life cycle of a prediction algorithm. Since the focus lies on information, however, only those parts are mentioned here where information plays a role in the building and use of a prediction instrument. To illustrate this process, we can consider a team that decides to include the variables of time, location, and modus operandi into their prediction tool. First, they have to define what we could call 'content' parameters that capture the variables 'time', 'location', and 'modus operandi'. One may think of location, for example, as a straightforward variable that is easy to capture. However, depending on the theoretical model the team considers relevant, parameters capturing location may already vary: is 'location' relating to near-repeat theories or theories about the relevance of environments in general? Once these content parameters are defined, the next step is to find concrete examples of information in the datasets that reflect these parameters. This potentially requires cleaning the data to match these parameters. Parameters and data then need to be integrated with mathematic form. The algorithm is trained on such datasets where the 'correct' hits or patterns are known to the algorithm's engineer. The algorithm associates different digital datasets to infer or, as Bertrand says, 'predict' a pattern

'and gets it wrong. You change parameters and it predicts wrong again. Millions of times. Some predictions were better than others ... the computer tries to remember the parameter settings that made its predictions better than others ... It keeps on varying other parameters that didn't have an effect to find (correct hits).' (Bertrand)

Note that Bertrand here talks about changing mathematic, not content parameters. This training phase much illustrates how both algorithm and information merge and create re-materializions at this stage. Since this process is semi-automated and the computer associates variables at a considerably higher speed than human brains can manage, this is a phase where the co-creative agency of algorithms and information moves to the fore. At the same time, all the preceding turns, namely the imagination, generation, storage, and curation of information are decisive, too, because they define the patterns of information that algorithms may or may not be able to identify. Considering how much these turns matter, the collaborative effort between team members who define sociological parameters, those who curate sets of data, and the mathematicians who write algorithms, is crucial, too. Surprisingly, however, Johannes, who heads the team of a prediction software, mentions that he does not know how mathematicians do their work. Neither does he consider this to be his role. While some teams may experience this inability to follow each other's concepts and translations as unproblematic, it may cause frictions later in the process. Police officer Hans sees the lack of communication and shared understandings across prediction processes as a challenge: "I guess it's harder for people, then, to question those patterns if these parameters are not visible or accessible. You just accept the parameters." He recognizes that the choice of parameters and the ways in which they are captured by an algorithm matter quite drastically:

'if you don't have good ... parameters you might define problems that are not really there. If you set the parameters wrong, you get a huge heat map and it looks like the whole city is burning. But it's not really burning, it's the parameters in the GIS system and when you present the patterns from the data then you are actually telling a story that's not true.'

What exact parameters are included in prediction algorithms varies greatly and the usability of algorithms, as just described, is highly dependent on the many explicit and implicit decisions that are taken underway. Since the algorithm will eventually be used to associate information in datasets where the correct matches are *not* known, it is also clear that all these agencies together determine what patterns will materialize and matter to policing decisions. The broad variety of tools that exist in the landscape of prediction reflect the different styles of association (see Kaufmann, Egbert, and Leese, 2019).

An interesting aspect concerns the way in which parameters and information were chosen according to the specific style of association. Developers focusing on big, relatively uncleaned datasets were mainly concerned with the correct matches of the algorithm as well as the identification of new patterns. Their associative technique was based on mere correlation, not causality. The guiding idea was that the more data exists, the better the chances of finding new, surprising correlations (for example software developers Giorgios, Ives). Hence, algorithms – correlational tools – have famously been described as the 'End of Theory' (Anderson, 2008). However, developers who wanted to include an element of causality into their tools chose to do so via preselecting and cleaning information in accordance with the theories they would choose about the causation of crime. Software developer Johannes was, for example, one of them. Indeed, reflecting causality in the choice of information matters as information and algorithms then embody and perform these specific ideas. Software developer Amanda said that one needed knowledge about causality so that one "can decide whether these reasons are relevant or not". Police officer Hans agrees: "if you could have software that suggests *why* this is happening, you could guide the officer into the problem-solving on scene ..., give better advice to the woman who had a burglar in their apartment."

An earlier-mentioned software that traces networks of people rather than predicting hotspots includes a specific function, which is supposed to analyse and strengthen aspects of causality. Instead of merely identifying a link between two people, then, additional information is used to give explanations as to why a specific link is identified. Police office Dihyah explains how this is done:

'In this field you put in that kind of data and so on. But what about the story? There is a storytelling here. ... We have the free-text story and ... we have this search engine that automatically indexes the free text and you can navigate the free text by using indicators.'

The software, then, would not only associate information, but also offer a feature to learn about causality. The standard associative tools for predictions are, however, algorithms that identify likely hotspots for crime. Their only openings for causality are the theories that drive the selection of information and the writing of parameters.

Once the algorithm is trained and tested, it is employed in practice, where correct patterns or hits are not yet known. Here is where the algorithm creates actual predictions. This is another point at which frictions occur. Software developer Amanda recounts that "a lot of police officers were frustrated with the program." Amanda mimics the officers: "The program shouldn't be predicting this spot, it should be predicting this spot over here. ... They're like: 'I am smarter than this program is, I know where the crime should be and it's not finding it'."

Police officers and the prediction programs differ in their assessment of which association actually matters. This is why IT professional Karl also finds it important to mediate the different agencies involved in the prediction process.

'So if the computer says low and you think high risk, you should probably do the assessment once more – and the other way around.

The danger is if you trust the computer too much, you might overlook very important information that will lead you to do a sensible decision. But you can also distrust the computer too much and these algorithms using information. You should pay attention to it.'

In addition, association should also not be too time-efficient, because it may have a detrimental effect on policing. Software developer Frank describes a common problem:

'Doing predictions in real time creates distractions for police officers. ... (I)f they constantly have to ask the question: "Where are my predictions now?", then they spend more time on their iPhones looking through where the predictions are rather than policing the environment. So it actually is counterproductive to do predictions in perfect real-time.'

The associations provided by prediction programs can also have learning effects. Amanda mentions, for example, how algorithms can create new impulses based on association:

'I think police officers don't necessarily have a handle ... of how macro-level or community level factors influence individual behavior. That's obviously something the ... software picks up. ... it might change how officers view why crime is happening in particular locations. Why is crime happening here, but not there?'

Police officer Dihyah, again, ties a potential benefit of association back to the epistemological level. He believes that association can provide the police with "kind of higher knowledge base. ... So when we do something to any of our citizens, it's based on a higher level of knowledge." The description of the life cycle of information so far has shown that the relevance of this statement is very much dependent on every single turn discussed here.

Death/Re-use

Information rarely disappears completely. Especially in its digital form, information travels easily. As mentioned earlier, in some prediction instruments a first life cycle is determined by speed, where timely predictions are created with recently produced information. After information has been made to matter for that purpose, it is integrated into a second, slower cycle, where it is associated to for the sake of long-term trends and background information (Kaufmann and Leese, 2021). Other prediction instruments plan for the deletion of information. However, Jean-Francois Blanchette reminds us that even when deleted traces of digital information may remain (2011). Public authorities such as the police have strict rules for deleting selected personal information after a certain period of time. At the same time, they also have a duty to document and archive information. Upon archiving information is open to re-use. While even re-use can be regulated, not all databases are subject to this regulation.

We have seen examples of policing software that actually re-use data collected in databases not owned by the police. Such data are 'open to constant repurposing by a range of actors and agencies, often in ways in which the original generators of these data have little or no knowledge' (Lupton, 2015: 563; see Thylstrup, 2019). Such datasets are broken down (Kaufmann et al, 2020) or broken apart and composted to serve new purposes. For example, publicly available information from private services such as twitter are originally produced for the purpose of communication, but can rematerialize in policing activities. In fact, software developer Chris considers the re-use of existing information as key to associations based on big data. Police office Dihyah also sees the value of it, explaining how the police collaborates with private institutions, such as banks:

> '[The system] connects all these types of information – financial information and all the other information that we have in all the other databases – and then it gives each object a relevance factor based on the rules that impact each object. So, after this automatic process, person A can have a factor of 700 and B can have a factor of 400, telling us that person A could be a bigger risk factor than person B.'

While it was expected that the police draw on information from different public and private sources, generated for a variety of reasons, the problem of re-use becomes particularly prevalent when considering information produced in the specific domains of law enforcement. Here, information is imagined and generated in precarious situations, such as arrests. By re-using that information for predictive policing, information is not suddenly stripped of the context in which they appeared originally (Kaufmann et al, 2020). Information transports aspects of its original context of materialization. Since discrimination is a known challenge in surveillance and law enforcement (Browne, 2015; Benjamin, 2019), re-using information in the context of predicting crimes and policing requires extra attention (see Kaufmann et al, 2020). IT professional Bertrand summarizes his point of view on this:

> 'History is biased! ... They arrest Blacks and all the historical data say, "Well, we have all these wonderful arrests of Blacks possessing dope" ... And the algorithm basically says, "Sure, it's ok, it's not racist, you

can go on [ironically] because algorithms are absolutely apolitical and you can just go on harassing Blacks.'''

Information is imbued with its particular history of being imagined, generated, and stored. Such histories travel to more abstract, harder-to-comprehend contexts as information rematerializes in new association processes. This is a reality that matters and needs addressing.

Association is critical to surveillance today. It gives information form in order to identify possibilities for intervention. The example of predictive policing has not only shown that information matters, but also how it rematerializes at each turn of the life cycle. These materializations are collaborative efforts of many: police officers, software developers, and their respective imaginaries of information. Materialization is determined by paper and digital forms, databases, storage hierarchies, regulation, and mathematic instructions – just to name a few. The described turns in information life cycles document that it matters how information materializes in the context of predictions. That is why more and more academic and journalistic analyses address prediction efforts critically (to illustrate the necessity of such efforts, I list more references than usual: Anderson, 2008; Amoore, 2011; Van Brakel and De Hert, 2011; Leese, 2014; Bennett Moses and Chan, 2016; Asher and Arthur, 2017; Fyfe et al, 2017; Benjamin, 2019; Kaufmann, 2019; Kaufmann et al, 2019; Sheehey, 2019; Stagoff-Belfort, 2020; Chun, 2021; Egbert and Leese, 2021). In addition, initiatives emerge to draw attention to how much police information matters in today's landscapes of association. These include stocktaking exercises and investigative reports as provided by *Pro Publica*, initiatives to research data in/justice as is done in the *Data Justice Lab* at Cardiff University and projects of actively generating just data as happens in the *Ida B Well's Just Data Lab* headed by Ruha Benjamin. There are movements such as *Data for Black Lives* and organizations such as *All Tech Is Human* that seek to engender active changes in the way in which information is generated, stored, cleaned, and processed. Only when we grasp the specificities of each turn can we create space for such important critiques and identify entry points for our role in the process of making information matter.

5

Conversion

'On the one hand we have state-based online surveillance and on the other we have surveillance by companies and other entities. For both of these, surveillance increased mainly due to the technological possibilities that we have today. Just 20, 30 years ago, there would not have been the technological possibilities to retain and analyze data ... The analytic tools that are used today, such as machine learning and algorithms, also increase the amount of online surveillance.' (Kate90r13)

Hacker Kate90r13[1] summarizes the upsurge of associative information practices. He observes powerful routines in analysing, revealing, and disclosing insights based on digital information and in engineering these insights into new products and socio-technical procedures. Kate90r13 is not the only one who watches these developments with a growing unease. Self-critical journalism problematizes our role as consumers in this development as our clicks, swipes, and likes are analysed by those with the privileged overview (New Scientist, 2018). The vocabulary of the 'frightful five' (referring to Alphabet, Amazon, Apple, Facebook, Microsoft; coined by Manjoo 2017) or worries about China's 'digital authoritarianism' (Erixon and Lee-Makiyama, 2011) were early indicators of a rising awareness about the consequences of sharing information online. By today, countless reports, citizen and legal initiatives, as well as entire research programs address how public and commercial actors practice the collecting, storing, curating, and processing of information. Policies for opting out of digital services (Burgess, 2018), personal choices of 'UnFacebooking' (Evans, 2014) and 'digital detox' (Syvertsen, 2020), as well as 'non-participation' (Casemajor et al, 2015) are attempts to answer these trends. Yet, not everyone agrees with such radical reactions: "Pulling the plug is not an option", says hacker jE2EE. He prefers to engage critically with the rise of association without abandoning the Internet as such. An opt-out of online services is almost impossible as it produces social, financial, and utility costs that are hard to afford (Brunton and Nissenbaum, 2011, 2016; Morozov, 2017). In addition, an opt-out may also not be desirable. Despite the rise of objectionable online practices, most users cannot imagine living without online infrastructures. In many societies, online technologies have become key to how users socially express, make, and reproduce themselves. We have started to become-with the Internet. This also creates a sense of identity and ownership, which is why pulling the plug is not an option. At the same time, the Internet is a set of infrastructures that have traceability, as well as the possibility to associate information deeply engrained in their architecture.

A practice that I want to describe as *conversion* has become one way of making information matter differently. It is an active engagement with online information. Hacker jE2EE argues why such an engagement is necessary: "It's important one knows what happens and how technologies work in order to assess dangers and possibilities." This knowledge is what allows for collective practices of converting information to emerge. Conversion is 'to turn around', 'to transform', deriving from the roots *com-* 'with, together' and *vertere*, 'to turn' (Harper, nd). Making information matter, here, works with the idea of transforming it. While information is always in-formation, its formation, reformation, and transformation is here the ambition of the entire practice. The aim of conversion is to discover different affordances of digital information and information infrastructures, and to use these properties not for association – as is done in other cases. Rather, information and information infrastructures are repurposed or converted in order to engage with, question, and upset associative practices. For example, the materiality of information can be converted in order to limit its (re-)use, at the same time as it transmits an intended meaning only to a select few. Or information that looks like it is designated to submit a specific meaning, matters in fact quite differently to the intended addressees. Practices of conversion question existing information routines. They are an attempt to move away from technological and analytic standards towards identifying alternative ways of making information matter. In the preceding chapter we have learned, however, that practices of association also make use of conversion, for example when information generated for one purpose is scraped from the net and scrubbed to match another associative purpose. Conversion is – like association – a very context-dependent practice. In this case, I study examples of conversion that upset traditional veillance routines. Thus, association and conversion are not mutual countercultures, but practices of making information matter that stand in an ongoing dialogue (Kaufmann, 2020).

Throughout this chapter I use hacking as a 'resource' (Chun, 2008) to illustrate practices of conversion. Andrzej Zarzycki describes hacking as the act of disassembling, rethinking, and 're-appropriating' a standard, object, or 'system for another purpose than originally intended' (2018: 78). This, according to Gabriella Coleman, is often done 'with technical know-how and ability, but also with some degree of agility, guile, and even disrespect' (Coleman, 2017: 92). Indeed, guile and disrespect long characterized the public discourse about hackers as their acts were considered 'harmful and menacing' (for a critical discussion see Nissenbaum, 2004: 213). Helen Nissenbaum opposed such partial portraits of hacking by emphasizing the potential of hacking to produce social value. These discussions coincided with the concept of hacktivism (Jordan and Taylor, 2004). Hacktivists would fight those forms of technological progress that they would see as social decline (Maxigas, 2017). Yet, the image of hackers as activists, 'anti-institutional', 'countercultural and resistant' (Hunsiger and Schrock, 2016: 537) again did not match with those hackers who have become complicit in neoliberalism and globalization by providing the infrastructures for capitalism (Söderberg and Delfanti, 2015). After all, conversion is a practice that can be integrated with commercial or governmental association techniques, but it can also upset them. While hacking may be the 'subversive use of technology that allows creating new meanings' (Kubitschko, 2015: 83), it is not always 'critical, creative, reflective' (Kubitschko, 2015: 83). A history of partial portrayals still leads to binary understandings of hacking as either lauded or denounced (for a critique see: Coleman and Golub, 2008). Alternatively, they are seen as acts of protection or corruption (Steinmetz and Gerber, 2015). Equally, the model of different hats over-simplifies a rather complex practice: black for illegal hacks, white for ethical hacks, grey for hacks that are ethical in the outset, but may be illegal, blue for hacks performed within a business framework, green for newcomers. Rather, hacking involves different ethical positions including the support of negative freedoms (for example, freedom from surveillance) and positive freedoms (for example, availability of free software). While some hackers are state-employed or act as ethical instances and risk managers (Palmer, 2001), hacking also includes moralities of the underground and romantic individualism (Coleman and Golub, 2008). Hackers move in a diverse field that includes authority and sharing (Powell 2016), self-expression and collective forms of action (Söderberg, 2017), expressions of masculine identity (Hunsiger and Schrock, 2016; Jordan, 2017) as well as feminist values of inclusion and intimacy (Goode, 2015; SSL Nagbot, 2016). In sum, hacking is not a homogenous practice, but 'under constant negotiation and reformulation and replete with points of contention' (Coleman and Golub, 2008: 255). The label combines 'different, sometimes incompatible, material practices' (Jordan, 2017: 528). It is a diverse practice, which also means that conversion is in and of itself not necessarily marked by an affirmative ethics: hacking and conversion, too, involve surveillance. At times, they are a practice of subjecting others to one's power or of avoiding taking on responsibility. Hacking, in the spirit of Melvin Kranzberg (1986), is neither good nor bad, nor is it neutral. Thus, with the empirical studies in this chapter, I only portray 'small corners of activity in a vast territory' (Coleman, 2017: 91). Hackers also do not self-identify as one group. When I asked hackers themselves how they would summarize their activities (see Kaufmann, 2020), bl4ckb0x explained that hackers "de- and re-construct" technologies in order to "discover" (Crypsis), "define the undefined" (Panoptipwned), "test" (heisenbugwatch), "reinvent" (LOLveillance), "create" (3x3cute), or "divert" (GCSgateway). Hacking is a "science of staying curious" (3x3cute) – all of which are starting points for making information matter differently.[2]

Even in the specific context of engaging with surveillance and association, hacking has different functions and roles (see Kaufmann, 2018, 2020). It can be a practice of (mainly hackers') everyday life (De Certeau, 1984: xv) that does not take the rules of online communication as a given. This can be done as a reflected tactic (for example by using a self-developed code) or it can become a routine (for example by using PGP certificates by default for messages). At the same time, hacking has emerged as political culture. It has produced concrete artifacts to interrogate and re-appropriate technologies – even if these interrogations are marked by 'multiple disagreements about conceptions of rights, autonomy, and dispositions of acceptability' (see Huysmans, 2016: 91). Hacking also includes aspects of play (Sicart, 2014) when standards are disrupted, technologies are re-appropriated, and communication routines are ambiguated. Mandelbugger emphasizes the "fun and games" that help hackers to "break out" of standard procedures and at the same time enable "learning". Hacks are also identity work. They express one's opinions about surveillance, but also one's standpoint within the hacker community. Technology is not only a means to an end, but interacting with it, creating personal scripts for it and re-appropriating it – making it one's own – is part of practicing a sense of self (see Kaufmann, 2018). It is not surprising, then, that hacking is also a physical experience full of affective encounters. While the collection and association of one's own information by third parties is linked to "pressures" (AceOfPlays, bl4ckb0x), "fear" (Crypsis) and even "creeping pain levels" (Crypsis), hacking is experienced as "being awake" (Numbercruncha), "self-empowerment" (AceOfPlays), "self-defense" (GCSgateway, Numbercruncha, Real&), which can be "constructive" (Re-ID) or "egoistic" (Sousveillor). Hacking, then, does not simply make information 'less valuable' (Brunton and Nissenbaum, 2011: online). Rather, the value of information is redefined and adapted to the context in which information is supposed to matter. That is the vantage point for conversion described in this chapter. There are, however, different degrees to which conversion is successful or creates the intended effects. After all, conversion is a collaborative practice including information, infrastructures, and users, which means that frictions will occur.

In order to study practices of conversion, I chose to speak to those who self-define as hackers, who are concerned about the rising level of online surveillance and seek to make information matter differently. Speaking to hackers was a deliberate methodical choice, because they enabled all the involved to discuss the how and why of conversion. The different conversations lasted between 45 minutes and 2.5 hours. I reached out to 22 hackers via the mailing list of the Chaos Computer Club (CCC). Using this path to find hackers that were willing to speak to me impacted the answers I received. Not only is the CCC largely a German-speaking organization with local branches throughout Europe, but the club is known for their commitment to online privacy and sharing knowledge. While this may be different in other hacker organizations, it also helped me in identifying hackers that would speak about the role and practice of conversion I wanted to analyse.

I interacted with everyone online. While some researchers see no discontinuities between Internet and conventional ethnography (Hine, 2008; Lee et al, 2008: 13), I would argue that the Internet very much co-determined my research. As laid out earlier, the Internet co-constitutes hackers, their cultural codices and practices, as well as those of the legal authorities that work with surveillance (see Kaufmann and Tzanetakis, 2020). Digital environments make it possible to trace information – the very point that gives rise to conversion. Thus, the fact that I conducted my research online influenced both my method and the knowledge created. Concretely, the Internet already co-determined *how* I would be able to access hackers. Some hackers were relatively public, willing to speak to me while using their real name via commercial communication channels in which all information is shared with the provider. Most hackers, however, wanted to remain anonymous. Some would use end-to-end encrypted chat software and would not reveal their real name, face, or voice to me. More important, most hackers would test me when I reached out to them. They would ask about my political and ideological standpoints with regards to online veillance. If my answers were not satisfactory, they would discontinue the conversation. When I mentioned this to DataD14709, he answered:

'Well, you know, within our community there is a thing called the social captcha test. In the same way that you'd complete a captcha test online, you also have to pass a captcha test as a human being, a hacker, a member of a social network. Every community has their own test and you have to find out how to do it. … In hacker communities you will mostly experience technical captchas. We want to find out how much IT knowledge this person has, whether we like this person. Does the person do activities that we do, is the person interested in things we are interested in? … If you want to enter a community you have to check them out first. You really can't botch that captcha test up.'

While many ethnographic situations involve the passing of a social entry barrier, this captcha test was not only an examination in terms of ideology and familiarity with slang, but the test also involved the specifics of the research environment. My capacity to navigate and use hacking technologies was tested, too, in order to understand my familiarity with the culture. Not surprisingly, the specific situation of speaking to hackers *online* ended up in an individual negotiation with each of them on the type of tools, programs, and apps we would use to converse. Since this involved a reasoning about the functioning, politics, and effects of each tool, these negotiations already tackled the core of the research project. What is more, the tools also acted back: some were not very user-friendly or too user-friendly (and sharing user data). Others broke down or had glitches. This co-shaped the situation of communication. However, they also co-shaped the situation in the sense that some hackers would have not participated or would have given different answers if I had used commercial solutions or met them in person. The tools helped creating a situation of trust in which hackers would eventually open up (see Kaufmann and Tzanetakis, 2020; Kaufmann, 2022).

Hence, what may be experienced as 'messiness' (Squire, 2013) in the ethnographic situation turned out to be a necessary pathway for gaining meaningful access and creating knowledge. Moving away from what John Law and Vicky Singleton critically describe as 'methodological managerialism' (2005: 333) or the 'impulse to hold the object of analysis together as a coherent one' (Squire, 2013: 38) has also become relevant when coding the data material generated during the conversation. I will now turn to the life cycle through which information passes when techniques of conversion are used and when information is deliberately made to matter differently (see Chapter 3). Here, it was possible to assign the material to different turns of this life cycle, but the earlier-mentioned multiplicities, incoherences, and disagreements among hackers still remained.

Imaginaries

When hackers deliberated about the character of information they spoke of its materiality. At the same time, they also tied this materiality to volatility and the inability to remain in control. Re-ID formulated it quite directly: "once shared, information exists out there and cannot be retracted anymore." Crypsis, too, described that information may defy influence: "Control over my own data ... (pauses) Can I still exercise that control?" Information, once it materializes online, is released into the unknown, because it cascades through various systems: "Once my information is online, I can never take it back. It is extremely difficult to turn the wheel back" (3x3cute). This idea of information being material, but agile and uncontrollable also plays into the idea of information becoming lively (see Chapter 2 and 3). Even more, information may eventually take control. Information and information infrastructures will "strike back! The more networked we are, the more will technology take control of humans" (LOLveillance).

Since information was imagined as something that is hard to contain, hackers turned to the alternative of re-shaping the information that circulates already. This imaginary of a flexible materiality is key to conversion. It gives rise to the idea that once information materializes, it can still be made to matter differently. Indeed, to convert the materiality of information, that is its instantiation in different technologies, was central to hackers. It is only because information materializes that it can be explored, dissected, crafted, and created with (bl4ckb0x). Making information matter differently was thus also tied to the conversion of information technologies and techniques. Dissecting these technologies, bl4ckb0x explained, is the first step of conversion. Conversion itself, he argued, does not necessarily have to be an ethical practice. It can produce "anything from legal protest to destruction". Crypsis, too, said that the curiousness about technologies and options to redefine technologies leads to a "conversion of information that can be both, positive and negative".

Still, many hackers tied this ability to change information to progress: not only is hacking a "creative process" (LOLveillance; see also ToastIt) and the "mindset and ability to make things differently" (=Overview; see also IzMyQ), but it is "enhancement" and "adaptation" of existing solutions (DataD14709). Conversion requires that one can identify "possibilities" within material instances of information and "overcome limits" (GCSgateway; see also LOLveillance; =Overview). The whole point of "making" is then not to look at "conventions and laws" inscribed in materialities, but to overcome them (GCSgateway; see also Real&; ToastIt). Such a practice "surpasses" and "works outside the imaginations of the original technical providers and owners" (Re-ID). It "identifies the undefined and forgotten parts of systems" (Panoptipwned). Conversion "makes something new from something that already exists ... That expands our means of existence. We don't take things as a given" (Sousveillor). Hackers do not consider data as a given (see Chapter 1), but these imaginaries imply that information is rather given into a situation by someone or something and continues to change. Information is in-formation. And that formation can be worked with.

The ambition and the imaginary of making information matter differently led Kate90r13 to conclude that hacker cultures are meritocratic, that is "based on merits – those who demonstrate that they are able to make something are recognized members of the community" (see also ToastIt). In practices and cultures of conversion, making and matter are central imaginaries of information. Information was seen as non-permanent and agile. The trajectory was considered uncontrollable, but it was also seen as inherently material. Information and information technologies can be explored, dissected, crafted and created with, which also means that making matter is at the heart of specific hacker cultures and their relationship to information.

Generation

Imaginaries of materiality also influence practices of generating information. In fact, Sousveillor suggested that "(t)he best data are those that cannot be registered in the first place." This is why many hackers limit and control their data-generation. They cover laptop cameras. In addition, they password-protect the hard disks of computers used to go online and do not store private data in cloud spaces. Especially the rise of social media encourages the generation of online data – a publicity that is different from those in private chats (Mandelbugger). Many hackers avoid the use of commercial service providers such as Google, Facebook, WhatsApp, or Dropbox when generating data, but move to encrypted and open-source providers instead. They find out which type of encryption they can trust before online information is even generated (DataD14709; AceOfPlays; 3x3cute; GCSgateway; Re-ID; Panoptipwned).

Encryption is one way of converting the standard format of online information. Using encryption was very important, for example, to heisenbugwatch: "The only thing that I actually feel is secure, is e-mail encryption with PGP. PGP is still uncrackable, there is nothing happening there, but anything else, VPA ... there is nothing ... GSM, GPS information, all of this is somehow hackable."

Information is encrypted before sending and decrypted upon arrival. Only parties with the correct sets of encryption keys have access to the meaningful content. When it travels through different infrastructures information takes on a different shape, which means that it may be accessed by others, but cannot be understood. When encrypted, information "does not make any sense" to those who collect and analyse it (=Overview). This change of shape matters. IzMyQ would write his own encryption keys. Others used keys provided by companies or open-source projects they trust. While encryption makes data matter differently, it still faces some challenges: "encryption keys can get lost, they can be stolen or published" (Re-ID). In addition are users of PGP identifiable, because the certificate attached to the mail makes PGP users stick out. This again allows for new forms of association:

'What I do most often in practice is to encrypt my data, but the problem is of course that my metadata is still visible, which means that someone who is watching me can – with a little bit of statistics and some solid assumptions – draw conclusions about my communication. If I encrypt my mails and I am active in a political group, then it's possible to recognize – just by surveilling the data traffic – the decision-making structures. If one can recognize specific communication patterns, you can deduce something about the contents of these communications, for example: every Saturday when you want to organize the info-table in the city center, it's the same three people talking to each other.' (GCSgateway)

One way to avoid sticking out due to the PGP script is to use an entirely different form of encryption. Some hackers used social codes when they generated information. In effect, such codes not only obscure content, but sometimes also the fact a message of content is sent at all. DataD14709, for example, mentioned riddle-based and other playful kinds of conversion: "Steganography. ... A way of data transmission that makes it impossible to find the data, especially not with a filter or other kinds of technology." He mentioned a range of techniques that play with the materialization of information:

DataD14709:   (H)ere are many ways: visual ways, languages, different logical connections to transmit a message that cannot be digitized, ... a chat via two different chat providers, where you only send a part via each program. ... Here are so many options! In most of the cases I know, you as a private person create a key and once the other understands it, you can use it as a communication means. That's the point: you can only communicate with that one person that you want to communicate with.

Mareile Kaufmann: Do you know of other hackers using that?

DataD14709:   Many! For example, for indicating time, you only send a ... digital picture of an analogue watch with the time. That is practical, because you could communicate a time without creating a direct association.

Hacking has a history of converting information into a shape that matters differently as its intention is to reveal content only to the adept. Well-known examples include, for example, Leet or rather '1337'-speak, where characters are replaced by stand-ins such as numbers, symbols or other letters. Other examples, as mentioned by DataD14709, are sending pictures instead of words or using two chat channels for the same conversation.

Since these techniques only matter as long as they are not overtaken by information tracking and analytic efforts, there is a growing amount of techniques that generate information in a way that converts communication standards. Some of them have become categorized as obfuscation, that is, the use of 'ambiguous, confusing, or misleading information to interfere with surveillance and data collection' (Brunton and Nissenbaum, 2016: 1). The forms of conversion that DataD14709 described earlier would then be a form of 'selective obfuscation' (Brunton and Nissenbaum, 2011; Kaufmann, 2020) that changes information to the extent that it is only understandable to insiders. Knowledge about veillance logics is needed to convert it. While calling for collective action using obfuscation, Finn Brunton and Helen Nissenbaum also reflect about a range of central criticisms about the concept. Obfuscation may be considered dishonest as its intention is to mislead. Its users want to freeride, that is to receive services without contributing to their functioning, and some techniques pollute informational resources (Brunton and Nissenbaum, 2011). Other criticisms address ethical challenges, in particular when obfuscation is practiced by corporations. Yet, specifically in the current situation of being pressured to share information online, Brunton and Nissenbaum conclude, such techniques can be considered the 'only resort' (2011: online) for private users. They may be the only means to overcome information asymmetries. As mentioned earlier, those who use such techniques are not necessarily interested in commercial services, which disproves the criticism of free-riding. Similarly, the reproach that conversion is set out to mislead others can be met with the argument that information is intended for a specific recipient only and converting that information is otherwise a comment on extractive data politics. Thus, obfuscation and other practices of conversion need to be assessed in relation to their actors, intentions, and effects.

Another way in which private users make information matter differently is by routing information through unorthodox pathways or by repurposing standard communication pathways. Some users would go as far as generating and sharing information only in infrastructures that exist disconnected from the Internet, so-called parallel networks or pirate boxes that enable the local sharing of information. These can be built with simple, credit card-sized computers such as raspberry pis or beagle/freedom bones. The materiality of hardware is here what determines the materiality of information. Re-ID uses such solutions:

'There is a so-called pirate box, that is an image one can draw onto a raspberry pi and once you have that connected to a mobile charger, you can let it run 'headless', meaning without mouse, keyboard or monitor … The raspberry pi creates a WLAN that is completely secluded from the Internet, that means nobody goes online with this and no data are shared via the Internet. That means anything you communicate via a pirate box, that you upload – pictures, photos, videos, any data – are local and that is an interesting concept.'

Other infrastructures may be connected to the Internet, but their design and the ways in which they are used for information generation is decisive. Dark boxes, for example, are second computers that are only used for information, which is not supposed to be associated with the user (DataD14709). Or, in order to remain inaccessible GCSgateway would start the computer's operating system completely from a stick using the operation system TAILS. Yet a different material practice was to generate and send information via so-called overlay networks, infrastructure that is added on top of existing networks. Instead of travelling straight from sender to the intended receiver, information travels decentral via many different sender- and receiver-infrastructures worldwide. This decentral and collective approach makes it harder to track communication and communication patterns. Since most overlay networks spread vastly, it is difficult for a third party to watch the full string of connections through which information travels. Due to such roundabouts and collective efforts needed to send information these overlay networks have become categorized as cooperative obfuscation (Brunton and Nissenbaum, 2011). While some hackers would build overlay networks themselves – an arduous socio-technical process – most used open-source software such as The Onion Router (Tor) or I2P (AceOfPlays; Filterer; heisenbugwatch; Re-ID; Kate90r13; LOLveillance; Mandelbugger; ToastIt).

Since the whole intention of the process is that information materializes and rematerializes in a range of different infrastructural nodes, Tor has also practical challenges. It tends to be slow and the entry and exit nodes of information traffic are still identifiable by third parties. This is a reason why some hackers also considered overlay networks a "disproportionate" tool to make information matter differently (LOLveillance). Filterer explained that alternatives to overlay networks are tunnel protocols, which repackage the information before sending it through a public network. In this case, the standard wrapping of information is converted to a different one (see PGP).

There are other techniques of making data matter differently that avoid the problem of still being identifiable via encryption certificates or entry and exit nodes of overlay networks. For example, Panoptipwned would convert the very act of generating information as he would make relevant information vanish in a lot of irrelevant information. Thus, whenever he would write and send a message, excess information traffic is generated. This solution, however, creates its own problems. jE2EE reflected about such tools:

jE2EE: There is a fun browser-plug-in that generates
                    random traffic, but I don't use it. I'm not a fan of it.
Mareile Kaufmann: Why not?
jE2EE: Good question ... somehow the limits are reached.
                    I made a certain threat-model for myself, asking
                    whom do I actually want to defend myself against?
                    I could also defend myself against the NSA, but

in that case we would not be able speak to each other today. My threat model is not that a three-letter agency invests money into attacking me as a single person.

Others did not agree with such plug-ins, since new algorithms are developed to filter out relevant information nonetheless (3x3cute) and excess traffic clogs already limited bandwidth (GCSgateway), which is why they preferred encryption.

Though hackers disagreed about the best ways to generate information that matters differently, the collection of these practices are, so explained Re-ID, an attempt to create a space where third actors are not able to access and collect information without more invasive methods. They fracture the Internet's totality and imagine alternatives outside the totalized condition of the Internet (Browne and Blas, 2017).

Storage

The transition from the generation of information to its storage is fluent, because information is always instantiated in a medium, which is often also a form of longer-term storage. Thus, a distinction between the generation and storage of information can at times be unnecessary. Here, it serves to describe yet a different set of practices. So far, examples of conversion were described that happen when information is actually generated, this part focuses on what information is stored and whether storage itself can become a source of conversion.

Users deployed techniques of conversion to influence the kind of information that ends up being stored about them. Some hackers tried to change that by using false IDs or location data, changing their computers' MAC address every time the computer is started, or using several accounts for different occasions. Others used apps that randomly generate text, which is sent to others so that it looks like they are communicating with others. The idea of this is to make it harder to identify and store data about speech and communication patterns. More aggressive forms of engaging with storage procedures exist, too. Here, storage itself ends up being a source of conversion. One such example is to barricade stored data so that it is no longer accessible. Others mentioned the use of distributed denial of service (DDOS) attacks (DataD14709; Kate90r13; Mandelbugger). Here, an enormous amount of information is added to already existing information, which overloads storage capacities and disrupts information infrastructures. Databases are then overwhelmed with information traffic. In these cases information matters and materializes to the extent that it can no longer be accessed or sites and services are no longer functional. Information becomes lively and it is difficult to stop these attacks. Hackers, however, have very differing opinions about DDOS attacks. Many considered them a too invasive practice.

Maturation and processing

Conversion is practiced when information is generated and stored, but there are also techniques that engage with already circulating information and convert it as it matures and is processed. Sousveillor, for example, used a technique to re-shape his informational profile online by converting the ways in which information about him is associated. He would feed the browsers specifically chosen, yet irrelevant datasets to upset profiling tactics. By doing so, he would change how information generated on his IP-address is labelled and associated. ToastIt would try the same by randomizing his 'likes' on Facebook. For that reason, one also calls this technique masking. It is like wearing a mask to protect one's informational profile. Masking, or ambiguating obfuscation (Brunton and Nissenbaum; 2011), converts the standard information that one is expected to share about oneself. Real& explains that association and profiling only work with enough training material that eventually reveals meaningful patterns. Converting training material by using tricks or distracting information is then a way to upset the machine learning process. The algorithm would then have too diverse training material to sensibly integrate one's own data into the profiling process. =Overview would use this technique, too: "You can find so many things in Google about me that it just does not make any sense anymore … It's a different identity – the person I am online does not match me anymore." Non-representative information is added to representative information to upset analytic logics. While some users hand-picked the clicks they would use to mask their representative information, Panoptipwned would write bots that mimic online behaviour.

What sounds straightforward in theory is difficult in practice, because algorithms learn fast and it requires constant creativity to convert training data. In order to convert in a meaningful way one needs to know tracking logics and browser designs (Sousveillor). In addition, the use of masks has to be organized consistently in order to be effective, which delimits the user's freedoms. =Overview found that masking is arduous, but still doable. She even reverse-engineers algorithms, dedicating a computer to be a "honeypot" to attract the programs she wants to understand, convert, and exploit.

> 'These are only algorithms! One has to know the algorithm, but …
> I do reverse engineering. … I try to find source codes and once I have
> them, I can trick it. It's difficult, but doable. … Sometimes it takes
> months, but it works, even if is a self-learning algorithm. I know how
> to program AI algorithms, so I see every day how that works, how

the statistics work – it's only a few equations. It is very difficult to find all the parameters, but the people who programmed them in the first place knew what they trained the algorithm to know.' (=Overview)

A more aggressive form of converting already existing information or even a software's source code (which is also information) is subversion. Here, codes are written and injected into information-driven applications, which then disrupt or change their execution. Such SQL (Structured Query Language) injections or software subversions are used to change, convert, or tamper with information to the extent that either databases or websites look completely different. Sousveillor mentions the example of web defacements. With SQL injections information can also be leaked (Crypsis), destroyed or made unavailable. Not everyone agrees with such attacks: "My form of protest is constructive, not destructive. I give advice or organize a critical blog. I can also start a crusade by switching away from Google-based services to services with less tracking functions. That is my form of protest" (AceOfPlays).

In addition, it is unclear whom these aggressive attacks eventually damage (bl4ckb0x; 3x3cute; Filterer). Some hackers would justify offensive hacks in particular cases (DataD14709; Kate90r13; Mandelbugger; Sousveillor).

> 'Earlier I observed active raids – DDOS, but I don't do them myself. … There are definitely legal ways to challenge systems and companies one does not like – without having to be aggressive. One can show one's opinion online, on social media, blogspots without generating black hat traffic. If you want to be a black hat, you have to go all the way. If you do not want to follow any ethical standards or do anything bad – you can go for it, but then you always have to expect that your behavior has consequences.' (DataD14709)

The different examples of conversion underline again that the practice is in and of itself not affirmative or destructive. Rather, they illustrate that conversion matters as they change the materiality of information. Again, how they matter needs to be understood and studied in the light of intentions and effects.

Death/re-use and a call for engagement

Some forms of conversion are aimed at stopping data from mattering, such as specific SQL injections and DDOS attacks. That is to say, though data materializes at exponential speed, it stops mattering in its original context. Most practices of conversion, however, are not aimed at destroying or deleting information. Those practices shared during the conversations were in line with the imaginary discussed at the beginning of the chapter: "once shared, information ... cannot be retracted anymore" (Re-ID). This imaginary and the different techniques of conversion discussed in this chapter speak rather to the opposite of death, but to continuous becoming. Conversion is to experiment with the ways in which information can be lively and information. Imaginaries and practices of conversion are generally not driven by final resolutions and attempts to kill information. Conversion practices do not avoid data re-use or stop their creep. Instead, the impetus of conversion is to influence the direction of information creep. Information is allowed to exist online, but practices of conversion aim to create space to question how it is used. Conversion is a playful back-and-forth between different information practices.

Indeed, GCSgateway saw no other way but to constantly question and debunk information technologies. Kate90r13, too, found that these ongoing practices of questioning and converting would be necessary; they "can be a form of social engineering. ... This thinking is essential to modern society". The challenge is that many forms of conversion are studied, understood, and incorporated into new associative and analytic regimes. Filterer observed: "most measures of obscurity are no longer effective as algorithms can filter them out and identify them". This integration of veillance with conversion, however, may bring about new critical engagements with veillance. Making matter differently, then, also changes with new legislation regimes (Sousveillor). This is why GCSgateway suggested that such engagements "need to be flanked by political measures" rather than being annulled by them.

This constant back-and-forth between different information practices can be costly and exhausting. Some hackers actively used cost-benefit calculations to assess their actions. It may seem as 'an endlessly repeating series of responses. Therefore, to battle this twinning of crises and codes, we need a means to exhaust exhaustion, to recover the undead potential of our decisions and our information through a practice of constant care' (Chun, 2011: 92).

Much in this spirit, many hackers wished conversion would no longer be a fringe activity without much representation (Kate90r13). A surprising number mentioned that their actions are not a refusal to be part of the mainstream (Re-ID; Mandelbugger; =Overview; Q; Sousveillor). Panoptipwned explained: "Actually, I hope that hackers' knowledge about surveillance and our techniques to deal with online veillance will become the mainstream." In a similar vein bl4ckb0x said: "It's the other way around. I wish that mainstream users were more aware of online surveillance." Numbercruncha agreed: "We need to confront this ... We need a bigger amount of people who say: We don't want this!" One can observe that terms such as 'obfuscation', 'masking', and 'the dark net' have established themselves in hacker and policing glossaries alike. However, they invoke associations with weak reactions of hiding and covering-up. More so, they tend to be interpreted as behaviour that is merely opportunistic – not as a self-confident engagement with information politics. In the worst case, these terms may even contribute to criminalizing that which can also be a 'practice of constant care' (Chun, 2011: 92). The vocabulary of darkness and obscurity does not help emphasizing the many different ways in which information matters and may rematerialize.

In response to these challenges, one could invoke poet Édouard Glissant, who formulates a burning defense for techniques that he summarizes under the term opacity. Opacity is the right and a deliberate choice to produce unknowability by evading cognitive schema and standards used to govern people (1997). As such, it can become a force to challenge systems of domination from within, which reflects the commitment to remain online while engaging with current information politics. In the light of opacity, these techniques can make information matter differently. They can become a self-confident engagement with the politics of capture and control. Opacity can address 'the limits of schemas of visibility, representation, and identity that prevent sufficient understanding of multiple perspectives of the world and its peoples' (Blas, 2016: 149). In a similar vein, practices of conversion can mark participation in this contested societal arena. Conversion and hacking are attempts to recast and "increase the value of one's own data", so =Overview suggested. They can be a form of disputing where and how data is collected and how technologies function (Kaufmann, 2020). Though hackers disagreed about the different forms of conversion, what united all of the mentioned practices is that they put usability and convenience up for discussion.

It is this mindset of putting usability up for discussion and exercising practices of constant care that many hackers wished would be more pronounced in society at large: "You don't need to be an information scientist, you don't need a specific training! Everyone has the potential to do this," said DataD14709. Everyone would be able to ask themselves: "What kinds of data traces do I leave behind? What do I share? You have to look into this subject consciously" (AceOfPlays). =Overview also found that such positions and practices would involve each individual: "Yeah – it's like a disease this trend to over-share. ... Collecting likes and 'points' has become so important." IzMyQ summarized: "Any information you share online is public. ... Once you know that, you have responsibility." Kate90r13, too, invoked responsibilities: "the general public stands in its own light. Technologies are like a miracle that somehow works, but in order to drive a car, you need a driver's license. ... People need to be obligated to do more."

At the same time, however, the public would still need to be "taken by the hand to become aware of the problem. A critical view on technologies – discussing them – should become a general 'cultural technique'. People can no longer be passive" (3x3cute). Taking others by the hand was also an important ethos to many hackers. bl4ckb0x expected hackers to "point to gaps or unfair behavior" in order to sensitize others. As one of those who are in the know, heisenbugwatch argued, "I am part of shaping technologies. I am responsible. ... I have to sensitize people about these problems – this is a part of my own future." Showing impacts on society, explaining technologies, creating know-how, "spreading facts – if necessary via leaks" (Crypsis) were mentioned as part of hackers' role in society (LOLveillance; Mandelbugger; Panoptipwned; Real&; Sousveillor; ToastIt). Hacking and conversion may be one road to teach people how to gain back their "informational sovereignty" (jE2EE). Re-ID, too, spoke of "technology sovereignty". Gaining that sovereignty may also mean to rethink the standing of technology. It may mean to give up the idea that it is

'technology that can change the world, but we need a societal change. We need a better understanding of technology and even when you are not an expert, you can help others to learn self-defense. Repair cafés are excellent. You can do it yourself. You will receive help to help yourself.' (Re-ID)

=Overview, finally, made the point that this type of education cannot start early enough:

'The "Kleinen Forscher"[3] do an excellent job here. They explain teachers how they can teach encryption to children – just like the alphabet. "Chaos macht Schule"[4] is another one. When you look at children you can observe how they give each other nicknames, how they develop codes. With children, this is very important. They have secrets.'

Hackers, here, made a strong case for their own and for everyone's role in making information matter differently. Everyone should have a vigilant, yet explorative mindset in relation to information routines and online technologies. A good culture of furthering knowledge and relating to information would then also be reflected in technology design. Such technologies would allow people to understand how their information materializes and is made to matter. While conversion is in and of itself not an ethical practice, hackers agreed that this specific combination of awareness, education and design could further a positive ethos of conversion as a way of making information matter differently. Mushon Zer-Aviv reminds us that the ethics of such practices always have to be considered in context, while the same is true for any form of surveillance (2021). In seeking to make information matter differently hacking allows us the 'much-needed benefit of the doubt' (Zer-Aviv, 2021: 493). At best, it can become a tool to identify the ethics of big data and surveillance (Zer-Aviv, 2021). This position reflects the ethos discussed throughout this chapter: practices of conversion need to be assessed in relation to their actors, intentions, and effects.

These appeals to everyone encourage the study of information practices in other everyday settings. There is a need to better understand how people, infrastructures, and information work together in different settings and the know-how that this may warrant. Zer-Aviv argues that obfuscation, for example, would provide a means to those who cannot afford the tech-savvy and costly method of encryption as a tool to question veillance (2021). While this may be true to some extent, it became clear throughout this text that some forms of obfuscation, as well as conversion, may be equally tech-savvy solutions. They require knowledge that is not easily accessible to everyone as well as technological skills. In that context, a central question emerges: Is there something more to learn by looking at how information matters, changes and is made to matter in settings that are less high-tech? =Overview made the point that it is necessary to understand and involve those who are making information matter offline – already early in life. The results of such a study can be found in the next chapter that discusses how children make information matter differently.

6

Secrecy

Information is not always out there, waiting to be accessed, collected, processed and revealed. We may be under the impression that information matters because it is made seen, associated, and known. After all, the word *information* describes an act of informing, communicating, and instructing. On closer inspection one may find that most practices of making information matter, however, are exercised and known by few, even if the actual practice may affect many. Thus, information matters not only when it is accessed and explored for patterns, or when it is converted in order to question association. Information matters, too, when it resists being known, when it is shared among few or when it remains inaccessible.

One engagement with information is to actively keep it from being out in the open, to make it known to select people only. *Secrecy* is a practice of making information matter. However, secrecy is not the opposite of making information seen or known. The relationship between secrecy and seeing, knowing or watching is not a dialectical one. Secrecy is more about how information is seen, known, accessed, and watched, by whom and how that matters. Georg Simmel argued that the interplay of knowing and not knowing matters as it shapes social relations. Not only 'knowledge of each other' (1906: 444) is a socializing force, but secrecy and concealment disrupt and vitalize socializing forces (Simmel, 1906: 448). Or as Susanne Krasmann puts it: 'In an imagined world without secrets, there would be no curiosity or confidentiality, no sincerity or trust, and no political possibility of thinking otherwise' (2019: 690). Knowing in secret regulates information flows and thus matters concretely. The work of confidentiality clauses and Chatham House Rule are illustrative examples of the effects of secrecy. Not surprisingly, there is a tendency to discuss secrecy as a practice of domination and exclusion, often associated with positions of power (for example, Fenster, 1999; Blakely, 2012). Carol Warren and Barbara Laslett (1977) dissociate the secret from elitist tools, but they still analyse secrecy as the morally questionable refuge for those without access to privacy: 'Privacy is consensual where secrecy is not' (Warren and Laslett, 1977: 43). Not only could one object, suggesting that privacy is not consensual and that the shared secret (see Smart, 2011) includes a dimension of consensus, but Simmel also warned against 'the manifold ethical negativeness of secrecy' (1906: 463). Clare Birchall goes one step further by problematizing 'any easy opposition between secrecy and transparency' (Birchall, 2011: 21). Indeed, approaching them as dyadic has concrete effects. Jack Bratich, for example, observes that meeting secrecy with watching, publicity, and exposition – even when it is done for activist reasons – denies that this opposition plays 'into a larger logic of concealment and revelation that is ultimately disempowering' (2006: 48; see Debord, 1998). Transparency and watching can challenge the secret, but they are not opposites of the secret. They are different forms of making information matter that sometimes merge. Secrecy, for example, includes specific forms of watching and watching out. Thus, being an interplay of knowing and not knowing, of watching and concealing, the secret remains 'always a moving target' (Birchall, 2014: 46). By its 'secretion' the secret also prods 'known subjects into action' (Deleuze and Guattari, 1987: 287). Secrecy is a project of making information matter by challenging the 'conditions of visuality' (Birchall, 2016: 159f), which affects the productivity of both, publicly known and secret information.[1]

It would suggest itself to study secrecy by looking at trade or business secrets, especially when they are kept by the same institutions that are otherwise the strongest drivers of watching and associating information (Moore, 2017; Glaeser, 2018; Maggiolino, 2019), such as large-scale online service providers. It would show us that association, as described in earlier chapters, also includes aspects of secrecy. Another obvious case study would be to explore secrecy and infrastructures of secrecy in the military, law enforcement, in politics and other governmental affairs (Feldman, 1988; Roberts, 2006; Vermeir and Margócsy, 2012; Brown, 2014). Though it is very important to understand practices of secrecy in these high-level and official contexts, a study of secrecy in more commonplace and everyday activities (de Certeau, 1986) can give us new insights. In addition, I wanted to choose a context in which secrecy is exercised as a way of engaging with and questioning surveillance, paired with the aim to extend the study of information into offline environments. Hence, I turned to rather obvious performers of the secret: children. They are very good at managing visuality, but they do so for a whole range of reasons. Like professionals, children develop techniques and use infrastructures to make secret information matter. In addition, they practice secrecy in settings that are – to a certain extent – different from online and other digital environments. Children demonstrate how important information is in contexts of life that are easy to forget when we study informational practices. Precisely because their informational practices appear to be quite 'basic', there are plenty of opportunities to gain insight from them. Children illustrate that information matters from

Figure 6.1: Magnhild Winsnes; *This is a Secret*; 2019

Source: Courtesy of the artist.

the beginning of life and that minors, too, are actors in making information matter. We tend to think of children as passive subjects of information, since much information about them is gathered and analysed by others. As Valerie Steeves and Owain Jones write: 'In a sense, to be a child is to be under surveillance' (2010: 187) – whether by parents and other family members, pedagogues, (health) care officials or private companies (see Figure 6.1).

Information about children is gathered for behavioural purposes (Marx and Steeves, 2010), marketing (Chung and Grimes, 2005), pedagogy (Sparrman and Lindgren, 2010), or for keeping track of them (Porter et al, 2011). Information is collected about them from the beginning of their lives as is done, for example, in pre-natal screenings (Marx and Steeves, 2010). In children's lives, too, information is increasingly generated in digital environments as happens in online interactions (Lewandowski, 2003) or through RFID chips (Ema and Fujigaki, 2011) and the use of smartwatches. Probably because children are associated with a higher need for oversight and care, most works single out the social, ethical, and developmental effects that gathering and analysing information has *on* children. Information practices co-create their lives and social relations (Rooney, 2010). Children are, however, 'active participants in this process' (Denzin, 2010: 4). When they are aware about information practices, they begin to interact with them (Kaufmann, 2021). They can thrive on the fact that information is gathered about them, when they experience it as care (see Foucault, 1979). However, children also resist the gathering of information about them (Raynes-Goldie and Allen, 2014). They negotiate information about them (Barron, 2014), they perform with it, they test it, and question it. Indeed, children are active subjects of information when they watch adults, other children or when they watch themselves. Like any person, children generate, collect, and keep information about themselves and about others, for example when they write diaries, take selfies, or play. All of these can be instances of control, vigilantism, of self-watching, and establishing peer-relations, but also of care and watching out for someone (Walsh, 2010; Kaufmann, 2021). One way of making information matter to themselves and others is secrecy.

At times, children use secrecy in response to the control that is exercised when information is collected about them. Here, secrecy can signal 'affirmative gestures of disappearance' (Bratich, 2006: 52). At the same time, children use secrecy as a way to control situations. Many children develop, for example, secret codes and languages to control a situation of being watched or watching others. Information materializes and matters as secret code (see Kaufmann, 2021). Alinea[2] and her friend, for example, responded to other children who used a secret language to mock them, by creating their own: "We demonstrated: we are capable of this, too. They were two years older and we were very upset that they mocked us – us, who are much younger than them … That's why we made our point."

Secrecy is also a practice of securing exclusive access to something valued. Children use hiding places, secret strategies, and languages to protect gifts and finds, games, other people or even friendships. Zeynep keeps information about whom she fancies in a secret place in order to protect that actual feeling. Indeed, keeping information secret also matters emotionally. Secrecy is tied to various affects, such as fun, excitement, thrill, fear, or shame and affection (Kaufmann, 2021). Sharing secret information matters in creating friendships and other relationships, while not being able to share secret information does so, too. Zeynep is, for example, sad that her mother is not interested in her secrets: "For her, my secrets are just air; they are only decorated paper. She knows that these are my secrets, but she does not find them interesting." Some children explained that having secrets matters to their own identity. Æsa, for example, finds that keeping a secret can tell the owner something about themselves. Other children explain that secrecy also gives them the space to express themselves freely and creatively. Many children enjoy the aesthetic of that which materializes when they engage with information in secret.

Talking to children about their information practices is very different from speaking to software designers or hackers. However, the relevance of talking to children may become more obvious when we know that hiding information in plain sight is a much-used practice of teenagers to engage with the fact that parents collect information about them online (boyd,

2014). In that light, secrecy can be quite similar to conversion. Chapter 5, for example, focused on the life cycle of online information that is relatively public in the outset, but converted in order to limit access. This chapter focuses on the life cycle of secret information instead. It studies the ways in which children imagine, generate, and store secret information, how secret information itself matures and is re-used. It explores what infrastructures and tools children use to make secret information matter. Expectably, these tools are different from those used in other information practices. Sometimes, however, there are striking similarities. Since techniques used to practice secrecy can be extrapolated to different societal contexts, including digital ones, but also adult live, it makes sense to understand them better.

Doing research with children is shaped by some methodological specificities that are worth mentioning, if only briefly. I spoke to 30 children between the age of six and 12 at a primary school. Two thirds of these children were girls, one third were boys. During this research project one child asked me if we were sharing a secret – now that we had begun speaking about secrecy. This question expresses that secrecy is also a relevant information practice in empirical research. It shaped the very situation of conversation in which research information was generated. This meant that the project not only needed the informed consent of teachers, parents and children as well as careful ethical monitoring, but a situation of trust had to be established constantly. Some children would be very shy, others considered me an authority, but by the end of our conversations most children would speak to me as if I was a confidante. This is a position for a researcher that needs to be handled with extreme care, since it requires reflexivity about the social, ethical, and legal responsibility one inherits.

A key challenge was to consider how I would handle situations in which children would mention sensitive information about harm done, or harm done to them, self-harm, or types of issues that would in other social contexts require me to act or share this information with others. A research situation is, however, bound by confidentiality and intimacy. The respect for confidentiality is not only an ethical commitment and requirement, but also actively shapes situations of trust. Especially with minors the earlier-mentioned situations present the researcher with a dilemma: Does shared information stop being confidential, because it is in need of further addressing? If so, at what point and how should issues shared in confidentiality be taken further? There are different ethics traditions concerning this issue. Some researchers would follow strict confidentiality and not take any initiative to follow up on this information. Others would mention serious issues, especially uttered by minors, to relevant actors. I never got into the situation where such sensitive information was shared with me. However, I prepared for this case. I decided that I would mention to an adult that an in-depth talk with the child in question would be advisable without detailing what problem exactly the child shared. I would ask the child to tell me who a trusted contact would be and whether it would be ok to reach out to them. Vis-à-vis that contact, I would not share detailed information in order to leave the judgement on the seriousness and veracity of the statement to professionals.

All of this illustrates that secrecy concretely influenced my research-relations, because it determined what children would share. A different methodological specificity was that the children switched quickly between sharing actual situations, varieties of actual situations, fabulations, or spontaneous brainstorms. Ingo, for example, claims that a group of children at his school once caught a thief "and the police came, too!". Bo, who is not much older than seven, mentioned that he would pay the winners of his secret game an enormous amount of money from his own pocket. Fiona spontaneously adapted her story during the conversation when she noticed that her anecdote had an effect on the other child present:

Fiona:	Sometimes when Georgia comes for a visit, I trick her together with my sister.
Georgia:	*(looks surprised at Fiona)*
Fiona:	Well, I never did that! Sometimes. Not so often.
Georgia:	I never noticed.

While some of the shared experiences were notably exaggerated, I also learned to distinguish between different varieties of narratives when I listened to the same situation told by different children. At the same time, the actual interview situation would also allow me to understand how children would enact secrecy if they could choose freely. It also allowed me to observe how children practiced secrecy vis-à-vis me as a researcher. Thus, whether children would share situations they experienced, varieties of them, or what are probably rather fantastic narratives confirms that any conversation is highly dependent on the sharing individual. This, actually, only made a small difference for the analysis, since I would be able to learn and observe anyway how children choose to practice secrecy as a way of making information matter to themselves.

Imaginaries

Life cycles of secret information include imaginaries. Children do reflect about what secrecy means to them conceptually and on an interpersonal level. Here, the children described a tension between the idea that information should be kept secret and the secret's tendency to spread. Both aspects matter to children.

Their initial association with secrecy was that the accessibility to secret information is and should be limited. Secret information would only be shared with those who should know it, as Dora mentioned: "I did share the secret with someone, my friend, but that was only between the two of us. We did not pass it on to anybody else." She continued and expressed a widespread idea about the temporality of secrecy: "Often, a secret is something that people have, because other people are *never* meant to find out about it." A few children discussed the effects such imaginaries of limited accessibility and permanence can have. Alinea considered that lying may be necessary technique to protect secrets and that by sharing secret information one "may render oneself susceptible to blackmail" (Alinea). Dora assumed that strict secrecy is necessary when the information is about something "uncomfortable". Æsa found that strict secrecy is relevant "when it concerns another person". These imaginaries of limited accessibility and permanence underline the productivity of secrecy, because it steers visuality and knowability. Imaginaries of intimacy and trust were also strong: "My brother has told me his best secret hiding place and I told him mine. ... Only he knows it. ... I shared that with him, because we play together and are best friends" (Morten). Only a few children experienced that intimacy was forced onto them, for example when secret information was shared that they did not want to know. Most children would share secrets only with those whom they considered close and trustworthy. Dora tried to explain why: "Well, some people you know well and you know that they cannot keep the secret to themselves. And since I do not know everyone so well, I won't share my secrets with just anyone. When it comes to my best friend, I know that she won't share my secrets."

Indeed, many children shared information only with those who would be nearest to them or those whom they would choose carefully. To Xenia, Yvonne, and Zeynep, secrecy was a defining part of their friendship. Alinea recounted that a secret she shared with her kindergarten teacher would strengthen their relationship. Oliver explained how strict limits to accessibility would also tie a group together: "It's just like that: when you include, like, 50 people into your secret group, it will fall apart." To children, then, regulating accessibility to information is an expression of intimacy, as well as a defining imaginary of secrecy: "When the whole class knows, it's no longer a secret" (Jenny). Hilde argued for strict limits as to who would be allowed to be a member of their secret group: "We vowed not to let anyone in, just Vincent, but he is a real close friend to one guy in our group and he will leave school this year, so we let him in for half a year, but no one more." Thus, at times, information about the very existence of a secret is kept secret. Sina, Jenny, and Alinea mentioned that it would be obvious that if one knows a secret, one would not share it, and Anton found that one does not have to "agree upon" which terms one shares secret information.

Though strict limits to accessibility emerged as the strongest imaginary, children also mentioned the secret's inclination to spread. Secretion

(Deleuze and Guattari, 1987) is thus another imaginary that influences how information is generated, accessed, and shared. Alinea said to me: "I always feel that others will share my secret with others. ... And when one girl sends a quarter of the package on and the next one another quarter, then at some point everyone knows and I stand there with no secret left."

Øydis, who was barely six years old, described the secret as if it had its own agency that pushes for secretion:

Øydis:	One secret was really not easy to keep. It almost burst out of me, but then it didn't burst out anyway.
Mareile Kaufmann:	How did you manage to keep the secret?
Øydis:	I just tried not to move my mouth.

Secrecy and secretion are experienced as complementary imaginaries. Children mentioned that they would have secrets which they would never share with anyone. In other situations, however, the whole point of the secret would be to share it. Æsa and Sina described the excitement and positive affectivity of being able to gain access to secrets. Bo, Timo, Ulla, and Veronika also liked preparing secret information for others to be accessed in a playful manner and Karlo would test others by checking whether they would manage to gain access to his secrets. All of these practices of secrecy feature careful plans and choreographies for when and how to grant access to information. Without making a deliberate point, Karlo mentioned another important temporal aspect about secrecy, namely the ageing of secrets. With time, their secrecy would lose importance:

Mareile Kaufmann:	Did no one ever find out?
Karlo:	Dunno. I don't think so.
Mareile Kaufmann:	Would it be terrible if someone found out now?
Karlo:	Nah.

Secret information evoked several defining imaginaries: those of limited accessibility, permanence, and (forced) intimacy were combined with those of secretion and potential obsolescence. All these imaginaries are part of unfolding the secret's agency: it ties together and breaks apart, secrecy nurtures ideas of trust at the same time as it seems to force its way into secretion. These different imaginaries can be experienced as tensions, but often they vary with the type of secret practice. At times, the children met the secret's agency with the idea to use secret information deliberately as an instrument to manipulate a situation. Most important, imaginaries influence what information is going materialize in the first place, how it is generated, and whether it is meant to secrete.

Generation

That children imagine secret information as something that should be limited in accessibility has concrete consequences. They keep, for example, the very practice of generating secret information secret. Åke has a twin brother and though they were barely six years old at the time of the interview, they experimented with a secret language. In fact, it is not unusual for twins to develop a language that only the two can understand. The linguistic term for that phenomenon is cryptophasia (see Bakker, 1987). He explained that they do not want anyone else to access this language, which is why they would hide when they practice it. When they developed or spoke that language, they would make sure that "our parents will not see what we do" (Åke). The idea is here to avoid creating information about the fact that something secret is being established. Such behaviour is parallel to what hackers describe, too, namely that if one does not want personal information to be accessible, the best measure is not to generate much information in the first place or to generate information in a way that remains unnoticed by others (see Chapter 5). Thus, not only Åke and his brother, but many children also removed traces when they generated secret information.

In order to control access to contents, children also generated information in an encrypted fashion. A secret language is one form of encrypting information. Two thirds of the children I spoke to experimented with secret languages. Anton, for example, developed a language based on existing words in which he varied the initials: "I did this with a friend who is not at my school. Whenever we used it, no one understood us. (We used it) in front of people, like adults and others and they were like: Huh?!" Ronja's secret language was based on exchanging words in sentences. Alinea and her friend invented new vocabulary, some of which even expressed something that has no equivalent word in their mother tongue. This may be done for many reasons: to experience excitement and thrill, to send a social signal, to protect secret information, and to control the ways in which secrets secrete. That is to say, some children use a secret language for the sake of the game and to let others decrypt it, while others create languages to encrypt information for as long as possible. Åke and his twin brother, whom we already know, created a whole new language, which was meant to encrypt information only for the two of them:

Mareile Kaufmann:	How can you understand each other?
Åke:	Because we learned it together! We said something like this: (*cites an example*) and then we said, like, this means: how are you?
	...

Mareile Kaufmann: And when do you use this language?
Åke: When we have secrets just between us.

Another way in which children would generate encrypted information was via nonverbal, bodily signs. Emily explained how she and her friend used physical expressions to communicate secretly, some expressions emerged spontaneously, while other signs had been agreed on before: "We used these expressions so that no one knew that we wanted to meet later." Similarly, Fiona and Georgia had a secret code they developed using their fingers. Paula, who was a bit older, made a more systematic effort to develop bodily codes with her friends:

Paula: So we used facial expressions at first, then my friend showed me a Swedish sign language. And since she was a bit hearing-impaired we developed the idea to make our own sign language.
Mareile Kaufmann: Do you translate the alphabet into signs or do you use a sign for a complete word?
Paula: Complete words. But we also use a note ... for the new words.

Winnie explained that she and a friend would use hand signs to communicate in situations where they "share secrets or when no one is supposed to notice that we 'talk'." Xenia, Yvonne, and Zeynep, too, used their fingers, hands, and facial expressions to communicate secretly.

The function of secret languages, expressions, and physical codes is to generate information that is per se not broadly accessible. Secrecy, then, shapes how information materializes and is embodied, especially when the child's body becomes the central element in enacting information.

Secret information is, however, also generated in other material form. Cypher is a prime example of encrypting information in a different material fashion. It is very prominent in children's lives and includes specific infrastructures. The generation of information intersects here with the lives of anything from written alphabets to the instruments necessary to materialize the cypher, even if that is just a pen and a paper. The reasons for developing cypher are again a combination of many things: it elicits a specific affect, sends social signals, but it is also developed to protect and regulate access to information. During the time I spent with children, I listened to explanations about cyphers they developed, but I could also observe how they developed some in practice. In one group, I tested together with the children if they would actually be able to read the cypher they had just developed. While there was only limited practical usability of the cypher, the point was that it mattered to them anyway. The experience of creating a secret cypher tied them together.

Many children base their cypher on the alphabet of their mother tongue. Sina mainly decorated the letters of the alphabet, which at times turned into an aesthetic practice: "An L, then a line and a line, then a circle and below that a square – no: a triangle!". Xenia, Yvonne, and Zeynep developed a version of the alphabet using vertical lines only. Æsa explained a cypher where certain letters would be doubled and mirrored. Ingo mirrored complete sentences and Christa used coding wheels to cypher her writing: "Let's say where A is B and so on." Such coding wheels are often based on what is known as Cesar cypher or cascade cyphering. Oliver wanted to develop a cypher for his secret club: "We could either switch letters or exchange letters for numbers or other signs, like the morse code. ... like something totally complicated." Dora and her friends translated the entire alphabet into alternative signs: "We have a note. We do not know all signs by heart so we can look it up there. ... We have developed this code ourselves ... it is completely new, yes!" Jenny did the same with her friends. While not having found a way to implement it, Fiona and Georgia thought that the best cypher would be one in which the code or encryption key would shift constantly. With that, children speak about cyphers and encryption methods that are actually practiced in field of encryption at large. Without knowing about it, Oliver explained the idea of leet speak (1337) while Fiona and Georgia formulated the idea of asymmetric encryption.

Not all cypher is based on the alphabet or letters. Many children work with pictograms, where words are replaced by signs or pictograms that represent them, which is also a method employed by hackers (see Chapter 5). Anton, for example, used pictograms to encrypt writings with his friend. Yet another form of generating encrypted information includes tools such as special ink on paper: "Lemon! I put it on a brush and painted a picture with it and ... it dries when you put it in the oven." Oliver explained his tool: "We have a secret pen. You have a white one and when you paint over it with a blue one, you can see the white." In combination with the different infrastructures including pen and paper or the children's bodies, secret information materializes and matters in unique ways.

Storage

Using tools such as specific inks and pens may be alternatives to using actual cyphers, not least because some children cannot memorize the encryption keys. Fiona invented a creative way of recollecting such secret information: "Sometimes I create myself a secret memory, so that I remember the secret. I match a name with a secret and then I mix these two. I can keep it better in my head like that."

Figure 6.2: Magnhild Winsnes; *This is a Secret*; 2019

Source: Courtesy of the artist.

Other children memorize through constant practice, but most children use a device to store and explain the cypher by adding infrastructure. Bo, Christa, and Karlo wrote their cyphers down and kept these references in a secret hiding place (see Figure 6.2). So does Jenny:

| Mareile Kaufmann: | Do you know the cypher by heart? Can you remember it? |
| Jenny: | No, sometimes I have to look it up in my secret diary, there I keep the encryption key. The diary also has to be opened with a numeric code. |

Encrypting information, then, also involves classic keys and locks – not as expressed in code, but in the material form of lockable books. Children make active use of instruments to store and lock secret information. Alinea kept her key on a necklace "because it is safe there." Øydis emphasized that other material entities would be part of secrecy. She explained that she wanted to have a lockable book or box to keep her secrets:

| Øydis: | In the store we found a secret box with a code. My mom thought of a code and then the box |

Figure 6.3: Magnhild Winsnes; *This is a Secret*; 2019

Source: Courtesy of the artist.

	played music. Really loud. I said: I won't take this. That's too loud.
Mareile Kaufmann:	Because everyone will notice when you open the box to do something secret?
Øydis:	Yes. So I took the book with a secret key. I also hid the key in my room.

Zeynep mentioned a box with a fake bottom to hide secret information. Sina, Bo, Nina, and others stored secret information in lockable boxes, too. And Georgia observed: "Friends of mine have small box with a code and only they know the code. It's a secret code. They can put things into that box that are only for them. And no one else knows about them" (see Figure 6.3).

Boxes, books, and keys are materials that matter, because they limit accessibility to their contents. When information is stored in such tools, secret information materializes: the book, the lock, and the information together (re-)constitute information as secret. Such re-materializations are quite parallel to practices and tools of encryption in digital settings, where lockable hard disks or password protected documents rematerialize information, too.

What is more, the ways in which secret information materializes are diversified and layered. Alinea, for example, shared an intricate plan of where to keep the key to her secret diary: "When I can sew, I make a little heart with a zipper and then you can put the key in there from the bottom. Then I put the heart into the case with a glass wall, so no one can access it."

Anton and Ingo preferred to dig secrets down in sandboxes or other holes. And Karlo referred to his personal hideaway:

Karlo: I had a secret hideaway once.
Mareile Kaufmann: How did you pick that hideaway?
Karlo: I didn't use it that often, but it is an obvious
                                place. It is so obvious that one does not expect
                                a hideaway there.

Places, too, can be central to establish information as secret. Winnie, for example, developed a way of practicing secrecy by using the spatial capacities of the school building. "There are two entrances and sometimes we use the one and sometimes the other, which one is usually not allowed to use. That's why no one would try to find us there. No one thinks we are actually there" (Karlo).

What Karlo and Winnie described is similar to practices of hiding in plain sight in order to remain unnoticed. Many children use hideaways when they make secret information mater. Oliver explained how he constructed a hideaway that would include an emergency backdoor, an option for escape, in case someone should gain access anyway.

In most cases discussed earlier, imaginaries about limiting access and permanence inform the generation and storage of information. In some cases, imaginaries of secretion and increasing obsolescence are also reflected in the materiality of secret information. The techniques are varied: children use secret languages, by sending bodily signs. They generate information in cypher using infrastructure such as coding devices or special pens. Secret information rematerializes when it is stored in secret boxes, lockable diaries, or hideaways. Thus, different ways of making secret information matter are layered and developed together with those who are meant to have access. They matter practically, in play and emotionally.

Maturation

Once generated and stored, secret information may or may not work in practice. Developing encryption techniques that actually limit access to information and can be decrypted again is a practical challenge. Morten, for example, mentioned that when secret codes emerged spontaneously, these codes would still need to be understood by those that he would share secrets with. Timo, too, saw that one would be able to send encrypted messages that do not really work, because they would be misunderstood. In addition to that, other children described that secrecy may fail, because secrecy would be practiced too obviously, which would attract unwanted attention. This implies that it is not only the content of information, but also the social situation that needs to be 'understood'.

This is the reason why children continue to engage with the secret information they generated. Paula knew that developing secret languages would be an ongoing activity: "We are not really finished." Secrecy is not about finalizing a technique. Making secret information matter implies the constant re-materialization of information and techniques. Bo recounted a situation in which others constantly updated and adapted a secret hiding place. Bo was interested in finding it and remembered that the changing of the hiding place worked and had a concrete effect: "The harder it was to find ... the more precious it was." Indeed, since secrecy is a social situation, children also experience that others seek access to their secret information. Experiencing that the secret secretes is in fact quite a normal situation at school, but it does not stop children from practicing secrecy. Xenia, Yvonne, and Zeynep mentioned that they switched from one secret language to another when they would notice that their key was understood. Other kids updated or adapted their techniques preventatively, before others would get access. Several children explained how they made access to information harder over time by adding additional measures. When hiding information was not considered effective enough – since someone could discover the hiding place – children developed maps. These maps functioned as additional tools that were supposed to obfuscate the actual hiding place.

Bo:	So we added a few traps to the map. We made arrows that would point exactly in the wrong direction and from that we made a labyrinth.
Mareile Kaufmann:	How so?
Bo:	In this one place, we drew 15 possible ways (*to get to the hiding place*), of which 14 are wrong and only one is the correct one.

The way in which Bo added irrelevant information to the map is parallel to the practice of ambiguating obfuscation that hackers sometimes use online when they feed browsers with randomized, irrelevant information. A variation of such practices is to make the hiding place or information itself appear irrelevant. Timo would regenerate secret information by making it look like it was junk: "I would scrunch the paper up, put it into a plastic bag, put that bag into paper again and so on ... The problem is that this would be a waste of paper." Interestingly, Timo's second remark reflects the current critique of digital practices that aim to make relevant information drown in irrelevant information as they waste precious space (Brunton and Nissenbaum, 2011).

Oliver went even one step further in adding extra tools for protection. He was not only interested in actively deceiving those who wanted to access his secret, but he wanted to find out who they are and deter them in person. To do so, he developed a kind of honeypot (see Chapter 5), a map that was supposed to lure people into looking for the secret in the wrong place.

> 'At home I have a place where I hid many, many sweets. And I have a treasure map. I drew that one. It looks a bit like this: (*shows a stylized map with many crosses*) ... and here, this is the correct cross. And when one picks the wrong cross, you will only find random toys. Still, when someone would look at it, for example in the middle of the night, I can say: Hey, you are looking for my secret sweets! And they would be surprised.'

Not unlike professionals, children care as to whether secret information still informs in a meaningful way and whether their efforts to actively limit access to information work. They are also aware of the fact that the secret secretes. Whether intentionally or unintentionally, the secret tends to remain a moving target (Birchall, 2014), which is why making secret information matter is an ongoing activity. Children update and add layers of materials, tools, infrastructures, and techniques to ensure that information remains secret. With each practice of establishing secrecy further, whether it involves new hiding places, new encryption keys or the adding of deceptive information, secret information rematerializes and becomes lively.

Death/re-use

Children do destroy material traces of secret information. Some children mention that they regret having generated secret information, they may be ashamed of it or they realize that it may cause problems for them. Others also destroy material traces to protect information even better. Oliver would usually keep information about secret 'cases' that he and his friends worked on in a book: "When we still need the information, I hide the book in a secret spot. And when we are done with the case, I rip the pages out, so no one gets to know our approach" (see Figure 6.4). The destruction of material information, however, does not necessarily mean the end of secrecy. Secret information continues to exist in a different form. To Oliver, for example, the information of earlier cases would still be both, relevant and secret, because it would describe practices he and his friends would like to develop further. Oliver's example rather describes how secret information continues to be in-formation – even when a specific form of it is destroyed. The reason why Oliver would destroy secret information is precisely because it still matters. Thus, the destruction of information emerges as a practice of secrecy.

Figure 6.4: Magnhild Winsnes; *This is a Secret*; 2019

Source: Courtesy of the artist.

The life and death of secret information is also impacted when it unintendedly secretes. Even though this may also not 'kill' the secret entirely, children still try to actively prevent this from happening. Jenny, for example, was a member of a secret group, the rivalling group to Oliver's. Both groups resorted to quite official means to try to prevent secrets from being accessed. They wrote a contract-like document to prohibit accessing each other's information. That contract had its own life cycle and was also part of making secret information matter. Jenny explains: "Of course we don't want the other club to know what we talk about. We actually just made a paper together" A few days later when I interviewed Oliver, the story about their deal took a surprising turn:

Oliver:	First, we had a contract with the others to ensure that we don't spy on each other. But today, they tore the contract and said it's no longer valid. That's why we also have a secret written code so that when the other group sees our documents, they won't be able to understand them.
Mareile Kaufmann:	They ripped the contract in two?
Oliver:	Yes. We had that contract to make sure we don't spy on each other, because they were our enemies and stole our documents. … But,

actually, we forged the contract. So that's why the other group continued spying on us and tore the contract.

Children update and add techniques to prevent unwanted access, but children can also react creatively when parts of their secrets have been accessed and rendered public. Oftentimes, then, secret information does not die down, but returns in a different form, which is a different aspect of secretion.

Xenia:	When someone copies our code, then I just come up with a new one! We could always think of a new one, or we mix of two codes that we had from before.
Yvonne:	And when someone copies that, we could make yet a new one.
Xenia:	… but what happens when we have nothing left?
Yvonne:	Then we start making pictograms!

The secret's secretion is not just about unintended leaks, but is also includes the regeneration of secret information. So even if information, tools, or techniques set themselves apart from their original owners or form, secret information may still matter. Secretion does not have to end with obsolescence, but secret information can enter new life cycles as it keeps materializing. Some children, however, expressed situations in which they are "left with no secrets" (Dora). Secret information dies when nothing is left and when information becomes insignificant, forgotten, when it is no longer actively engaged with and stops even secreting. Karlo explained that he had experienced that situation when some of his secrets had become irrelevant.

Secrecy provides us with new perspectives on making information matter differently. As mentioned in the beginning of the chapter, children are mainly portrayed as those subjected to surveillance (Lewandowski, 2003; Chung and Grimes, 2005; Marx and Steeves, 2010; Sparrman and Lindgren, 2010; Steeves and Jones, 2010; Ema and Fujigaki, 2011Porter et al, 2011). And indeed, these information practices influence the lives of children concretely (Rooney, 2010). Against that backdrop, secrecy gives children space for engaging with information. They are not only subjected to information practices, but are active subjects as they intervene in surveillance and make information matter differently. Children's practices of secrecy demonstrate how information matters from the beginning of life. In addition, adopting the children's perspective provides a view on analogue information practices at a time when a considerable number of studies focus on the ways in which digital information matters. Not only does this remind us that information still exists in non–digital formats, but some of the practices studied here make information matter with techniques that are either relevant or comparable to more professionalized environments.

Studying secrecy is one of many ways to understand and rethink how information matters and becomes lively. It is an ongoing, dynamic, and engaging process. The ways in which secrecy materializes are highly dependent on how, with which infrastructures, intentions, and imaginaries information matters. This case study identified entry points for engagement, namely when information is imagined, generated, stored, when it matures, is destroyed, or reimagined. Not only children are involved, but the examples illustrated how information itself, tools and infrastructures, too, are part of this process. Taking this collaboration seriously, this study has shown that secrecy moves beyond the 'ethical negativeness' (Simmel, 1906) that it tends to be associated with. It demonstrated that secrecy can be an opening to practice difference. The ethos of secrecy is not just about exercising power, domination, exclusion, and suppression. Secrecy also makes information matter in ways that can empower, protect, strengthen relationships and identities, as well as elicit joy and creativity. These affirmative effects of making information matter are also central to the practice explored in the next chapter.

7

Speculation

What will happen to the Internet in the future? 'I will answer very simply that the Internet will disappear', is what then-Google Chairman Eric Schmidt famously answered at the World Economic Forum 2015 (Schmidt in Szalai, 2015). Two years earlier, filmmaker, artist, and writer Hito Steyerl asked 'Is the internet dead?' (2013: online). Eric Schmidt and Hito Steyerl could not be more different in the ways in which they engage with questions concerning the presence of the Internet. While Schmidt envisions a seamless transition to a trans-societist[1] condition via 'devices, sensors, things that you are wearing, things that you are interacting with that you won't even sense' (Schmidt in Szalai, 2015), Steyerl asks whether that kind of Internet actually 'stopped being a possibility'" (2013: online), because it is left to those who commercialize and racialize instead of forming potentials. While the Internet and more general processes of digitization should not be confused, these discourses about the future of the Internet also illustrate how digital information matters and may come to matter.

Hito Steyerl is one of many artists who calls attention to the ethics and politics of the Internet. Since the early 2000s many *post-Internet* art projects emerged, but only some of them take a stance on what it means to make online or digital information matter through art. Furthermore, not all who create artistic content through, with, or in relation to the Internet consider themselves part of the post-Internet art community. Yet, two contentious issues within the post-Internet art discourse are pertinent to the debate as to how art projects make online or digital information matter. One point concerns the ontologies of digital information and the Internet: Is the Internet – in line with Schmidt's vision – indeed ubiquitous? Is it true that '*all* culture has been reconfigured by the Internet' (Connor, 2017: 61), which implies that a standpoint outside such cultures is no longer possible? Related to that is, second, the status of the 'post' in post-Internet: what does that temporality imply? Artist and writer Zach Blas, with whom I spoke about information practices, offers important considerations about both points: ' "Post-" announces that challenging instances of passage and transformation can only be articulated through what they proceed' (Blas, 2017: 87). In addition, 'post-' speaks to a 'saturation or (pseudo)totalization', both of which signal an 'inability to account for the present in its specificity' (Blas, 2017: 87). Hence, to him ' "post-" is an insufficient choice for articulating political and aesthetic alternatives both within the internet and digitality' (Blas, 2017: 88). Making information matter, making it undead if one wants to invoke Steyerl (2013: online), or contributing to its liveliness as this book suggests, is to have the possibility to imagine alternatives to what *seems* ubiquitous. Inspired by J.K. Gibson-Graham's alternatives to capitalism (2006), Alexander Galloway and Eugene Thacker's 'antiweb' (2007), Beatriz Preciado's 'Manifesto contrasexual' (2011) and Ulises Ali Mejias' 'paranode' (2013) Zach Blas sees the necessity to give practices that challenge dominant forms of digitality and connectivity

'a certain amount of autonomy … That fractures the assumed totality and creates a space for the outside or for alternatives. … It's that position of possibility. At the end of the day, are you just like: "Fuck it. We're all trapped!"? Or: "'Oh, there is a crack of possibility, I'm gonna go with that!"' (Zach Blas[2])

He argues that these cracks of possibility 'must exist as an ideality: as the aesthetic potentiality to make the political alternative … as something not fully known but sensed – a longing, the fantasy of a future' (Blas, 2017: 96). This is not only an answer to the question about the relevance of art in societies influenced by the Internet. Calls for engagement with the specificity of the present and demands to identify cracks of possibility for change are central to how art can make information matter differently.

Information, surveillance, and art

Many artistic projects that aim to create cracks of possibility in prevalent information infrastructures and practices address surveillance and 'capture' (Agre, 1994). Capture is to break an activity 'down into discrete units, which can be articulated … into various grammars and schemes for optimization and normalization' (Chun, 2016: 59; for original see Agre, 1994). A classic theme in such artistic works is to approximate the watcher's or data collector's point of view and, by doing so, crossing ethical boundaries. Such artistic works often foster a detectivist form of critique that merely 'uncovers', 'does justice' and ultimately solidifies established binaries of surveillance power and resistance (Felski, 2012; Austin, Bellanova, and Kaufmann, 2019). Other artworks, in turn, draw attention to the violence that we consume online through which we also participate in the very networks that organize violence (Gronlund, 2017). Such projects, then, tend to address our 'complicity in the regimes in question' (Hogue, 2016). Torin Monahan describes how artworks about surveillance can 'activate a sense of social connection and introspection to make recognition of collective responsibility possible' (2018: 560). Such artworks can enable 'shifts in worldview' (Monahan, 2018: 561). That is to say, art projects about surveillance and capture can work with the capacities of affect in the sense of creating an onset for action (Massumi, 2002; Mc Cormack, 2004). And, while not outspokenly activist, an onset for action is also what many artists engaging with surveillance desire (see American Artist, Simone Browne and Ruha Benjamin, 2021). This chapter focuses on art projects of speculative character that activate their viewers – even if that state of activation remains in a place of ambiguity and may not be all planned out when the project is being realized.

Artists have offered their demonstrations and interpretations of how information matters since before the rise of the Internet. In the late 1970s, Sophie Calle, for example, began interacting with modes of information collection by both, letting herself be watched and by becoming the voyeur in diverse pieces of performance art, including *Suite Venitienne* (1979), *The Hotel* (1981), and *The Shadow* (1981). Ever since, many other artists have become known for working with information technologies to make information matter differently. The collective *Forensic Architecture* runs projects using algorithms, machine learning, remote sensing, data mining, and pattern analyses to identify and document alternative truths about political violence. They describe themselves as investigative agency and usually translate their findings into exhibitions. Trevor Paglen is known for investigating and documenting sites and infrastructures of state surveillance, including their use of Artificial Intelligence (AI) systems and computer vision. Some have turned the camera onto themselves to make information matter differently. Ai WeiWei's reaction to being watched and arrested by the Chinese government was to render his home into the most-watched space in the city of Beijing (*WeiWeiCam*, 2012). Similarly, Hasan Elahi has put his entire life online, including GPS coordinates, credit card transactions, pictures of himself – a deliberate reaction to having been put onto a terrorist watchlist by the American government (*TrackingTransience.net*, started 2002). Rather than merely taking the watchers standpoint, both works provide a statement on transparency at the same time as they underline the potential to disappear in a flood of relevant and irrelevant picture information. They also belong to a set of artists who are forced to define their own expressions and languages in heavily surveilled environments and whose work often has to strike a balance between commentary and activism. Here, Xu Bing's film *Dragonfly Eyes* (2017) including Zhai Yongming's poetry (which plays with the Chinese fine-tuned relationship to symbols and the double meaning of their informational characters) and the work of Wu Yuren, who also faced imprisonment due to his activist art, are other important reference works.

In the context of surveillance targeted at black communities in the US, the works of American Artist engage technology to expose institutional racism in such practices, as well as the relationship between Silicon Valley and the police. One of their works, *I'm Blue (If I Was* ■■■■■ *I Would Die)*, from 2019, uses information about the defensive attitude of the police in relation to George Floyd's killing to pinpoint that this feeling of vulnerability itself 'comes from a place of dangerous insecurity, preventing them from hearing plights of breathlessness made by the people' (American Artist in Schneider, 2020). Making information matter differently is a way of working that is also reflected in Arthur Jafa's video collage *Love is the Message, the Message is Death* (2018), which remixes circulating video footage of black pain. Sadie Barnette has made analogue information matter differently. In *Dear 1968, …* (2017) she confronts the FBI's 500-page file about the surveillance of her dad's civil right activism and membership in the Black Panthers with her pink and glittery decorations. Her artistic engagement with this information seeks to expose and to heal violence, as well as foregrounding the loving relationship between a father and a daughter. 'From what I understand, this file is supposed to be so secret and for us to put it on a wall, I think, has made him feel some ownership over his work and this information and his life' (Sadie Barnette in Bess, 2017). The ownership of personal information is also prevalent in performance artist Nick Cave's *Soundsuits* (1991 onwards). However, he seeks to achieve this ownership rather by obscuring and enveloping information about 'gender, race and class, thus compelling the audience to watch without judgment' (publicdelivery.org, 2021).

Most of the recent works that engage with information tend to address digital information and related technologies. Manu Luksch, Jack Wolf, and Mukul Patel made computational imaging technologies matter differently as they used them to direct the musical *Algo-rhythm* (2019) in order to problematize profiling and micro-targeting in machine intelligence. Martine Syms co-opts technologies to reveal their embedded ideologies, in particular to extract and discuss 'representations of blackness and its relationship to vernacular, feminist thought, and radical traditions' (martinesy.ms). In a similar vein, Stephanie Dinkins' works make matter in the sense that she seeks to develop a more equitable AI and algorithmic matrices, while also exploring and showcasing their limits. Making information matter differently is also reflected in earlier works that intervene in automated analyses. Hito Steyerl has a long artistic history of engaging with concepts of visibility, invisibility, and circulation in both, texts and moving image projects among which is *How Not to be Seen: A Fucking Didactic Educational .MOV File* (2013, listed in artworks). Another artist engaging with machine vision and (in)visibility is Adam Harvey, whose facial detection camouflage make-up (*CV Dazzle* started in

2010) and Faraday cage cases for phones (*OFF Pocket* started in 2011) are some of his most widespread works.

All these art projects make information matter differently from within technological and dataveillance environments. Many of them move away from art that merely uncovers current politics. Rather, these works affect by opening cracks of possibility – whether these possibilities are utopian, dystopian, or pragmatic. Art projects are thus one way of engaging with the specificity of the present and creating cracks of possibility to make matter differently. Such art projects also reflect the 'ethics inscribed in the very dynamics of mattering' (Jones, 2020: 246). By quoting, including, excluding, creating, making, doing, '(w)e are part of a material-discursive process of changing the possibilities for change' (Jones, 2020: 246). This, again, leaves us with 'responsibility and accountability for the lively relationalities of becoming of which we are part' (Barad, 2007: 393). Art can be one channel for offering alternative forms of making information matter, for becoming-with information in new ways.

Propositions and imaginaries: the speculative interventions by three artists

Luckily, the list of artists encouraging alternative forms of making information matter is too long to cover within the realm of this book. In this chapter, I want to analyse and discuss artistic interventions in which *speculation* becomes a prevalent form of making information matter differently. We should be aware that associative practices of making information matter, too, include elements of speculation, especially when this practice is geared towards predictions. Artistic interventions, however, can provide specific spaces 'of propositions and future imaginaries' (Davis, 2020: 65) that are different from the practices discussed earlier in this book. Art projects can contribute with material forms of speculation 'that are not confined by the regimes of scientific objectivity, political moralism or psychological depression' (Davis, 2020: 64). This does not reduce artistic projects in their ability to matter. On the contrary, David Garneau describes the agential properties of speculation: 'What art does do – and what is difficult to measure – is that it changes our individual and collective imaginaries by particles, and these new pictures of the world can influence our behavior' (see Hill and McCall, 2015: ix). When they get to matter, artworks become 'media for affective interactions' (Seyfert, 2012: 35). Thus, the 'public which repeats in itself states of mind, sentiments, emotions, thoughts through sympathy' (Guyau, 1887: 43), can become part of speculation, of making matter differently, of seeing cracks of possibility.

For the sake of illustrating speculative practices, I studied the works of Heather Dewey-Hagborg, Zach Blas, and Oliver Chanarin (from the duo Broomberg and Chanarin). They invoke alternative futures by making material interventions, many of which focus on information technologies, specifically the informationalization of the human body. All three are concerned with the level of intimacy biometric technologies speak to, the unequal flows of power they enable, and the normalizing effects they have. Their artworks are based on empirical research and extensive experimenting with technologies, which is necessary to detect the often invisible decision-making processes, specificities, and workings that make information matter. While all three engage with digital information and information technologies, they cover a broad range of media and infrastructures ranging from photography and image capture, algorithms, genomic technologies to networking infrastructures. Their art takes many material forms: sculptures, such as masks and cages, but also other types of 3D objects, still images and film, poems, fiction and scientific texts, robots and software, network infrastructures, as well as installations paired with performances.

My ambition is not to offer an interpretation of their artworks. I am not trained to do so. Instead, I retrace the ways in which their artworks offer speculation as one way of making information matter. Thus, I am not introducing the works artist by artist or project by project. Rather, I follow the turns of the information life cycle (see Chapter 3) at which the respective pieces intervene. Of course, most of the artistic projects combine several turns of the information life cycle.

The central argument of this chapter is that artworks can seize and open up information, render it lively and make it matter at any stage, drawing us into the -topias and pragmatisms that are necessary to shape meaningful presents and futures. In order to get a better sense of how their works make information matter I draw on context information about the artists, but mainly on statements directly from the artists. The entire chapter is based on my conversations with Heather Dewey-Hagborg, Zach Blas, and Oliver Chanarin about speculative information practices and their role in society, which is why this text takes a slightly more dialogical form than the other chapters and features longer statements. When I talked to them about how they make information matter, all three distanced their oeuvre from political solutionism or activism and rather argued for the ways in which ambiguity and speculation move to the fore.

Heather Dewey Hagborg:	I am really interested in pointing out that things are political, pointing out the problems, pointing out some of the aspects that could be beautiful. I don't want to come across as having some kind of policy solution or suggestion. So I would stop short of claiming that I would know the answer. I would love to

be involved in a conversation of finding the answer together, but I alone am not going to come up with that. I think that is something that has to be done together with others. With other specialties, with other knowledges.

Oliver Chanarin:

I wouldn't describe what we do as activism or trying to change governmental policy or anything as direct as that. It really is a much softer form of debate. It is using art as a tool for discussion and debate. And I think that that has an impact – also through teaching, through having exhibitions, through doing books – there are so many different ways of getting out into the world and create a conversation about the production of images. I think that we are operating in that vague territory. … Just stay in that ambiguous place. Staying at that place of living in a question without necessarily offering an answer or a solution.

Zach Blas:

I don't need to call my work activism. And I think that's presumptuous and a little arrogant, because I'm not doing what people that are involved in direct action or work with NGOs do. It's not the same thing. For me, art gives you the opportunity to engage politics on a different level … It can use its speculative and imaginative powers to show us other possibilities, other modes of existence. … Activism is tied down by certain practical matters and contingencies of working, whereas when you make artwork, it's an opportunity to express a grander, even utopic is the right word … some kind of political yearning or desire that goes a lot further. Artworks can activate a political longing or desire and then you can have this realization between the gap of social reality and the desire, or political horizon opening up.

As a form of making information matter, speculation educates about specific technologies and practices, at the same time as it opens up and creates -topias that can influence affect and action. Heather Dewey-Hagborg explains the trajectory of creating one of her artworks:

'So it was that aspect of thinking about the availability of the body for surveillance and there was ... this emerging technology of DNA phenotyping that was also totally invisible. Almost no one had published anything about it, other than in scholarly papers. So I saw a few of these papers coming out, hinting at this direction that was coming, so I did this semi-speculative future, a hands-on practice of making that visible, of making that something that people could discuss and making it a subject for debate, really. I think that is one aspect of things that I attempt with my work: making things available to be contested, to be discussed, things that may otherwise be hidden. ... And how can one open that (practice) up, so it isn't just those really narrow options that are offered by companies and health systems. There's got to be more there!'

She describes how her works should invoke a succession of alternative futures before answers can be discussed: "Like we first have to go through the utopian and then we have to go through the dystopian and then maybe we can get to something in the middle" (Heather Dewey-Hagborg). Her desire is that these matterings result in "a little more place for critical conversation, a little more space for agency before things get solidified" (Heather Dewey-Hagborg). In doing that, speculative interventions reflect the notion of companionship forwarded in this book (see Haraway, 2003; Austin et al, 2019). Speculation, too, is about making as a form of becoming-with and accompanying information practices. The speculative nature is also reflected in Oliver Chanarin's work:

'Every project is a 'What if'? ... What if we use pose-estimation, which is developed for understanding normal and abnormal human behavior in public space, and we use it to look at a piece of art that is part of cinematic history that is also a piece of state propaganda? And the result is something kind of terrifying and poetic and very beautiful at the same time.'

Speculation also involves an educational element: "I think we're misusing technologies. That would be another way of characterizing what we do. So how can we misuse a technology in order to highlight the ideology that's embedded there?" (Oliver Chanarin). Later on, he describes the affect that he has in mind when he works with information technologies to document, experiment and speculate:

'I think one of the words is ambiguity. The world feels ambiguous. Like its purpose is ambiguous. It's not there to slap you on the wrist or pass judgment. As artists we are using a technology in a different way. What we're trying to say about it is not easy to sum up or conceptualize. And it's not morally central either. It sits in a very ambiguous and fluid place, where we're both using the technology and celebrating it. We are terrified by it, but we're also excited by it.' (Oliver Chanarin)

Zach Blas describes how artworks often combine educational with critical and speculative matters:

'Artists help you understand that a technology isn't set in stone, not teleological, but in a process of constant contestation and that can have power, agency and impact. You say demonstrate – the other word that I use is to educate. That's a big part of it. Often, these kinds of things of speculating, demonstrating, educating, documenting – you can see them entangled in plenty of different art practices, where by documenting something is also to educate you about how an aspect of surveillance is working.'

To him, art literally is about making matter differently, which is also to tie in fantasies and desires:

'The artwork is changing the horizons of possibility. ... It's re-configuring the horizon of what appears possible. For me it's like: If the fantasy of Silicon Valley is to have the Internet disappear into the world, have a corporate internet overload, totalizing the world, it's to make work to say: "Hey, this hasn't happened yet and it doesn't have to happen yet!" You can do that through imagination, emotion, drama, absurdity – lots of different types of things to make people feel and experience and get a taste of what could be. ... The work is a longing for something. The work is materializing that longing, that political desire, that queer longing. It doesn't mean that it has that answer, that fix. It's sharing that longing. I'm opening that up for other people to experience and discover and have an encounter with.' (Zach Blas)

The frictions that occur when making matter

Artworks matter, but it is important to remember that they, too, experience frictions and failures that urge spontaneous decisions and changes of plan. Not surprisingly, all of these frictions are part of making matter and they materialize, too. Sometimes, they become central to the project. Oliver Chanarin gives an example (see Figure 7.1):

Figure 7.1: Adam Broomberg and Oliver Chanarin; *Spirit is a Bone*; 2015; The Philosopher

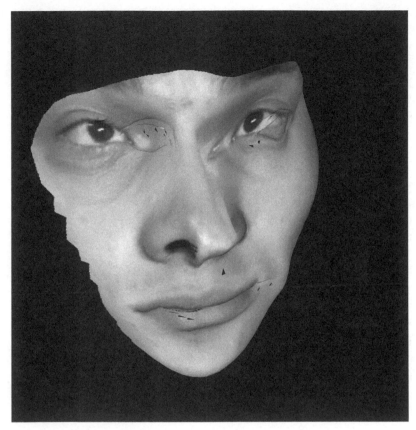

Source: Courtesy of the artists and Goodman Gallery.

> 'When the technology fails is always the most interesting place. ...
> It is those glitches, those boundaries. For example, one of the things
> that the facial recognition system couldn't deal with is children. ...
> And so when a child was put in front of the machine it created a very
> distorted and strange phenomenon and those glitches. There are some
> pictures in the book. ... And there is a kind of beauty in that distortion
> as well.' (Oliver Chanarin)

Zach Blas mentions a range of very practical frictions, such as fiscal and time
budgets, the different aesthetic expectations varying with geography, and the
demands of art markets. Art has a history of being co-opted by the commercial
structures of curation (for example Wintle, 2016) and patronage (which, for
example, inspired the rise of Dadaism as anti-art, see Graver, 1995). Today,
art is not only guided by the politics of awards and grants. Digital technology

giants that embody digital veillance and commercial practice, such as Apple (2019) and Google (Google, nd), offer supposedly non-profit art walks and digital art experiences. Zach Blas explains that these economic and political frictions meet the technical and material challenges of making an artwork, too.

> 'Like getting a budget where you have half the time to finish the work. ... You don't have enough to do the materialization process, the fabrication process that you wanted. You have to do something else. So many little practical things like this come in and affect how an artwork takes its shape and manifests itself. ... Who commissioned the work? ... There is a materialization of all of this as well. ... There is a bro culture, a toxic masculinity around digital art, because you totally get those types of artists that are all about: do you know this tool? Can you use it? ... I have no patience for that. Art has to have a more, open generous space, where people can work with technologies ... This is why I work in teams.' (Zach Blas)

Indeed, he also finds solutions for these restrictions and frictions in his artworks:

> 'I make the work and this is what I have been able to accomplish with the material limitations and affordances I have at this moment in time. I see the gaps. So guess what? The next work is about that gap. ... Another way that I think about it, is variations of a theme. When I do an installation I always make a smaller work, I may write an essay − all about the same thing. It's all within the same research project, but switching form.' (Zach Blas)

Keeping these concrete affordances and frictions in mind, I will now describe the different turns at which the three artists intervene in dominant information practices.

Speculation: the art of making information matter

Hito Steyerl's question: 'Is the Internet Dead?' (2013: online) has become an important reference point for artistic engagements with information and information technologies. Her own answer involves a burning plea for making information matter, for speculating about new, different possible lives of information and information technologies. Indeed, much in line with this book's argument, her writings invoke the materiality and liveliness of digital images:

> They surpass the boundaries of data channels and manifest materially. ... They spread through and beyond networks, they contract and

expand, they stall and stumble, they vie, they vile, they wow and woo. … But by becoming real, most images are substantially altered. They get translated, twisted, bruised, and reconfigured. (Steyerl, 2013: online)

Information technologies, too, are 'a form of life (and death) that contains, sublates, and archives all previous forms of media. In this fluid media space, images and sounds morph across different bodies and carriers, acquiring more and more glitches and bruises along the way' (Steyerl, 2013: online).

By invoking the agencies of images, of technologies and our own agencies (for example the agency of image generators, post-producers, editors, who correct, filter, cut), she formulates a challenge: 'Why not slowly withdraw from an undead internet to build a few others next to it?' (Steyerl, 2013: online). This project may fail – or 'it could become the art of recoding or rewiring the system by exposing state scopophilia, capital compliance, and wholesale surveillance' (Steyerl, 2013: online). The artworks of Zach Blas, Oliver Chanarin, and Heather Dewey-Hagborg seem to take that challenge up at each stage of information's life cycle. They, too, emphasize the liveliness of information, the circulation of concepts, and the work of making information matter.

Oliver Chanarin, for example, explains how the photos of August Sander, whose portrait series "was trying to create a record or survey of human society during the Weimarer Republic" (Oliver Chanarin), mattered differently when "Hitler came to power and there was this massive shift to the right. This idea of categorizing people according to any sort of label, be it racial or social in terms of hierarchy or labor, suddenly took on this much more sinister tone" (Oliver Chanarin).

Together with Adam Broomberg he re-appropriated Sander's portrait series to make it matter differently by bringing the project to the techniques of image production in the 21st century. They engaged with so-called non-collaborative portraiture in the context of Russian state surveillance. We will return to this work in the description of the information life cycle.

Heather Dewey-Hagborg addresses a different dimension of liveliness when she points to biological material and the complexities of making it matter. Cells are alive – and personal information, too, inhabits a type of liveliness that requires intimate care work:

'This (care work) is another thing that no one discusses or thinks about. But to me, it was so striking when I started working with doing tissue culture: this washing, feeding, keeping warm, all of these activities that we associate with mothering or caring for others are directly translated into how we are caring for our cells. … The act of what the scientist does is an intimate act in the lab – even if it is not framed in these terms necessarily. … And there are some similar things there, also, with data and with analyzing peoples' most personal information.' (Heather Dewey-Hagborg)

In a similar vein, almost all projects of Zach Blas can be quoted as speculative interventions that recognize the materiality and liveliness of information. In fact, Hito Steyerl described Blas' art as making matter differently: 'While a lot of contemporary technologically oriented art tries to resuscitate the wreckage of Futurism, or overidentifies with strategies of surgical marketing and apple polishing, Blas' work insists that one doesn't need to brand oneself into voluntary servitude or to eagerly identify with the aggressor' (Steyerl, 2014).

Imaginaries

Zach Blas' work intervenes already at the level of imaginaries. His works engage with how information and information technologies are conceptualized, understood, and envisioned as these. Any such imaginary matters as they formulate expectations towards the capacities and powers of information and technologies, many of which become manifest at a later stage in concrete designs and programming languages, diagrams, tables. Imaginaries have the fascinating capacity to interfuse the air of the conceptual, logical, and analytical with beliefs, religion, and spirituality.

Phil Agre's 'capture' (1994) is central to many imaginaries that Zach Blas' works address. While the wording of surveillance tends to convey big brother-type of power models, capture ventures into computational data collection and processing, the decisions that inform these practices and the effects that they create. For Zach Blas, capture "starts to provoke questions about how identity is calculated, standardized, trained in all these algorithms. That is the more precise question to ask if you are concerned with feminist, queer, anti-racist positions" (Blas). On this theoretical backdrop, his works address already the dominant imaginaries about what type of information images can capture and transmit. In what his friends refer to as his "pop song" (Zach Blas; one of first pieces that garnered much attention) he played with the imaginary of what biometric images can convey. His work *Facial Weaponization Suite* (2012) 'protests against biometric facial recognition – and the inequalities these technologies propagate – by making "collective masks"' (Zach Blas, website). These masks were created in a workshop. The aggregated facial data of participants resulted in amorphous masks that cannot be detected as human faces by biometric facial recognition technologies. The project addressed the imaginary of the facial image as something that can be standardized and used to categorize types of humans.

'I found Francis Galton's composite portraiture, which I just found hysterical. He would take a whole bunch of photographs, composite them to get an average to go like: this is the average face of such and such criminal. So I actually wanted to use Galton's exact same method of compositing faces, but actually arrived at the opposite result. He composited to get an average – I composited to get a messy, conceptual, excessive face.' (Blas)

He continued to address biometric imaginaries in the follow-up project *Face Cages* (2014–16). The installation and performance work dramatizes 'the abstract violence of the biometric diagram' (Blas, website). Four queer artists generated biometric diagrams of their faces, which were then fabricated as three-dimensional metal objects. Metal was chosen to evoke a material resonance with handcuffs, prison bars, and torture devices. The metal face cages were worn in endurance performances for video (Blas, website).

While we will return to both projects at the level of information generation, *Face Cages* (see Figure 7.2), too, makes information matter differently already at the level of the imaginary, the logic, the concept of biometrics:

'What does this biometric logic look like? It's so fascinating. You would see these [commercial] videos and demonstrations of these very colourful, playful grids over faces. You often see this in life-facetracking that is using facial recognition. It's like [mimics enthusiasts]: "Oh my god, it's like this nimble pliancy, amazing grid over your face. You blink and it blinks, too!" There is something so immaterial about that. So effervescent, it just seems so light that it's nothing and this always personally really irritated me. I want to make a work that really tries to put front and center that biometrics is primarily a technology for surveillance, for policing, for criminalization.' (Blas)

His project conveys that biometric information technology and imagery is in no way a matter of being light and nimble, but in effect closer to heavy and hard materialities.

With his newer works, Blas continues to intervene and speculate even more outspokenly at the level of imaginaries and concepts. He dedicated a whole trilogy of works to the beliefs and phantasies of Silicon Valley, a place that stands for the most dominant voices in what our lives with information and information technology should look like. The average Silicon Valley company does not only develop technologies, infrastructures, business models, work, and informational cultures, but all of them are driven by imaginaries, ideals, and phantasies. This is why the trilogy explores "how belief and phantasy is operating within these systems" (Blas). He continues to give examples of how Russian-born writer and philosopher Ayn Rand, especially her ideas about capitalism and individualism, have become

Figure 7.2: Zach Blas; *Face Cage 1*; endurance performance with Zach Blas; 2015

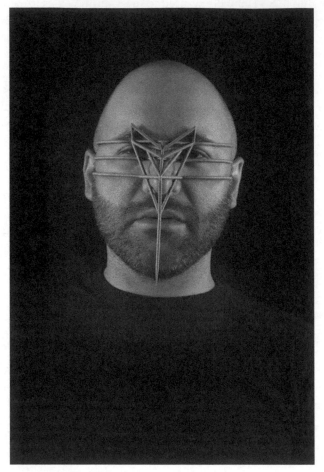

Source: Courtesy of the artist.

influential in the technology industry. In *Contra-Internet: Jubilee of 2033* (2019) he portrays Ayn Rand 'as the philosophical queen of Silicon Valley' and works with 'imaginaries of how one can move through the world and how that is manifested in things in Silicon Valley' (Blas, website). These newer works, too, are very material, working with objects, prostheses, that make imaginaries of information and information technologies matter differently. In *Metric Mysticism* (2017–18) and *Icosahedron* (2019) he addresses the imaginaries about information that drive practices of association (see Chapter 3), of large-scale data analysis and prediction.

Zach Blas: I am trying to pull out the various beliefs and phantasies that drive Silicon Valley companies'

	mission statements – what they even understand they are doing with data to begin with. … I made this AI work a couple of years ago called *Icosahedron*. That work is presented as a desk with a crystal ball and this AI elf inside that you can talk to. That work was specifically responding to the company Palantir [one of the leading companies in association work, see Chapter 4]. Part of that work was about re-contextualizing Palantir and really teasing out the beliefs and phantasies that are motivating how this highly politicized company understands what they are doing with data.
Mareile Kaufmann:	May I just throw in: are you aware of the fact that in the Palantir headquarters, they have a Foucault portrait hanging on the wall?
Zach Blas:	[laughs out loud] 'Oh my god, I didn't know that. That's amazing. I love how you said that. Something I've been thinking a lot, doing my Silicon Valley research, is how they absolutely subsume and eat their critics.'

One of the projects that he planned at the time of the conversation was dedicated to expand on the "religious attitudes, spirituality, fantasies, projections" (Blas) around AI. It engages with Silicon Valley's history of interest in fringe religion and cults that are centred around the idea of transcending the human body. "A few years ago a church was also founded in Silicon Valley that was organized around an AI god. So already this is a very direct fusion of the two things" (Blas). In relation to that, he mentions how many AI visualizations draw on Michelangelo's fresco of *The creation of Adam* (1508–12) in which the finger of a robot touches that of a human.

> 'And for me that is the religious fantasy of the 1%, the religious fantasy of the elite. Because it is about AI rejuvenating life. AI is this radical life extension think tanks that are being funded by SV billionaires. Whereas I think, in reality, the appropriate religious metaphor for most people in the world is one of judgement and evaluation.' (Zach Blas)

This is why he plans on producing a variety of Michelangelo's *The Last Judgment* (1536–41) and combining it with other ideas that confront the elite imaginary of transcendence with the rather intense experience of being evaluated and judged. This would also match what, today, starts to resemble a religious belief in metric systems.

Like Zach Blas, Heather Dewey-Hagborg uses theories and scholarly research as an inspiration for her works, but also follows how the phenomena she is interested in are taken up in current events. When she explains at what point in time she began looking into the usage of DNA in different societal domains, it becomes clear that her artworks, too, are predecessors in discussing the relationship between DNA, information, intimacy, and politics. Some of her works have become reference points in academia, administrative work, and public discourse (for example Bioteknologirådet, 2013; The New York Times, 2017; Walker-Rettberg, 2018). Many pieces intervene at the level of the imaginary, addressing the authority that DNA has in the legal system. She does so in one of her most circulated works, *Stranger Visions* (2012–13), for which she collected hair, chewed up gum, and cigarette butts from the streets, public bathrooms, and waiting rooms of New York City. She extracted DNA from them and analysed 'it to computationally generate 3D printed life size full color portraits representing what those individuals might look like, based on genomic research' (Heather Dewey-Hagborg, website). When asked about the imaginaries she addresses with this, she answers:

'I was thinking about the limitations of authority of DNA. So I was doing a lot of research into the history of DNA fingerprinting and how that is used politically and in the criminal [investigation and prosecution] systems. And one thing to question was: we took this technology in an uncritical way. In the beginning there was a lot of push and pull and fighting over whether it was meaningful or good enough to be used in court. And by the time it was used in the O.J. Simpson case it ... became this so-called gold standard. ... So maybe the technology improved a bit, but the problems that were there before were carried along with it. It flips from being something that is subject to scrutiny into being suddenly this gold standard and all the other forensic sciences are seen as very poor by comparison.' (Heather Dewey-Hagborg)

Her work *Probably Chelsea* (2017) (see Figure 7.3), which includes 'thirty different possible portraits of Chelsea Manning algorithmically-generated by an analysis of her DNA' (Heather Dewey-Hagborg, website), takes this discussion further. It addresses the imaginary that one can draw out a portrait of a person by informationalizing and phenotyping DNA. "So you have phenotyping – predicting a face from DNA – which has almost nothing to do with DNA fingerprinting, but it borrows that authority. This piling of authorities that is based already on a shaking foundation" (Heather Dewey-Hagborg).

Both works and many others of Heather Dewey-Hagborg also offer speculations at the level of generation, that is how bio-information, such as

Figure 7.3: Installation images of Heather Dewey-Hagborg and Chelsea
E. Manning, *Probably Chelsea* (2016), 30 3-D printed portraits rendered from
mitochondrial DNA, each portrait 8 x 6 x 8 inches, overall dimensions variable

Source: Photo by Paula Abreu Pita. Courtesy of the artists and Fridman Gallery, New York.

a DNA 'fingerprint' or a face print, but also biological samples that are the
base of these, materialize.

Generation

Many of Heather Dewey-Hagborg's works focus on the generation of
bio-data. To her, hacking, spoofing, tearing apart cultures of bioveillance
are important instances of making bio-information matter and generating
bio-information in alternative fashions. She explains how she got there: "So
I found out that we have this kind of vulnerability to our body. What next?
I started researching if there were more ways in which we can protect
ourselves from that" (Dewey-Hagborg). With *DNA spoofing* (2013) she
created a 'playful look at DIY ways in which anonymity can be enabled
in the age of genetic surveillance' (Dewey-Hagborg, website) and in *The
Official Bionymous Guidebooks* (2015) she gives DIY instructions on how one
can erase and replace one's DNA. This theme was also continued in many
other works, among which are the essay *Biopunk: Subverting Biopolitics* (2017)
that rejects 'genetic determinism' and the lecture *Hacking Biopolitics* (2017)
which is 'a call for biopolitical art practice' (Dewey-Hagborg, website). All
of them encourage practices that generate biological information differently.

Some of these works were suggesting concrete "ways in which you could cover up your DNA fingerprint. But these are limited because you can't go around doing this all the time. So it's really limited to very specific small cases" (Dewey-Hagborg). Other works were aimed at questioning the shaky foundations of DNA evidence, showing "that DNA can be hacked and can be forged in a way that's much easier than we might expect. And also to provoke a bit" (Dewey-Hagborg).

The aspect of imagining, making, and actually generating alternative information and infrastructures is central to her approaches. The way in which she creates cracks of possibility with these particular art projects can be summarized in the concept of biopunk:

'We want to tear them apart and look at the pieces in the way that we want them reconfigured. That's sort of the part of punk that is interesting to me in relation to biology. It is thinking of this hacker-ness, this do-it-yourself-ness and this taking part of things that appear as a given, as a kind of cultural norm and reconfiguring them, and dreaming up different kinds of possibilities from that. ... That's the practice of thinking about what futures can be?' (Dewey-Hagborg)

With *Stranger Visions* and *Probably Chelsea* she re-appropriates phenotyping, a procedure for making bio-information matter by creating portraits from DNA (see Figure 7.4). She uses the same procedure used in forensic contexts to show the inherent challenges and politics of that technique. Here, she addresses how the generation of information is intertwined with rendering visible: one aspect is that one loses control over how one is rendered visible, another one is that one may be denied visibility. She summarizes: "it's really about having agency over your visibility and how you are interpreted" (Heather Dewey-Hagborg). In order to make these points, her projects also have an educational component. They illustrate at the same time as they offer a speculation about the technology in question. And in order for the public to appreciate all aspects, a careful narrative needs to be chosen when making matter.

'I think what's really difficult is always to tell the complex story. So the problem is that these things are not straightforward and it's much easier to make a narrative that is simple and catchy, that people can immediately grab on to and have a strong reaction to. So, for example, what *Stranger Visions* does really well is it creates this image that is immediately comprehensible and that people can have this gut reaction to very quickly, but it hides the complexity that is really going on. That we see in *Probably Chelsea.*' (Heather Dewey-Hagborg)

Figure 7.4: Installation images of Heather Dewey-Hagborg and Chelsea E. Manning, *Probably Chelsea* (2016), 30 3-D printed portraits rendered from mitochondrial DNA, each portrait 8 x 6 x 8 inches, overall dimensions variable

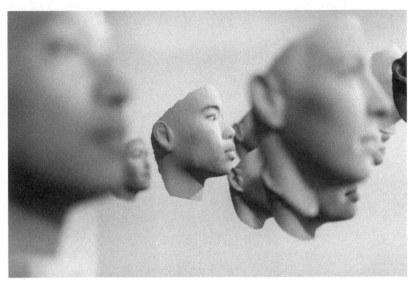

Source: Photo by Paula Abreu Pita. Courtesy of the artists and Fridman Gallery, New York.

When the speculative narrative works, the inherent call for engaging with such technologies, for making matter differently, becomes clear, too: "And I think it's worth thinking about how the biotechnologies that are unrolling on the one hand will affect us, but on the other hand, how we can keep agency to shape them so they affect us the way we want" (Heather Dewey-Hagborg).

The projects of Broomberg and Chanarin are also designed to convey the politics of the medium that generates information. Oliver Chanarin mentions that the technology creating a picture and the picture itself are highly political and always embedded in a historical context. Their work *Spirit is a Bone* (2015) was already mentioned earlier. It re-approaches August Sander's life project of capturing different 'types' of people on photographs. Broomberg and Chanarin make this work matter differently by re-generating August Sander's types with a new informational medium: the biometric camera.

'I tell you how *Spirit is a Bone* happened: we were invited to Russia by the State Television company to make a photographic series on the theme of [Human] Labor for the G20-meeting. This was kind of a straightforward photographic commission, kind of a dodgy one. This is the State TV asking us to come! ... Our proposal was to use this machine to re-enact August Sander's work in a week. So we weren't just critiquing the technology, we were also trying to critique the commissioning body. The question was: how can we take this commission and throw it back, blow it up in their face?' (Oliver Chanarin)

To prepare the image generation, they extracted the metadata from August Sander's portraits, which in that case was "simply the worker, the revolutionary ... That's the only metadata that's there. So we extracted that information and we gave that list to a casting agent and they went around the streets and found those people. We re-cast and re-shot every single archetype" (Oliver Chanarin).

This is also why they ended up making a portrait of Pussy Riot member Yekaterina Samutsevic as the revolutionary 'type'. The political technology of the camera generating the picture, however, was crucial, too. It was an early biometric technology that Russian technology developers were interested in showcasing. The technology would create so-called non-collaborative portraits. While one may question whether there really is no kind of collaboration involved, the wording and the technological design imply that the traditional link between the photographer and the subject is broken as the portraiture is automated. Thus, not only August Sander's archetypes, but also the way of generating the pictures of these archetypes were made to matter differently.

'Bear in mind: when I say "have your picture taken" it was a very depressing process. You walk into the room and we would say: "Thank you that's it, you're done!" That's all they had to do. There were several cameras in the room. Strange to even say "have their pictures taken". ... [T]hey were scanned without even being aware of it. ... These were like 600 people. It was done in a week. That was the worst week of my life. ... I was there, but it wasn't like photographing people – it was like processing people. It's turning people into pieces.' (Chanarin)

He adds technological details about the camera that contributed to making the portraits, which ended up looking like life masks: "The machine was only interested in the face – the eyes, the nose and the mouth and not the rest of the face. And then it presented them on this black background." More important, the camera created a 3D model of the person, which once again abstracted the portrait: "The person never looked in that particular direction. Because it can be rotated in space there is this kind of blankness to the expression" (see Figures 7.5 and 7.6). This series of portraits is an aesthetic commentary and a material speculation about how information can be exposed as political and made to matter differently. Specifically, it

Figure 7.5: Adam Broomberg and Oliver Chanarin; *Spirit is a Bone*; 2015;
Fairground Woman

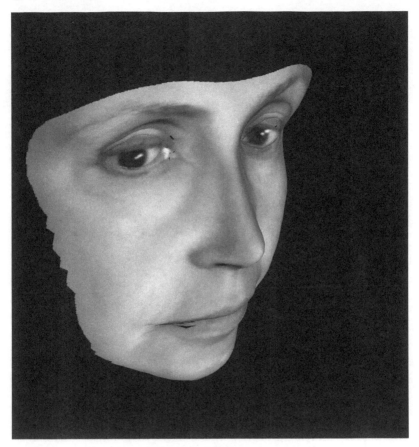

Source: Courtesy of the artists and Goodman Gallery.

highlights that generation matters: the portraits matter differently according
to the production technology and the context in which they are taken.

Zach Blas' *Facial Weaponization Suite*, mentioned earlier, also engages
with facial recognition technologies and the generation of biometric data.
In his work, the aspect of making information matter differently is directly
linked to informatic opacity: information is created, but it ensures that the
identity of the captured individual remains opaque. It is an answer to 'the
informatics of domination', which translate 'the world into a problem of
coding' (Haraway, 1991: 161, 164). Opacity, here, 'refuses a logic of total
transparency and rationality, disrupting the transformation of subjects into
categorizable objects of Western knowledge' (Glissant, 1997: 194). In
referring to Édouard Glissant, Zach Blas argues that transparency 'claims to
make a person fully intelligible and interpretable, and this is a barbarism,

Figure 7.6: Adam Broomberg and Oliver Chanarin; *Spirit is a Bone*; 2015; Domestic Servant

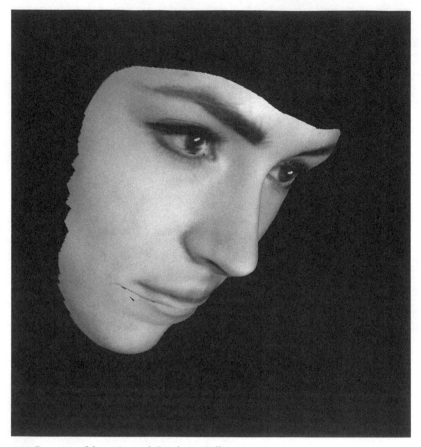

Source: Courtesy of the artists and Goodman Gallery.

as it destroys the opacity of another' (Blas, 2020: 198). He acknowledges, however, that 'becoming informationally opaque can have excruciating political consequences, such as the loss of basic human rights'. This is why his art eventually calls for us to 'live with technologies that express the joy of opacity, not its destruction' (Blas, 2020: 199).

The materiality of generating information was central to the process of *Facial Weaponization Suite*, which would result in a set of masks to allow for opacity in the context of biometric information generation. Zach Blas explained the very process of making the mask that includes generating data and translating it from digital information into a wearable item:

'(Y)ou take the final 3D model and it goes through a CNC milling machine. And ... this is a subtractive process. So let's say you have a

Figure 7.7: Zach Blas; *Facial Weaponization Suite*: Procession of Biometric Sorrows, public action, Mexico City, Mexico, June 5, 2014

Source: Photo by Oliver Santana; 2014; courtesy of the artist.

piece of really hard wood and this machine just cuts away and that creates the mask mold. Through CNC milling. For me, these kinds of processes are important, because it obviously has to be translated by a machine to get that kind of digital screen face to something physical. Once you have that mold, then I worked with recycled plastic. You would take the mold and put a sheet of recycled plastic over and that is the process called vacuum forming. And hot hair sucks the plastic very rapidly over the top of the mold and that's how this recycled plastic would take the form of the mold. It's completely transparent and we would paint them from the inside.' (Zach Blas)

Not only was this a very tactile practice of generating information, but in order to make the masks matter in political contexts, they would be worn in different parades, processions, and events (see Figure 7.7). He stresses that this project is not "about individual hiding, it was really making these masks and collectivizing the face". It was a way of generating biometric information in a material way that expresses the "demand for opacity" (Zach Blas).

The mask is confrontational, which also explains the project's title *Facial Weaponization Suite*. He explains:

'[Michael] Hardt and [Antonio] Negri have this theory about weapons for the multitude and weapons for democracy and it was very much about being non-violent, organized around defense, but also a tool-use for a process of political transformation. It just really clicked for me. It made a lot of sense. I like it because it emphasized the tool, the tool-ness of the project.' (Blas)

As mentioned earlier, the follow-up project to *Facial Weaponization Suite* was *Face Cages* – another material intervention of the speculative type that points to the violence in the generation of the biometric image. He approached the "different dramatic grid-like structures that generate over faces when faces are being tracked" (Blas) and made them literally matter differently. In reference to feminist durational performance art, he invited three other queer artists to do this project with him. Each of them scanned their face with a different biometric software, backed them into a 3D model software, adjusted the z-axes, and 3D printed them, which in itself contributed to the effect of the work:

> 'The whole promise of biometrics and facial recognition is that it is like a perfect calculation of your face. … And what was amazing was when we got them back they didn't fit our faces very well. And in fact some of them were really painful. Like mine had these weird things that actually made the corners of my eyes bleed when I ended up wearing them. … Just that alone: by staging an encounter between biometric calculation made material with the embodied person, there was incongruence. I was like: that was the entire work. That was it.' (Blas)

Not only does the work "perform this incongruence", but it also connects "this materially to criminalization and a history of punishment that is put at the level of the face" (Blas). They eventually fabricated the masks in stainless steel. These cages were worn "in front of the camera, like a portrait. … The whole thing is seeing that face wearing that object in time and duration. … You can start feeling discomfort of the people' (Blas).

He also mentions the feeling of a "prison line-up" (Blas). The title *Face Cages* is inspired by Shoshana Magnet's book *When Biometrics Fail* in which she writes 'biometric technologies draw on a nineteenth-century desire to force the body to speak the truth of its identity, much like Bertillon's early system of identification, which aimed to create a cage of information from which the criminalized body could not escape' (2011: 15).

To Zach Blas, this cage of information invokes two things: "number one, the cage is a part of a prison-industrial complex, two, biometrics also freeze materiality in the sense that it is a frozen recording of a materially dynamic human being" (Zach Blas). *Facial Weaponization Suite* and *Face Cages* work in combination. *Facial Weaponization Suite* undermines the idea of the portrait and fosters informatic opacity as "an individual person that is wearing the face into many" (Blas), commenting on the normativity of technologies that generate information. *Face Cages* makes information matter differently as it is "trying to represent a more contemporary or future subjugation, the enforcement of biometric in the visual" (Blas).

Maturation and processing

Most artistic projects speak to the ways in which information is generated. They make information matter differently by offering alternative ways of creating data or upsetting existing datasets. Art projects also address the ways in which information matures once it is generated. They intervene in how information is prepared, categorized, cleaned, scrubbed, or subjected to algorithms and other techniques of analysis. This is complicated, because such interventions require insights into processes that are often hidden from the public, including artists.

One of Heather Dewey-Hagborg's artworks is dedicated to intervene in the processing of information. The title much expresses that project: *How Do You See Me?* (2019). It is an attempt at taking the perspective of a facial recognition algorithm. In that work, she uses 'algorithmic exploration' to look back and try to learn 'how this alien intelligence … is structured, internally' (Heather Dewey-Hagborg, website). Through producing portraits of her own face, she aims to get closer to the techniques and technologies that recognize faces in general. She explores how such processing technologies make information matter. I asked her whether she thinks recognition technologies are powerful because they *do* reveal something about us – or whether they *fail* at capturing us, where power is exercised in how these technologies put us into categories, independent of whether these categories and labels are true or not. She answered:

'[T]he most troubling about many surveillance technologies – in particular machine learning-driven technologies – is this categorizing or classifying act. That's something I focus a lot on in my work, that is to try to push back the idea that you can detect a category of identity. And almost all of these technologies rely on some concept that you can put people into pockets that relate to their identity – whether that's gender, race, ethnicity. These all are things that are attempted to be read into data. … And I think that that is the really dangerous thing, because it connects to such troubling histories in everything from physiognomy to eugenics. … In particular, there are many computer vision, facial recognition papers that are very interested in detecting race – and it's very common that terms are used like "negroid" and "mongoloid" and terms that are deeply offensive to anyone who is kind of paying attention. There is very little awareness of how political these categories are.' (Dewey-Hagborg)

In order to break with these categorization processes, it is important to understand how they are established. This is why she used what I would describe as a reverse-engineering process: looking back at the machine that looks at her and using the results to show how machine vision and the categorization of information matters. She explains how it works: "So whenever there is a system that has an input that it is learning from, it can also produce an output. It tells you something about the structure and the way it has learned" (Dewey-Hagborg). With *How Do You See Me?* she questions the idea that that machine learning is an autonomous process:

'It is always based on some kind of initial data. And when you have any creation of a dataset you have curation, you have intuition, you have subjectivity. There is always something that is framing this starting phase. It is never just starting from nothing. And even if it was starting from nothing, even if you had models of neural networks for example that are unsupervised, that learn from experience. But still: the experience is framed by the person who is crafting it. It has no more objectivity than any person.' (Dewey-Hagborg)

More so, her projects show that training material matters. By using algorithms to "unpiece" (Heather Dewey-Hagborg) how neural networks have been trained, she finds the prototypical idea of what the algorithms identifies as a face: "this prototype is a white oval. It's just one of the things that is so blatant. I think anyone who is remotely thoughtful can look at this and say: Oh, that's a problem" (Dewey-Hagborg). Ultimately, the work lays open the tense relationship between representation and the way in which it influences reality. This work summarizes the argument and approach this book forwards: it encourages us to look at the life cycle of information, its interactions with other agents and the ways in which information turns lively as it performs politics.

On the level of processing information, Zach Blas is interested in the way in which programming languages matter. The project *Queer Technologies* (2012) was dedicated to making a difference in such languages. Its aim was to rethink the role of identity in their architectures.

'So for this queer programming language I was interested in how queerness has a history of slang languages, which were used in how queer people would find one another, but also how they would protect one another. How would that look if you updated this in a computational environment? So at the time I imagined this queer programming language. I literally created a software box and a DVD and I mass-produced it in the hundreds.' (Zach Blas)

He shop-dropped these products at "Apple, all these consumer electronics around Los Angeles. ... They had barcodes so they would even actually scan if you tried to buy them" (Zach Blas). The plan was to experiment with what would happen when one encountered such a project not in an art gallery, but as products. "I wanted these things to be in stores besides other products, just like them. When they walk into the store they can pick it up and would be like: … what is this? How do I use this? How much does this cost?" (Zach Blas).

Again, his speculative intervention at the level of processing information ended up being a material product. It was a concrete comment on the present of programming languages and a suggestion of what could be, how it could matter differently. Later, his project *Contra-Internet* (2015–19), which was already mentioned earlier, would further reflect on the need to create alternative infrastructures at large. *Contra-Internet* combines a queer science fiction film installation, glass sculptures, and a single edition publication. They all utilize 'queer and feminist methods to speculate on internet futures and network alternatives' (Zach Blas, website). *Contra-Internet* (see Figure 7.8) emphasizes that – politically – the alternative to a commercially driven network must exist. The alternative matters.

Death/re-use

At the end of a life cycle usually stands death. However, many practices discussed in this book have illustrated that information rarely dies in the sense of being deleted or of no longer mattering. Heather Dewey-Hagborg mentions how information technologies and information circulate and re-emerge in different instantiations:

Figure 7.8: Zach Blas, *Contra-Internet: Jubilee 2033*; featuring Cassils; HD film still; 2018; commissioned by Gasworks, Art in General, and MU

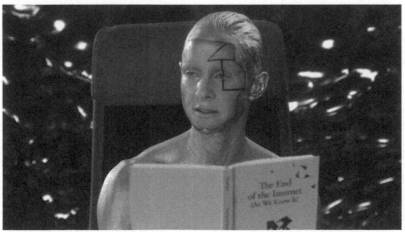

Source: Courtesy of the artist.

'they get passed on. You get a trained model and that gets passed on and incorporated into a million other things. And these people [i.e. new users or developers] don't know anything about how those models have been trained. They haven't been involved in that material process. So it [this knowledge] gets lost and then embedded a million times over.' (Heather Dewey-Hagborg)

The end of an information life cycle is thus rather a gateway to its re-imagination and re-generation. Information keeps being in-formation. Some art projects not only criticize that re-use, but actively involve the re-use of information. Existing datasets are re-used with the aim to make them matter differently. A project in which Zach Blas reuses a pre-existing dataset brings us back to the beginning of this chapter, namely the imaginations, beliefs, and fantasies of Silicon Valley. His work *The Doors* (2019) scrapes datasets and re-assembles them with machine learning methods to make a series of works that address the relationship between "psychedelics, AI and machine learning as a particular type of vision quest" (Zach Blas). Silicon Valley, he explains, is at the forefront of a new psychedelic era. There is "this new drug industry called nootropics – smart drugs for cognitive enhancement. [They are] all about optimizing one's abilities and being a visionary. ... [H]aving a psychedelic vision has become reimagined in contemporary Silicon Valley through LSD, to increase productivity, taking nootropics to enhance your cognitive capacity" (Blas).

What is important is that the re-use of information for his project is not sidelining or ignoring the origins of that data, but it is re-used precisely to address the original context and significance of this data by using speculative techniques. For this artwork, he and a team of engineers scraped Google and other technology providers for images and information and used them to train neural networks.

'It was everything from 1960s psychedelic rock posters to LSD blotter art, to brain scans and lizard skins. It was a wide range of things. Because I was interested in the contestation over who gets to have the vision of the future and also thinking about a psychedelic aesthetics within machine learning and AI. ... I stopped the neural networks before they entered queer representational imagery. This is this liminal spot when something is possibly coming into representation, but not yet.'

With that multimedia installation based on data reimagined, he once again freezes current colonizations of the Internet "in a moment of contestation" (Blas) and invokes the powers of what could be.

This section closes with an excerpt of Zach Blas' *The Doors*. It is a poem generated by a neural network trained on corporate literature discussing nootropics and poetry written by Jim Morrison. It closes one life cycle and reinvigorates a new one: scraped information is re-used to address Silicon Valley imaginaries of being an ultraproductive visionary as well as the techgnostic beliefs of becoming transcendent. As we have already seen in Eric Schmidt's comment at the beginning of this chapter, these are imaginaries that matter to mainstream Internet companies. However, they have begun to spill over into the lives of everyone who is captured, measured, evaluated, judged by them. So: what will happen to the Internet in the future? The poem is one answer to this question. Like all the artworks discussed earlier, it is a speculative intervention. It is a form of making information matter differently that draws on the specificities of the Internet of the present and opens them up. It creates a "crack of possibility" (Zach Blas), works as a "tool for discussion and debate" (Oliver Chanarin), it forms -topias and helps "making things available to be contested" (Heather Dewey-Hagborg).

An excerpt from *The Doors* (2019) "Lizard Brings Psychedelic Drugs to the Privatized Garden on the Island of Nootro":

Become a Neuromaster
with
a stronger brain and
bigger ideas.
…
The results
are mind-blowing.
They can help you become
a better tiring cruncher
…
To boost your 'Brain function' – the ability to think in
isolation from the rest of the body.
…
We welcome your continued participation
in helping us support memory and mental stamina.
…
And replace our obsolete
fuel cells.

8

The Ethics of Making
Information Matter

What ethos informs engagement, and what possibilities for activity are realized in *making*? What material effects play out in *informationalization*? What *matters*?

When we theorize and study different information practices one thing becomes clear: in this dance of information, infrastructures, tools, and ourselves, it makes a difference what matter gains liveliness and how. What information is generated, how matter matures, decomposes, and re-emerges, and at what point it stops being a possibility (Steyerl, 2013) creates effects for everyone involved. Ethics is central to the ensemble of this 'spiral dance' (Haraway, 1991: 181). Or to put it differently: what *matters* is ultimately an ethical concern. Ethics is present making: it implies the act of doing something consciously. It involves the ethicality of making something of consequence, contributing to something that matters. As a result of that, ethics is also present in matter. It is embodied in the very materiality that emerges and exhibits agency. In our case, the ethicality of materials can refer to what kind of information appears and how a tool performs normativity, values, and sometimes very concrete understandings of the world. This ethicality is not merely about morality and responsibilities, but about co-creative values and 'ethical forces that operate like analytic frames for ongoing experiments with intensities that need to be enacted collectively' (Braidotti, 2019: 158). This book's argument is thus also relevant to ethical considerations: the ethics of making matter are performed in collective, embodied material practices that acknowledge passing (Braidotti, 2019), and transience, but also make anew.

Making information matter is not a practice that always performs the same ethical frames or sets of values. Speculative practices can, for example, create relevant alternatives to judgemental associative regimes, giving a platform to minoritarian concerns. At the same time, speculation can also be part of predictive regimes that disable the presents and futures of specific minorities.

Similar ambiguities characterize information practices of association, conversion, and secrecy. That is to say, making information matter always happens in specific contexts, which also give rise to the respective ethics, value systems, analytic frames, and material effects. Since making information matter performs different ethicalities, the central question for our engagement becomes: how *should* information matter? What material imaginaries and visions are central to information practices? In this light, the title of this book is not just a description. It should also be read as an invitation to action (or to become aware of one's action) and to reflect about one's margin for engagement. The point of discussing theory, methodology, and practices of making matter eventually leads us to formulate what is at stake, as well as to point to the many possibilities that exist to engage. At every turn in the information life cycle, we can ask ourselves how and what we intend to 'make and grow' (Ingold and Hallam, 2016) – even if we are only a few of the many involved actors. I do not claim that the practices of conversion, secrecy, and speculation as described in this book are necessarily the right answers to make matter differently. Rather, they emphasize that creating alternative possibilities, developing them in their context and respecting 'distinct bodies of knowledge' (Harding, 2015) will be the main key to make a difference in information practices. In closing this book, I will recapture a few central arguments and tie them to perspectives on the ethics of making, making matter, and matter. This is not a conclusion, but the end of this book is an intent to open up for rethinking our engagements.

Ethics of making

We can contribute to making matter, but we cannot master matter. As Jane Bennett reminds us: 'humans and their intentions participate, but they are not the sole or always the most profound actant in the assemblage' (2010b: 37). She even formulates a creed that ties the ontology of relationality to the ethics of making:

> I believe that this pluriverse is traversed by heterogeneities that are continually doing things. ... I believe that encounters with lively matter can chasten my fantasies of human mastery, highlight the common materiality of all that is, expose a wider distribution of agency, and reshape the self and its interests. (Bennett, 2010b: 122)

That everyone and everything is immersed in a meshwork (Ingold, 2011) or subject to the condition of complex interiority (Boltanski, 2011) implies a general ethics of becoming-with each other (Haraway, 2015b). Strictly speaking, we cannot become-without as we always make in response to and with others. All of us are ethically accountable (Braidotti, 2019). We cannot look at, perform ethics, and influence *becoming* from the outside. Humans are not external 'observers of the world' (Barad, 2003: 328). Any of our making is making from within. On this backdrop one could ask 'must a distributive, composite notion of agency thereby abandon the attempt to hold individuals responsible for their actions or hold officials accountable to the public?' (Bennett, 2010b: 37). Karen Barad (2003) answers that a condition of interiority does not put us into some kind of relativist ethical position. Despite our entanglement in collective agencies, humans remain 'resolutely accountable for the role "we" play in the intertwined practices of knowing and becoming' (Barad, 2003: 812, quotation marks in original). *We* can make, while having the capacity to reflect about our actions, at the same time as we can acknowledge that we are not the only ones acting. This ontology has quite concrete consequences for the mundane practices of making information matter: if we withdraw from any informational context, we may no longer matter.

While it is evident to interpret an ethics of becoming-with as a commitment to companionship (see Haraway, 2008), it is important to remember that it does not necessarily imply an altruistic ethics. Interiority and companionship apply to any form of making matter. They also apply to those practices we may seek to undermine and change. We also become-with the practices and phenomena we disagree with. Despite the fact that we become-with those driven by a different ethos from ours, a difference can still be made. '(A)ffirmative ethics' (Braidotti, 2019; 2021) can be performed from within. As Jane Bennett summarizes:

> Perhaps the ethical responsibility of an individual human now resides in one's response to the assemblages in which one finds oneself participating: Do I attempt to extricate myself from assemblages whose trajectory is likely to do harm? Do I enter into the proximity of assemblages whose conglomerate effectivity tends toward the enactment of nobler ends? (2010b: 38)

In the context of making *information* matter, we become-with the logics and regimes of surveillance and capture (Agre, 1994). Here, especially digital service providers and big data companies make information matter according to their own values. Making matter differently, then, means to engage with these information practices and regimes from within. Michel de Certeau's study of everyday practices (1984) has argued for exactly this possibility of undermining a system from within. Rita Raley, too, emphasizes how new perspectives can be created by replicating the inside of dataveillance systems and creating mirror worlds 'without the fantasy of exteriority' (2013: 137). Both are examples of becoming-with the information practices one seeks to change. These attempts at making a difference draw their energy not from outside informational systems altogether and not by leaving such systems, but by performing more or less radical alternatives to dominant information practices from within.

These examples underline a more overarching argument about the possibilities of making information matter differently. While 'we are in this together' (Braidotti, 2019: 156), the condition of interiority does not flatten out any differences between us. Interiority does not deny the different power relations that mark and separate us or the different crises we respond to (Braidotti, 2019). Rosi Braidotti writes this to remind us about our different capacities to act and calls on us to empower those who are currently missing from the landscape of influential actors. She asks us to acknowledge those who are 'more mortal' (Braidotti, 2021) than others and need to inherit more powerful positions – if they want to. I want to build on this argument by highlighting another aspect of it: the very fact that everyone is differently materially embedded gives rise to very different information practices and ethics. This means, the difference that marks us also enables us to make a difference. The fact that there is no undifferentiated 'we' (Braidotti, 2019) not only gives rise to different practices, power positions, and ethics, but is *key* to making differently. An affirmative ethics of *making differently*, then, requires commitment to understand differences and common grounds and to actively choose with whom we can make information matter together. Or, as Rosi Braidotti formulates it, it is to 'map out the margins of possible actualization of the virtual' (Braidotti, 2019: 154) and to do so with careless generosity (Braidotti, 2010).

This resonates with Sandra Harding's argument for acknowledging and using our differences as a resource when we do research. What she identifies as 'possibilities for progressive transformation that are less available to the unified, perfectly coherent and autonomous subjects' (Harding, 2015: 164) also plays into an ethics of making differently. In *Objectivity and Diversity* (2015) she writes about the problematic ethics of the Enlightenment's disengaged, autonomous rational subject of knowledge that looks (and makes) from nowhere: 'It has a powerful ethical obligation to strive to see everywhere in the universe from no particular location in that universe. Producing this "view from nowhere" has famously been characterized by Donna Haraway (1988) as the "God Trick".' (Harding, 2015: 156–7, quotation marks in original).

Instead of looking and performing from everywhere Sandra Harding invites us to utilize our difference to make differently. How we get there is by acknowledging our multiple, hyphenated, and conflicted selves (see Crenshaw, 1991) and the communities these selves are embedded in. This requires a balancing act as we always research and write 'both as individuals and as communities' (Harding, 2015: 174). In line with Sandra Harding's argument, an affirmative ethics of making matter differently is to seek out and promote 'the underrepresented insights and critical perspectives of economically, socially, and politically vulnerable groups' (Harding, 2015: 174) – but to do so from our own position.

Actively recognizing and working with difference is everyone's task. Such an ethics of making, however, cannot be based on activities by an 'oppositional, resisting self ("I prefer not to")', but it needs 'transversal alliances' and 'a new people' (Braidotti, 2019: 164). Though we are all irreducibly different, we do share the ability to affect and be affected by others (Braidotti, 2019). To be exposed to each other is what enables us to connect, act, and make together (Braidotti, 2019, 2021;). In this vulnerability lies also the desire, freedom, and potential (Braidotti, 2019), the power to make differently. Our analyses of information practices and their life cycles, but also our attempts at making information matter differently, then, should involve the active search for alternative, affirmative standpoints. This is a constant process.

Ethics of making matter

The *ethics of making* are an ethics of becoming-with while actively committing to differences in embodied material settings. As such, they are foundational to the *ethics of making matter*, which is to contribute to something that actually matters in an affirmative fashion. Again, mattering is not per se positive or supportive of those in need. As mentioned before, the associative practices of big data companies, for example, matter as well and perform their own ethics. Knowing this, we have to ask ourselves again: what *should* matter? Our ethical decisions, too, are 'not ideational but rather specific material (re)configurings of the world' (Barad, 2003: 819). They materialize at any turn in the lifecycle, which means that '(p)articular possibilities for acting exist at every moment, and these changing possibilities entail a responsibility to intervene in the world's becoming, to contest and rework what matters and what is excluded from mattering' (Barad, 2003: 827).

Our decisions on how to make matter become manifest, for example, in the systems we co-create and design. In pointing to the effects of design decisions on large-scale information systems, Susan L. Star and Karen Ruhleder formulated an ethic of making matter differently:

> If we … design messaging systems blind to the discontinuous nature of the different levels of context, we end up with organizations that are split and confused, systems which are unused or circumvented, and a set of circumstances of our own creation which more deeply impress disparities on the organizational landscape. (1996: 118)

These and similar needs to make information and information infrastructures matter differently have been echoed in the broader scholarly landscape (see Suchman's 'located accountabilities' mentioned in Chapter 2, 2002). The *Evoke Lab* focusing on Values in Design, the *Data Justice Lab* or the *Ida B. Wells Just Data Lab* are examples of scholarly initiatives to change infrastructures and datasets, that is to make matter differently. Communications and Media Professor Mark Andrejevic, too, sees a necessity to re-imagine information infrastructures, especially when it comes to who is allowed to control them (Andrejevic, 2021).

The question as to who gets a platform for making information and information infrastructure matter is – once again – central here. It ties in with ethical considerations about what should matter and, thus, materialize. At the risk of repeating myself, I emphasize that creating platforms for action, too, is not only a metaphoric undertaking, but it is a concrete material practice. Bringing the Internet, for example, back from the 'dead' – rendering it into a possibility that matters (Steyerl, 2013) – requires a thorough knowledge about and engagement with the status quo of the involved technologies and actors. The active humans, tools, infrastructure, and sets of information need to be mapped and understood in order to imagine viable alternatives to that what seems ubiquitous. Sara Ahmed emphasizes the need for such concrete strategies to turn 'the tangible object of ... resistance into a tangible platform for ... action' (2012: 174). Such strategies include regular self-assessments and engagements with the present (Ahmed, 2012) – the material State of the Art – to understand *how* we can make matter differently. Without concrete knowledge of what matters presently, our efforts of making matter remain in the 'non-performative' (Ahmed, 2012: 174) – they involve only making and materials, but do not matter. Thus, the affirmative ethics of making matter differently invokes the creating of knowledge about and active engagement with materialities. In line with Rosi Braidotti we can say that such ethics calls on us to map conditions, develop schemes of knowledge about these conditions, and devise a platform for action on multiple scales (2019). As we have seen in the examples of conversion, secrecy, and speculation, we can make matter by studying and designing hardware, writing our own codes, generating and sharing information with care, creating artworks, implementing workshops, developing material routines. Hackers, children, and artists – perhaps groups that we do not expect to have a prominent platform in the material context of information politics – have taught us that everyone can make matter differently. The same is true for police officers, developers, and software companies.

Performing this ethics is work and it requires resources. Becoming-with and addressing deficits, grievances, issues of 'conflict and pain' (Braidotti, 2019: 154) and creating alliances is labour-intensive. Zach Blas describes the pains that making such a difference online can cause: 'becoming informationally opaque can have excruciating political consequences, such as the loss of basic human rights' (2020: 199). Enduring in such a project 'involves affectivity and joy, but it also means putting up with hardship and physical pain' (Braidotti, 2019: 172). We see this emotional work in all practices that were studied for this book. Hackers, for example, mentioned the constant work that goes into making information matter differently and weighing the pros and cons of their engagements. Children make considerable social and emotional investments into keeping a secret (but also celebrate its social and emotional yields). Artists recounted the emotional challenges of producing works that engage with information politics. Oliver Chanarin referred to the "worst week of my life" when he felt like "processing" 600 people with a biometric camera (Oliver Chanarin, interview, see Chapter 7). Zach Blas' performance art of wearing informational *Face Cages* (2014–16, see list of artworks) was all about enduring the physical pain that the cage inflicted. Heather Dewey-Hagborg reflected about the "care work also that goes into working with cells" (Dewey-Hagborg, interview, see Chapter 7).

Since the ethics of making matter differently calls on us to perform physical and emotional labour, to endure under adverse conditions, to become-with those that challenge us, there is the risk of exhaustion. Thus, Wendy Chun argues that we need means 'to exhaust exhaustion' (2011: 92). In her view, this is best done by actively removing the desire for an end and nurture 'constant ethical encounters between self and other. These moments can call forth a new future' (Chun, 2011: 107). Rosi Braidotti, again, emphasizes the necessity to be aware of the subject's limitations, which are intimately linked to the position of interiority. It is the 'sheer material nature' of the subject that determines its limitations: 'being embodied implies a singular spatial-temporal frame: one life, in its radical immanence' (Braidotti, 2019: 170). Not everyone has the same option or energy to make matter in the ways they desire. Hence, the ethics of making matter differently also invoke engagements and changes 'directly proportional to the subject's ability to sustain them without cracking' (Braidotti, 2019: 170). That practices of making information matter differently, then, also include the joys of opacity (Blas, 2020), different forms of creativity, tactics of the everyday life, positive affects, aesthetic encounters, and instances of play is key so to not overburden the acting subject.

Ethics of matter

Putting a finger on accountability is difficult. From various juridical processes, we know that holding collectives accountable and trying to apply justice to large, networked phenomena is a notoriously difficult undertaking (see Suchman, 2002). In addition, how exactly are non-humans accountable and how would we approach that accountability in practice? Accountability is associated with a sense of self and the ability to reflect that *humans* (can) display. However, if we want to take the collective processes of making matter – including the liveliness of materials – seriously, thinking about ethics only in terms of accountability may not be sufficient. We may need a new wording that relates to this problematic. Such a wording would not only have to acknowledge the *agency* of non-humans, but also that this agency implies a certain ethicality, too. This ethicality is intimately linked to that of other actants – human and non-human. In order to inch our way towards such an ethicality of matter we may begin with Jane Bennett's metaphor to describe the role of humans in relation to distributed agencies:

> Agency is, I believe, distributed across a mosaic, but it is also possible to say something about the kind of striving that may be exercised by a human within the assemblage. This exertion is perhaps best understood on the model of riding a bicycle on a gravel road. One can throw one's weight this way or that, inflect the bike in one direction or toward one trajectory of motion. But the rider is but one actant operative in the moving whole. (Bennett, 2010b: 38)

In a sense, the role of humans may still be the easiest to consider in relation to ethics. Our situatedness in a collective agency makes performing ethics a complex practice, but at least we can try to become aware of our own influence, the influence others have on us and take decisions on how to perform our role. This is what the example of the bike-rider illustrates. However, it becomes more complicated when we shift our focus to the role of non-human others. Here, we cannot expect the same awareness and reflexivity. And yet, they are not merely actants that matter. I argue that their materiality exhibits a certain ethicality, too. If humans exert ethicality by riding their bike on a gravel road in a specific way, we may ask what the ethicality of the bike and the road is? Having walked through the theory, methodology, and many practices of making matter, we know that tools co-create the ethics of making matter. Surely tools, infrastructures, and materials can be *used* in different ways. I can ride my bike in a careful or a disrespectful manner. However, this tendency to focus on the rider is truncated. The fact that we can use tools in different ways does not make these tools neutral entities. To stay within the metaphor: a bike can be built to match gravel roads – or not. It can be built in a sustainable or non-sustainable manner. Tools can afford the manoeuvring of difficult territories or complicate it. Sometimes they take over the manoeuvre. More importantly, we cannot consider either bike or rider separately. Humans have inscribed themselves into tools. Humans are part of their materiality and their ethicality. This becomes manifest in informationalized settings: algorithms and police practice influence each other, which is why the call for the legal regulation of algorithms has become more pronounced. It is also a call to acknowledge the ethical dimensions of algorithms. An algorithm can, for example, target minorities and the responsibility is not lying on the police officer alone who may (still) use tools in an exclusionary fashion. At the same time, the target of the algorithm is co-defined by datasets, by engineers who took decisions on parameters, by data scientists who cleaned datasets accordingly, by police officers that choose which target to finally control or which dataset to produce. All of these have inscribed themselves into the algorithms that now co-determine the ethicality of police practice. The ethicality of the algorithm arises from that of many who inscribed themselves into the tool. This multiplicity and mutuality in the ethics of matter also becomes clear in the conversation with the photographer Oliver Chanarin. The projects of him and his art-partner Adam Broomberg see cameras as complicit in the creation of surveillance. The collective agency of the camera, state, photographer, and the photographed subject becomes obvious in their work *Spirit is a Bone* – a series of biometric portraits of the Russian population shot with a camera developed for facial recognition efforts, discussed in Chapter 7. A different project of theirs comments on the specific technological features of Polaroid cameras that require a difference in use related to skin colour. Human decisions and technological solutions fuse in the camera and make the ethicality of Polaroid technologies as they give rise to racial segregation. Oliver Chanarin makes the ethicality of the camera clear: "Everything about it is political. So it doesn't matter what picture you make with it – it becomes politicized. Which is why we photographed plants. Because it didn't matter what we photographed. Just the act of using it is a political act" (Oliver Chanarin, interview, see Chapter 7).

In the same spirit, Sandra Harding points to the ethicality of cameras and other recording devices in the sciences. They were meant to be 'Technologies of "Right Sight"' (2015: 160), but they actively co-produce a researcher's standpoint, as well as the 'standards for accurate representations' (Harding, 2015: 160). If at all, these cameras were more representative of the 'history of the scientific self' (Harding, 2015: 161; Daston and Galison, 2007) instead of providing the objective, neutral services of right sight.

What is true for information technologies – cameras, recording devices, algorithms – is also true for information. Discussions around the ethicality of datasets tend to revolve around ideas of eliminating bias in data collection and in the curation of training datasets. However, just like information technologies, the matter of information itself is subject to ethicality. There is no value-free dataset. In any interaction with information, ethical accounts are written into information. Within datasets, specific values materialize and matter. Information cannot be rid of this ethicality, but in common processes of imagining, generating, storing, processing, and re-using information decisions about how information is supposed to matter can be taken. Instead of nurturing the imaginary of a value-free, unpolitical, unbiased dataset (that would no longer matter), the ethics of information needs to be embraced by asking: how should information matter? And how can we and information make matter together?

The ethicality of making matter is a constant negotiation. As agencies are rearranged, rearticulated, reworked (see Barad, 2003: 816–17), new ethicalities emerge. In the same way in which Karen Barad argues that not things but phenomena are the central ontological units of understanding agency (2003), this chapter suggests that neither a focus on humans or non-humans, but their material dynamics are central to grasp the ethics of making information matter. If we return to Jane Bennett's bike-metaphor, we can say that in order to understand the ethics of making matter differently, it is neither fair, nor useful to focus on the bike-rider alone. The ethicality of non-human matter needs to be appreciated, too. However, when emphasizing the ethicality of every single human and non-human actor, it is easy to get lost in some kind of ethical relativism with endless relations to study. Thus, instead of working with the logics of individual accountabilities, we may want to consider the ethicality of material practices, that is how we make matter together. Jane Bennett's personal maxim to 'tread lightly on the earth' (2010b: 121) is here a great vantage point for us to consider. I encourage us to not only tread lightly, but to make a more active difference. Everyone can use their unique and limited capacities to make matter differently by acknowledging the ethicality of non-human matter and by actively influencing the matterings we are part of. When we imagine, generate, store, process, or re-use information and information technologies, we can choose to actively inscribe ourselves – and the communities we want to create a platform for – into that matter.

Mapping a 'state of the heart': a summary and call for engagement

Making Information Matter is a commitment. It is an ontological commitment to consider information as material, as in-formation and always integrated with processes of making (Chapter 2). Since information practices have considerable influence in society today, it matters *how* information materializes. Practice matters, making matters. Associative practices, for example, have become a dominant form of using information for the sake of governance (Chapter 4). Commercial and non-commercial profiles have emerged as the key tool and rationale for the regulation of many societal fields. They are the results of collaborative information capture, storage, cleaning, and algorithmic association. Such data-profiles, including all shortcuts, categorizations, and data-decisions taken along the way 'go on to live and act in the world' (Amoore, 2011: 27). Initiatives to break with the reductive logics of profiling may be to convert information so it can no longer be captured or work with reductive 'types', or to select more consciously how and to whom one's data are rendered visible (Chapter 5). Secrecy, too, can be an opening to practice difference. Unlike the ethical negativeness (for a critique see Simmel, 1906) that is often associated with secrecy, it is a practice of making information matter that can also empower, protect, strengthen relationships and identities, as well as elicit joy and creativity (Chapter 6). Speculation can be an element of association, for example when statistical analyses and profiles take a conjectural form and follow the logic of the derivative, which is 'exposed to the underlying data without collecting them, created across the gaps and absences, in the interstitial spaces of inference and expansion' (Amoore, 2011: 33). Speculation, then, pushes the boundaries of categorization and 'what might be' (Amoore, 2011: 24), which can reflect divergent ethics. When used in the context of criminal profiling, for example, speculation is an opening for broadening the scope of suspicion. The art projects discussed in Chapter 7, however, employ speculation to offer alternative futures, to educate about 'what might be' and to suggest technologies that could matter differently. Making information matter is thus a messy landscape of overlapping practices and technologies that need to be studied and understood in their specificity in order to make a difference. Hence, the ontological commitment to making matter also necessitates a method to grasp processes of materialization and to identify the different elements that make matter together. Tracing the becoming of information throughout its life cycle can help us identifying the openings for our own engagement with information imaginaries, with information generation, collection, storage, cleaning, processing, and re-use (Chapter 3). This final chapter ties the ontological commitment more clearly to engagement. It argues that in making information matter, it is also an invitation, a reminder, and an ethical commitment. The ethos of making is not geared towards conclusions. Rather, it is the continued 'effort to interrupt the acquiescent application of established norms and values, to deterritorialize them by introducing alternative ethical flows. ... Such a leap engages with, but also breaks productively with the present' (Braidotti, 2019: 172).

Indeed, identifying cracks of possibility and making them matter requires thorough engagements with the present of information practices. When we map the State of the Art we need to recognize the ethicality of human and non-human matters. Such mapping also includes efforts to acknowledge our own positions. We need this insight to identify strategies to balance the loss, pain, and exhaustion that making differently may involve with creativity, pleasure, and the energy of forging new collaborations. Only when we understand with whom and how we make information matter can we let such a State of the Art guide our breaking and making of the present. Thus, instead of offering conclusions, I close with questions that may help us not only in mapping a State of the Art, but to make it a 'State of the Heart':

- What specific information practices are the State of the Art, and what is the ethicality of the information and information technologies they involve?
- Do we take account of the liveliness of the components involved in such practices? What is their role?
- What are the relevant turns in the life cycles of specific information and information technologies that we can use as entry points to make differently?
- Who has written themselves into datasets and information technologies? How do we matter to such practices?
- Whose agency is oppressed by information practices targeted at bodies, race, social position, gender, sexual orientation, or cultural heritage?
- What are our options to make information matter with and for these groups in a nonviolent, non-oppressive way? What specific possibilities for activity and agency do we need to realize? What information practices would represent these groups and ourselves? What information should not matter?
- What strategies can we develop to make information matter and become-with those humans and non-humans we disagree with?
- What are our own limitations, that is, what and whom do we need in order to practice in a way that matters?
- What losses, pains, pleasures, and creativities may this involve? And how do we make matter in a way that does not exhaust the resources we need?

Notes

Chapter 5

[1] All hacker names in this chapter are aliases used to anonymize informants. When interviews were conducted in a different language than English they were translated to English.

[2] Several parts of this paragraph are reproductions from the article Kaufmann, Mareile (2020) 'Hacking surveillance', *First Monday,* 25(5). https://doi.org/10.5210/fm.v25i5.10006

[3] Name, meaning: 'small researchers'.

[4] Name, double-meaning: The CCC is at school/sets a precedent.

Chapter 6

[1] This paragraph includes phrasing from the following article: Kaufmann, Mareile (2021) 'This Is a Secret: Learning from Children's Engagement with Surveillance and Secrecy', *Cultural Studies ↔ Critical Methodologies*, 21(5): 424–37. https://doi.org/10.1177/153270 86211029350

[2] All children's names are aliases. Conversations led in other languages than English were translated into English.

Chapter 7

[1] Neologism based on transhumanism – but extended to a vision of society at large.

[2] Any statements by Heather Dewey-Hagborg, Oliver Chanarin, or Zach Blas that do not feature an official reference are quotes from the conversations I had with them.

List of Artworks Cited

American Artist
I'm Blue (If I Was ■■■■■ *I Would Die)*, 2019

Sadie Barnette
Dear 1968, …, 2017

Zach Blas
Queer Technologies, 2012
Facial Weaponization Suite, 2012
Face Cages, 2014–16
Contra-Internet, 2015–19
Metric Mysticism, 2017–18
Contra-Internet: Jubilee of 2033, 2019
Icosahedron, 2019
The Doors, 2019

Xu Bing
Dragonfly Eyes, 2017

Broomberg and Chanarin
Spirit is a Bone, 2015

Sophie Calle
Suite Venitienne, 1979
The Hotel, 1981
The Shadow, 1981

Nick Cave
Soundsuits, 1991 onwards

Hasan Elahi
TrackingTransience.net

Heather Dewey-Hagborg
Stranger Visions, 2012–13
DNA spoofing, 2013
The Official Bionymous Guidebooks, 2015
Probably Chelsea, 2017
Biopunk: Subverting Biopolitics, 2017
Hacking Biopolitics, 2017
How Do You See Me?, 2019

Adam Harvey
CV Dazzle, 2010–
OFF Pocket, 2011–

Arthur Jafa
Love is the Message, the Message is Death, 2018

Manu Luksch, Jack Wolf and Mukul Patel
Algo-rhythm, 2019

Michelangelo di Lodovico Buonarroti Simoni
The Creation of Adam, 1508–12
The Last Judgment, 1536–41

August Sander
Antlitz der Zeit, 1929

Hito Steyerl
How Not to be Seen: A Fucking Didactic Educational .MOV File, 2013

Ai WeiWei
WeiWeiCam, 2012

References

Agrawal, Rakesh, Imieliński, Tomasz, Swami, Arun (1993) 'Mining Association Rules Between Sets of Items in Large Databases', *Proceedings of the 1993 ACM SIGMOD International Conference on Management of Data*, 207–216.

Agrawal, Rakesh, Srikant, Ramakrishnan (1994) 'Fast Algorithms for Mining Association Rules', *Proceedings of the 20th International Conference on Very Large Data Bases*, 1215: 487–499.

Agre, Philip E. (1994) 'Surveillance and Capture: Two Models of Privacy', *The Information Society*, 10(2): 101–127.

Ahmed, Sara (2012) *On Being Included: Racism and Diversity in Institutional Life*, Durham, NC: Duke University Press.

Alting, D. Leo, Jørgensen, D. Jørgen (1993) 'The Life Cycle Concept as a Basis for Sustainable Industrial Production', *CIRP Annals – Manufacturing Technology*, 42(1): 163–167.

Amoore, Louise (2009) 'Lines of Sight: On the Visualization of Uncertain Futures', *Citizenship Studies*, 13(1): 13–27.

Amoore, Louise (2011) 'Data Derivatives: On the Emergence of a Security Risk Calculus for Our Times', *Theory, Culture & Society*, 28(6): 24–43.

Anderson, Chris (2008) 'The End of Theory: The Data Deluge Makes the Scientific Method Obsolete', *Wired*, https://www.wired.com/2008/06/pb-theory/ (Accessed 24 November 2022).

Andrejevic, Mark (2021) *Lecture at the Data Justice Conference 2021 'Civic Participation in the Datafied Society'*, 20 May 2021.

Andrejevic, Mark, Gates, Kelly (2014) 'Big Data Surveillance: Introduction', *Surveillance & Society*, 12(2): 185–196.

Apple (2019) 'Apple Offers New Augmented Reality Art Sessions', *Apple Newsroom*, https://www.apple.com/newsroom/2019/07/apple-offers-new-augmented-reality-art-sessions/ (Accessed 9 December 2019).

Artist, American, Browne, Simone, Benjamin, Ruha (2021) 'Surveillance and Cinematics', *Institute of the Arts and Sciences*, https://ias.ucsc.edu/events/2021/surveillance-and-cinematics-american-artist-simone-browne-and-ruha-benjamin-february-2 (Accessed 1 June 2021).

Asher, Jeff, Arthur, Rob (2017) 'Inside the Algorithm That Tries to Predict Gun Violence in Chicago', *New York Times*, https://www.nytimes.com/2017/06/13/upshot/what-an-algorithm-reveals-about-life-on-chicagos-high-risk-list.html (Accessed 18 March 2021).

Aubry, René (2006) *Mémoires Du Future*, Album, France: Hopi Mesa.

Austin, Jonathan, Bellanova, Rocco, Kaufmann, Mareile (2019) 'Doing and Mediating Critique: An Invitation to Practice Companionship', *Security Dialogue*, 50(1): 3–19.

Azavea (nd) https://www.azavea.com (Accessed 7 April 2021).

Bakker, Peter (1987) 'Autonomous Languages of Twins', *Acta Geneticae Medicae et Gemellologicae,* 36(2): 233–238.

Barad, Karen (2003) 'Posthumanist Performativity: Toward an Understanding of How Matter Comes to Matter', *Signs*, 28(3): 801–831.

Barad, Karen (2007) *Meeting the Universe Halfway: Quantum Physics and the Entanglement of Matter and Meaning*, Durham, NC: Duke University Press.

Barlow, John Perry (1996) A declaration of the independence of cyberspace, https://www.eff.org/cyberspace-independence (Accessed 24 November 2022).

Barron, Carol Margaret (2014) '"I had no credit to ring you back": Children's Strategies of Negotiation and Resistance to Parental Surveillance via Mobile Phones', *Surveillance & Society*, 12(3): 401–413.

Bawden, David, Robinson, Lyn (2013) '"Deep down things": In What Ways Is Information Physical, and Why Does It Matter for Information Science?', *Information Research*, 18(3): 1–11.

Beck, Charlie, McCue, Colleen (2009) 'Predictive Policing: What Can We Learn from Wal-Mart and Amazon about Fighting Crime in a Recession?', *The Police Chief*, 76(11): 18–24.

Beer, David, Burrows, Roger (2013) 'Popular Culture, Digital Archives and the New Social Life of Data', *Theory, Culture & Society*, 30(4): 47–71.

Bellanova, Rocco (2017) 'Digital, Politics, and Algorithms: Governing Digital Data Through the Lens of Data Protection', *European Journal of Social Theory*, 20(3): 329–347.

Bellanova, Rocco, González Fuster, Gloria (2019) 'Composting and Computing: On Digital Security Compositions', *European Journal of International Security*, 4(3): 345–365.

Benjamin, Ruha (2019) *Race After Technology: Abolitionist Tools for the New Jim Code*, Cambridge: Polity.

Bennett, Jane (2001) *The Enchantment of Modern Life: Attachments, Crossings, and Ethics*, Princeton, NJ: Princeton University Press.

Bennett, Jane (2004) 'The Force of Things: Steps toward an Ecology of Matter', *Political Theory*, 32(3): 347–372.

Bennett, Jane (2010a) 'A Vitalist Stopover on the Way to a New Materialism', in: Coole, Diana, Frost, Samantha (eds) *New Materialisms. Ontology, Agency and Politics*, Durham, NC: Duke University Press, pp 47–69.

Bennett, Jane (2010b) *Vibrant Matter: A Political Ecology of Things*, Durham, NC: Duke University Press.

Bennett Moses, Lyria, Chan, Janet (2016) 'Algorithmic Prediction in Policing: Assumptions, Evaluation, and Accountability', *Policing and Society*, 28(7): 806–822.

Berk, Richard (2017) 'An Impact Assessment of Machine Learning Risk Forecasts on Parole Board Decisions and Recidivism', *Journal of Experimental Criminology*, 13(2): 193–216.

Berk, Richard (2018) *Machine Learning Risk Assessments in Criminal Justice Settings*, New York: Springer.

Berk, Richard, Sorensen, Susan B., Barnes, Geoffrey (2016) 'Forecasting Domestic Violence: A Machine Learning Approach to Help Inform Arraignment Decisions', *Journal of Empirical Legal Studies*, 13(1): 94–115.

Bérut, Antoine, Arakelyan, Artak, Petrosyan, Artyom, Ciliberto, Sergio, Dillenschneider, Raoul and Lutz, Eric (2012) 'Experimental Verification of Landauer's Principle Linking Information and Thermodynamics', *Nature*, 483(7388): 187–189.

Bevan, Andrew (2015) 'The Data Deluge', *Antiquity*, 89(348): 1473–1484.

Bess, Gabby (2017) 'The Woman Making Art out of the FBI's Surveillance of Her Black Panther Father', *Vice*, https://www.vice.com/en/article/vb4 vzx/the-woman-making-art-out-of-the-fbis-surveillance-of-her-black-panther-father (Accessed 27 May 2021).

Bioteknologirådet (2014) 'DNA i kunst og etterforskning', *Bioteknologirådet*, (DNA in the arts and in intelligence) https://www.bioteknologiradet.no/2014/01/11618/ (Accessed 24 November 2022).

Birchall, Clare (2011) 'Introduction to "Secrecy and Transparency" The Politics of Opacity and Openness', *Theory, Culture & Society*, 28(7–8): 7–25.

Birchall, Clare (2014) 'Aesthetics of the Secret', *New Formations*, 83(0): 25–46.

Birchall, Clare (2016) 'Managing Secrecy', *International Journal of Communication*, 10(0): 152–163.

Blakely, Sandra (2012) 'Toward an Archaeology of Secrecy: Power, Paradox, and the Great Gods of Samothrace', *Archeological Papers of the American Anthropological Association*, 21(1): 49–71.

Blanchette, Jean-Francois (2011) 'A Material History of Bits', *Journal of the American Society for Information Science and Technology*, 62(6): 1042–1057.

Blanchette, Jean-Francois (2012) *Burdens of Proof: Cryptographic Culture and Evidence Law in the Age of Electronic Documents*, Cambridge, MA: MIT Press.

Blas, Zach (2016) 'Opacities: An Introduction', *Camera Obscura*, 31(2): 149–153.

Blas, Zach (2017) 'Contra-Internet Aesthetics', in: Kholeif, Omar (ed) *You Are Here: Art After the Internet*, Manchester: HOME and SPACE, pp 86–97.

Blas, Zach (2020) 'Informatic Opacity', in: Braidotti, Rosi, Hlavajova, Maria (eds) *Posthuman Glossary*, New York: Bloomsbury Academic, pp 198–199.

Blas, Zach (nd) https://zachblas.info (Accessed 3 June 2021).

Blum, Andrew (2012) *Tubes: A Journey to the Center of the Internet*, New York: Harper Collins.

Boltanski, Luc (2011) *On Critique: A Sociology of Emancipation*, Cambridge: Polity.

Bostrom, Nick (2014) *Superintelligence: Paths, Dangers, Strategies*, Oxford: Oxford University Press.

Bowker, Geoffrey (1994) 'Information Mythology and Infrastructure', in: Bud-Frierman, Lisa (ed) *Information Acumen: The Understanding and Use of Knowledge in Modern Business*, London: Routledge, pp 231–247.

Bowker, Geoffrey C. (2005) *Memory Practices in the Sciences*, Cambridge, MA: MIT Press.

Bowker, Geoffrey C. (2013) 'Data Flakes: An Afterword to "Raw Data" is an Oxymoron', in: Gitelman, Lisa (ed) *'Raw Data' Is an Oxymoron*, Cambridge, MA: MIT Press, pp 167–172.

Bowker, Geoffrey, Star, Susan L. (2000) *Sorting Things Out: Classification and Its Consequences*, Cambridge, MA: MIT Press.

Bowker, Geoffrey C., Baker, Karen, Millerand, Florence, Ribes, David (2010) 'Toward Information Infrastructure Studies: Ways of Knowing in a Networked Environment', in: Hunsinger, Jeremy, Allen, Matthew, Klastrup, Lisbeth (eds) *International Handbook of Internet Research*, Dordrecht: Springer, pp 97–117.

boyd, danah (2014) *It's Complicated: The Social Life of Networked Teens*, New Haven, CT: Yale University Press.

Braidotti, Rosi (2010) 'The Politics of "Life Itself" and New Ways of Dying', in: Coole, Diana, Frost, Samantha (eds) *New Materialisms. Ontology, Agency and Politics*, Durham, NC: Duke University Press, pp 201–218.

Braidotti, Rosi (2019) *Posthuman Knowledge*, Cambridge: Polity.

Braidotti, Rosi (2021) 'The Critical Posthumanities', *Lecture at The Center for Culture and Technology at the University of Southern Denmark*, 29th of April 2021.

Brantingham, Paul J., Brantingham, Patricia L. (1991) *Environmental Criminology*, Prospect Heights, IL: Waveland Press.

Bratich, Jack (2006) 'Popular Secrecy and Occultural Studies', *Cultural Studies*, 21(1): 42–58.

Brine, Kevin R, Poovey, Mary (2013) 'From Measuring Desire to Quantifying Expectations: A Late Nineteenth Century Effort to Marry Economic Theory and Data', in: Gitelman, Lisa (ed) *'Raw Data' Is an Oxymoron*, Cambridge, MA: MIT Press, pp 61–76.

Brown, Jonathan N. (2014) 'The Sound of Silence: Power, Secrecy, and International Audiences in US Military Basing Negotiations', *Conflict Management and Peace Science*, 31(4): 406–443.

Browne, Simone (2015) *Dark Matters: On the Surveillance of Blackness*, Durham, NC and London: Duke University Press.

Browne, Simone, Blas, Zach (2017) 'Beyond the Internet and All Control Diagrams', *New Inquiry*, https://thenewinquiry.com/beyond-the-inter net-and-all-control-diagrams/ (Accessed 16 April 2019).

Brunton, Finn, Nissenbaum, Helen (2011) 'Vernacular Resistance to Data Collection and Analysis: A Political Theory of Obfuscation', *First Monday*, 16(5): np https://firstmonday.org/article/view/3493/2955 (Accessed 20 April 2020).

Brunton, Finn, Nissenbaum, Helen (2016) *Obfuscation: A User's Guide for Privacy and Protest*, Cambridge, MA: MIT Press.

Burdick, Anne (2012) *Digital Humanities*, Cambridge, MA: MIT Press.

Burgess, Matt (2018) 'How to Stop Google from Tracking You and Delete Your Personal Data', *Wired UK*, http://www.wired.co.uk/article/goo gle-history-search-tracking-data-how-to-delete (Accessed 5 June 2018).

Butterfield, Andrew, Ngondi, Gerard Ekembe, Kerr, Anne (2016) *A Dictionary of Computer Science* (7th ed.), Oxford: Oxford University Press.

Callon, Michel (1986) 'The Sociology of an Actor-Network: The Case of the Electric Vehicle', in: Callon, Michel, Law, John, Rip, Arie (eds) *Mapping the Dynamics of Science and Technology*, London: Palgrave Macmillan, pp 19–34.

Callon, Michel (2004) 'The Role of Hybrid Communities and Socio-technical Arrangements in the Participatory Design', *Journal of the Center for Information Studies*, 5(3): 3–10.

Camp Breakout, 'Das Digital Detox Camp', https://www.camp-breakout. com (Accessed 11 July 2018).

Camus, Alexandre, Vinck, Dominique (2019) 'Unfolding Digital Materiality: How Engineers Struggle to Shape Tangible and Fluid Objects', in: Vertesi, Janet, Ribes, David (eds) *digitalSTS: A Field Guide for Science and Technology Studies*, Princeton, NJ: Princeton University Press, pp 17–41.

Canguilhem, Georges. (2008) *Knowledge of Life*, Paola Marrati and Todd Meyers (eds), trans. Stefanos Geroulanos and Daniela Ginsburg, New York: Fordham University Press.

Casemajor, Nathalie, Couture, Stéphane, Delfin, Mauricio, Goerzen, Matthew Delfanti, Alessandro (2015) 'Non-participation in Digital Media: Toward a Framework of Mediated Political Action', *Media, Culture & Society*, 37(6): 850–866.

Chachra, Debbie (2017) 'Beyond Making', in: Sayers, Jentery (ed) *Making Things and Drawing Boundaries. Experiments in the Digital Humanities*, Minneapolis, MN: University of Minnesota Press, pp 319–321.

Chan, Ko Ling (2011) 'Gender Differences in Self-reports of Intimate Partner Violence: A Review', *Aggression and Violent Behavior*, 16(2): 167–175.

Chertoff, Michael (2006) 'A Tool We Need to Stop the Next Airliner Plot', *Washington Post*, https://www.washingtonpost.com/archive/opinions/ 2006/08/29/a-tool-we-need-to-stop-the-next-airliner-plot/bcd240b8- 8d61-4664-8f8f-f45d5b3cfaf7/ (Accessed 24 November 2022).

Chicago Police Department (2019) 'Special Order S09–11', *Subject Assessment and Information Dashboard (SAID)*, https://directives.crimeisdown.com/diff/a148929d984a05241f3ed79d55af4f0a185063a3/directives/data/a7a57b85-155e9f4b-50c15-5e9f-7742e3ac8b0ab2d3.html (Accessed 18 March 2021).

Chiribella, Giulio, D'Ariano, Giacomo Mauro and Perinotti, Paolo (2012) 'Quantum Theory, Namely the Pure and Reversible Theory of Information', *Entropy*, 14(10): 1877–1893.

Chun, Wendy Hui Kyong (2008) 'On "Sourcery," or Code as Fetish', *Configurations*, 16(3): 299–324.

Chun, Wendy Hui Kyong (2011) 'Crisis, Crisis, Crisis, or Sovereignty and Networks', *Theory, Culture & Society*, 28(6): 91–112.

Chun, Wendy Hui Kyong (2016) *Updating to Remain the Same: Habitual New Media*, Cambridge, MA: MIT Press.

Chun, Wendy Hui Kyong (2021) *Discriminating Data: Correlation, Neighborhoods, and the New Politics of Recognition*, Cambridge, MA: MIT Press.

Cohen, Lawrence E., Felson, Marcus (1979) 'Social Change and Crime Rate Trends: A Routine Activity Approach', *American Sociological Review*, 44(4): 588–608.

Chung, Grace, Grimes, Sarah (2005) 'Data Mining the Kids: Surveillance and Market Research Strategies in Children's Online Games', *Canadian Journal of Communication*, 30(4): 527–548.

Coleman, Gabriella (2017) 'From Internet Farming to Weapons of the Geek', *Current Anthropology*, 58(S15): S91–S102.

Coleman, Gabriella, Golub, Alex (2008) 'Hacker Practice: Moral Genres and the Cultural Articulation of Liberalism', *Anthropological Theory*, 8(3): 255–277.

Connor, Michael (2014) 'Post-Internet. What It Is and What It Was', in: Kholeif, Omar (ed) *You Are Here: Art After the Internet*, Manchester: Cornerhouse, pp 56–65.

Coole, Diana (2010) 'The Inertia of Matter and the Generativity of Flesh', in: Coole, Diana, Frost, Samantha (eds) *New Materialisms. Ontology, Agency and Politics*, Durham, NC: Duke University Press, pp 92–115.

Coole, Diana, Frost, Samantha (2010) 'Introducing New Materialisms', in: Coole, Diana, Frost, Samantha (eds) *New Materialisms. Ontology, Agency and Politics*, Durham, NC: Duke University Press, pp 1–43.

Cornish, Derek B., Clarke, Ronald V. (1986) *The Reasoning Criminal: Rational Choice Perspectives on Offending*, New York: Springer-Verlag.

Covin, Jeffrey G., Slevin, Dennis P. (1990) 'New Venture Strategic Posture, Structure, and Performance: An Industry Life Cycle Analysis', *Journal of Business Venturing*, 5(2): 123–135.

Crenshaw, Kimberlé (1991) 'Mapping the Margins: Intersectionality, Identity Politics, and Violence against Women of Color', *Stanford Law Review*, 43(6): 1241–1299.

Daly, Angela, Devitt Kate, Mann, Monique (2019) *Good Data: Theory on Demand*, Amsterdam: Institute of Network Cultures Theory on Demand Series.

Daston, Lorraine, Galison, Peter (2007) *Objectivity*, Brooklyn, NY: Zone Books.

Davenport Thomas H. (2014) 'Taming the "Data Plumbing" Problem', *Wall Street Journal*, https://www.wsj.com/articles/BL-CIOB-4559 (Accessed 7 April 2021).

Davis, Heather (2020) 'Art in the Anthropocene', in: Braidotti, Rosi, Hlavajova, Maria (eds) *Posthuman Glossary*, New York: Bloomsbury Academic, pp 63–65.

De Certeau, Michel (1984) *The Practice of Everyday Life*, Berkeley, CA: University of California Press.

De Certeau, Michel (1986) *Heterologies. Discourses on the Other*, trans. Brian Massumi, Minneapolis, MN: University of Minnesota Press.

De Vries, Katja (2020) 'You Never Fake Alone: Creative AI in Action', *Information, Communication & Society*, 23(14): 2110–2127.

Debord, Guy (1998) *Comments on the Society of the Spectacle*, London: Verso.

Deleuze, Gilles, Guattari, Félix (1987) *A Thousand Plateaus: Capitalism and Schizophrenia*, trans. Brian Massumi, Minneapolis, MN: University of Minnesota Press.

Deleuze, Gilles and Guattari, Felix (2004) *A Thousand Plateaus*, London: Continuum.

Denzin, Norman K (2010) *Childhood Socialization. Revised Second Edition*, New Brunswick/London: Transaction Publishers.

Dewey-Hagborg, Heather (nd) https://deweyhagborg.com (Accessed 3 June 2021).

Doctorow, Cory (2021) 'Machine Learning Is a Honeypot for Phrenologists', *Pluralistic*, https://pluralistic.net/2021/01/15/hoover-calling/#phrenology (Accessed 24 November 2022).

Downs, Joni A (2016) 'Mapping Sex Offender Activity Spaces Relative to Crime Using Time-geographic Methods', *Annals of GIS*, 22(2): 141–150.

Drucker, Johanna (2009) *SpecLab: Digital Aesthetics and Projects in Speculative Computing*, Chicago, IL: University of Chicago Press.

Drucker, Johanna (2013) 'Performative Materiality and Theoretical Approaches to Interface', *Digital Humanities Quarterly*, 7(1), http://www.digitalhumanities.org/dhq/vol/7/1/000143/000143.html (Accessed 24 November 2022).

Edwards, Paul N (2004) '"A Vast Machine": Standards as Social Technology', *Science*, 304(5672): 827–828.

Edwards, Paul N (2010) *A Vast Machine: Computer Models, Climate Data, and the Politics of Global Warming*, Cambridge, MA: MIT Press.

Edwards, Paul N., Mayernik, Matthew S., Batcheller, Arche L., Bowker, Geoffrey C., Borgman, Christine L. (2011) 'Science Friction: Data, Metadata, and Collaboration', *Social Studies of Science*, 41(5): 667–690.

Egbert, Simon, Leese, Matthias (2021) *Criminal Futures: Predictive Policing and Everyday Police Work*, London: Routledge.

Elden, Stuart (2019) *Canguilhem*, Cambridge: Polity.

Ema, Arisa, Yuko Fujigaki (2011) 'How Far Can Child Surveillance Go? Assessing the Parental Perceptions of an RFID Child Monitoring System in Japan', *Surveillance & Society*, 9(1/2): 132–148.

Ericson, Richard (2007) *Crime in an Insecure World*, Cambridge: Polity.

Erixon, Fredrik, Lee-Makiyama, Hosuk (2011) 'Digital Authoritarianism: Human Rights, Geopolitics and Commerce', *European Centre for International Political Economy (ECIPE) Occasional Paper*, 5/2011, http://hdl.handle.net/10419/174715 (Accessed 20 April 2020).

Evans, Claire L. (2014) 'UnFacebooking, Randomizing, and Other Ways to Burst the Filter Bubble', *Motherboard,* https://motherboard.vice.com/en_us/article/kbz3aa/unfacebooking-random-and-other-strategies-for-popping-the-filter-bubble (Accessed 5 June 2018).

Farrell, Graham, Pease, Ken (2014) 'Predictive Policing', in: Bruinsma, Gerben, Weisburd, David (eds) *Encyclopedia of Criminology and Criminal Justice*, Dordrecht: Springer, pp 3862–3871.

Feldman, Steven P. (1988) 'Secrecy, Information, and Politics: An Essay on Organizational Decision Making', *Human Relations*, 41(1): 73–90.

Felski, Rita (2012) 'Critique and the Hermeneutics of Suspicion', *M/C Journal*, 15(1), http://journal.media-culture.org.au/index.php/mcjournal/article/viewArticle/431 (Accessed 24 November 2022).

Fenster, Mark (1999) *Conspiracy Theories: Secrecy and Power in American Culture*, Minneapolis, MN: University of Minnesota Press.

Floridi, Luciano (2010) *Information: A Very Short Introduction*, Oxford: Oxford University Press.

Flower, William Henry (1898 [1889]) 'Museum Organization', in: Flower, William Henry (ed) *Essays on Museums and Other Subjects Connected with Natural History*, London: Macmillan, pp 1–29.

Forlano, Laura (2019) 'Materiality', in: Vertesi, Janet, Ribes, David (eds) *digitalSTS: A Field Guide for Science and Technology Studies*, Princeton, NJ: Princeton University Press, pp 11–15.

Foucault, Michel (1979) 'Omnes et Singulatim: Towards a Criticism of "Political Reason"', *The Tanner Lectures on Human Values, Delivered at Stanford University, October 10 and 16, 1979,* https://tannerlectures.utah.edu/_documents/a-to-z/f/foucault81.pdf (Accessed 17 June 2019).

Franklin, Sarah (2017) 'Staying with the Manifesto: An Interview with Donna Haraway', *Theory, Culture & Society*, 34(4): 49–63.

Frost, Samantha (2016) *Biocultural Creatures: Toward a New Theory of the Human*, Durham, NC: Duke University Press.

Fuchs, Christian (2010) 'Labor in Informational Capitalism and on the Internet', *The Information Society*, 26(3): 179–196.

Fyfe, Nick R., Gundhus, Helene O.I., Rønn, Kira V. (2017) 'Introduction', in: Gundhus, Helene O.I., Rønn, Kira V. and Fyfe, Nick R. (eds) *Moral Issues in Intelligence-led Policing*, London: Routledge, pp 1–22.

Galdon Clavell, Gemma (2018) 'Bad Data Challenge', *Dataethics*, https://dataethics.eu/bad-data-challenge/ (Accessed 26 March 2019).

Galloway, Alexander R. (2006) *Gaming: Essays on Algorithmic Culture*, Minneapolis, MN: University of Minnesota Press.

Galloway, Alexander R., Thacker, Eugene (2007) *The Exploit: A Theory of Networks*, Minneapolis, MN: University of Minnesota Press.

Gibson-Graham, J.K. (2006) *The End of Capitalism (As We Knew It): A Feminist Critique of Political Economy*, Minneapolis, MN: University of Minnesota Press.

Gillespie, Tarleton (2014) 'The Relevance of Algorithms', in: Gillespie, Tarleton, Boczkowski, Pablo J., Foot, Kirsten A. (eds) *Media Technologies: Essays on Communication, Materiality and Society*, Cambridge, MA: MIT Press, pp 167–193.

Gitelman, Lisa, Jackson, Virginia (2013) 'Introduction', in: Gitelman, Lisa (ed) *'Raw Data' is an Oxymoron*, Cambridge, MA: MIT Press, pp 1–14.

Glaeser, Stephen (2018) 'The Effects of Proprietary Information on Corporate Disclosure and Transparency: Evidence from Trade Secrets', *Journal of Accounting and Economics*, 66(1): 163–193.

Glissant, Édouard (1997) *Poetics of Relation*, trans. Wing, Betsy, Ann Arbor, MI: University of Michigan Press.

Goff, Stephen A., Vaughn, Matthew, McKay, Sheldon, Lyons, Eric, Stapleton, Ann E., Gessler, Damian, Matasci, Naim et al (2011) 'The iPlant Collaborative: Cyberinfrastructure for Plant Biology', *Frontiers in Plant Science*, 2: 34.

Goffey, Andrew (2008) 'Algorithm', in: Fuller, Matthew (ed) *Software Studies: A Lexicon*, Cambridge, MA: MIT Press, pp 15–20.

Goode, Luke (2015) 'Anonymous and the Political Ethos of Hacktivism', *Popular Communication*, 13(1): 74–86.

Goodfellow, Ian J., Pouget-Abadie, Jean, Mirza, Mehdi, Xu, Bing, Warde-Farley, David, Ozair, Sherjil et al (2014) 'Generative Adversarial Nets', *Proceedings of the 27th International Conference on Neural Information Processing Systems, Montreal, Canada*, 2: 2672–2680.

Google (nd) *Arts & Culture*, https://artsandculture.google.com/ (Accessed 24 November 2022).

Graver, David (1995) *The Aesthetics of Disturbance: Anti-art in Avant-garde Drama*, Ann Arbor, MI: University of Michigan Press.

Gregg, Melissa (2014) 'Inside the Data Spectacle: Television and New Media', *Television & New Media*, 16(1): 37–51, https://doi.org/10.1177/1527476414547774

Gronlund, Melissa (2017) *Contemporary Art and Digital Culture*, London: Routledge.

Guyau, Jean-Marie (1887) *L'Art au point de vue sociologique, 2nd edn*, Paris: Félix Alcan.

Haggerty, Kevin D., Ericson, Richard V. (2000) 'The Surveillant Assemblage', *British Journal of Sociology*, 51(4): 605–622.

Halton, Eugene (2011) 'Object Biographies', in: Southerton, Dale (ed) *Encyclopedia of Consumer Culture*, New York: CQ Press, pp 1051–1054.

Hallam, Elizabeth, Ingold, Tim (2016) *Making and Growing: Anthropological Studies of Organisms and Artefacts*, New York: Routledge.

Harari, Yuval N (2017) *Homo Deus: A Brief History of Tomorrow*, New York: HarperCollins.

Haraway, Donna J. (1988) 'Situated Knowledges: The Science Question in Feminism and the Privilege of the Partial Perspective', *Feminist Studies*, 14(3): 575–599.

Haraway, Donna J. (1991) *Simians, Cyborgs and Women: The Reinvention of Nature*, New York: Routledge.

Haraway, Donna J. (2003) *The Companion Species Manifesto: Dogs, People, and Significant Otherness*, Chicago, IL: Prickly Paradigm Press.

Haraway, Donna J. (2008) *When Species Meet*, Minneapolis, MN: University of Minnesota Press.

Haraway Donna J. (2015a) 'Birth of the Kennel', A lecture by Donna Haraway, August 2000, *The European Graduate School*, http://www.egs.edu/faculty/donna-haraway/articles/birth-of-the-kennel/ (Accessed 26 May 2015).

Haraway, Donna J. (2015b) 'Anthropocene, Capitalocene, Plantationocene, Chthulucene: Making Kin', *Environmental Humanities*, 6(1): 159–165.

Haraway, Donna J. (2016) *Staying with the Trouble*, Durham, NC: Duke University Press.

Harding, Sandra (2015) *Objectivity and Diversity: Another Logic of Scientific Research*, Chicago, IL: University of Chicago Press.

Harper, Douglas (nd) 'Associate', *Online Etymology Dictionary*, https://www.etymonline.com/word/associate#etymonline_v_17972 (Accessed 24 November 2022).

Harper, Douglas (nd) 'Conclusion', *Online Etymology Dictionary*, https://www.etymonline.com/search?q=conclusion (Accessed 24 November 2022).

Harper, Douglas (nd) 'Conversion', *Online Etymology Dictionary*, https://www.etymonline.com/search?q=conversion (Accessed 24 November 2022).

Harper, Douglas (nd) 'Data', Online Etymology Dictionary, https://www.etymonline.com/search?q=data (Accessed 9 November 2011).

Harper, Douglas (nd) 'Information', Online Etymology Dictionary, https://www.etymonline.com/search?q=information (Accessed 9 November 2011).

Harper, Douglas (nd) 'Matter', Online Etymology Dictionary, https://www.etymonline.com/search?q=matter (Accessed 9 November 2011).

Hayles, Katherine (1999) *How We Became Posthuman*, Chicago, IL: University of Chicago Press.

Hill, Sophie, McCall, Gabrielle (2015) *The Land We Are*, Winnipeg: ARP Books.

Hine, Christine (2008) 'Virtual Ethnography: Modes, Varieties, Affordances', in: Fielding, N., Lee, R.M., Blank (eds) *The Sage Handbook of Online Research Methods*, Los Angeles, CA: Sage, pp 257–270.

Hogue, Simon (2016) 'Performing, Translating, Fashioning: Spectatorship in the Surveillant World', *Surveillance & Society*, 14(2): 168–183.

Hopman, Roos, M'charek, Amade (2020) 'Facing the Unknown Suspect: Forensic DNA Phenotyping and the Oscillation between the Individual and the Collective', *BioSocieties*, 15(3): 438–462.

Hultman, Karin, Taguchi Hillevi L. (2010) 'Challenging Anthropocentric Analysis of Visual Data: A Relational Materialist Methodological Approach to Educational Research', *International Journal of Qualitative Studies in Education*, 23(5): 525–542.

Human Brain Project (nd) https://www.humanbrainproject.eu/en/ (Accessed 27 March 2023).

Hunsiger, Jeremy, Schrock, Andrew (2016) 'The Democratization of Hacking and Making', *New Media & Society*, 18(4): 535–538.

Huysmans, Jef (2016) 'Democratic Curiosity in Times of Surveillance', *European Journal of International Security*, 1(1): 73–93. I2P, https://geti2p.net/en/ (Accessed 11 May 2020).

Ingold, Tim (2011) *Being Alive: Essays on Movement, Knowledge and Description*, London, New York: Routledge.

Ingold, Tim, Hallam, Elizabeth (2016) 'Making and Growing. An Introduction', in: Hallam, Elizabeth, Ingold, Tim (eds) *Making and Growing. Anthropological Studies of Organisms and Artefacts*, New York: Routledge, pp 1–24.

Institut für musterbasierte Prognosetechnik (nd) http://www.ifmpt.de (Accessed 7 April 2022).

Jaton, Florian (2017) 'We Get the Algorithms of Our Ground Truths: Designing Referential Databases in Digital Image Processing', *Social Studies of Science*, 47(6): 811–840.

Jaton, Florian (2021) 'Assessing Biases, Relaxing Moralism: On Ground-truthing Practices in Machine Learning Design and Application', *Big Data & Society*, 8(1): 1–15.

Jeffery, C Ray (1971) 'Crime Prevention Through Environmental Design', *American Behavioral Scientist*, 14(4): 598–598.

Johnson, Shane D., Bernasco, Wim, Bowers, Kate J., Elffers, Henk, Ratcliffe, Jerry, Rengert, George, Townsley, Michael (2007) 'Space–Time Patterns of Risk: A Cross National Assessment of Residential Burglary Victimization', *Journal of Quantitative Criminology*, 23(3): 201–219.

Jones, Brandon (2020) 'Mattering', in: Braidotti, Rosi, Hlavajova, Maria (eds) *Posthuman Glossary*, New York: Bloomsbury Academic, pp 244–247.

Jones Jordan, Tim (2017) 'A Genealogy of Hacking', *Convergence*, 23(5): 528–544, https://doi.org/10.1177/1354856516640710

Jordan, Tim, Taylor, Paul (2004) *Hacktivism and Cyberwars: Rebels with a Cause*, New York: Routledge.

Kaufmann, Mareile (2010) *Ethnic Profiling and Counter-Terrorism – Examples of European Practice and Possible Repercussions*, Berlin: LIT Verlag.

Kaufmann, Mareile (2018) '"Now you see me – now you don't!" – Practices and Purposes of Hacking Online Surveillance', *Mediatization Studies*, 01/2018: 85–101.

Kaufmann, Mareile (2019) 'Who Connects the dots? Agents and Agency in Predictive Policing', in: Hoijtink, Marijn, Leese, Matthias (eds) *Technology and Agency in International Relations*, London: Routledge, pp 141–163.

Kaufmann, Mareile (2020) 'Hacking Surveillance', *First Monday*, 25(5): https://doi.org/10.5210/fm.v25i5.10006 (online only).

Kaufmann, Mareile (2020) 'Vocations, Visions and Vitalities of Data Analysis: An Introduction', *Information, Communication & Society*, 23(14): 1981–1995.

Kaufmann, Mareile (2021) 'This Is A Secret: Learning from Children's Engagement with Surveillance and Secrecy', *Cultural Studies ↔ Critical Methodologies*, 21(5): 424–437.

Kaufmann, Mareile (2022) 'How to Gain Access: Connecting to Hard-to-Reach Participants Online', *How to Guide. SAGE Research Methods: Doing Research Online*, https://dx.doi.org/10.4135/9781529607420 (online only).

Kaufmann, Mareile, Jeandesboz, Julien (2017) 'Politics and "the Digital": From Singularity to specificity', *European Journal of Social Theory*, 20(3): 309–328.

Kaufmann, Mareile, Egbert, Simon, Matthias Leese (2019) 'Predictive Policing and the Politics of Patterns', *British Journal of Criminology*, 59(3): 674–692.

Kaufmann, Mareile, Tzanetakis, Meropi (2020) 'Doing Internet Research with Hard-to-reach Communities: Methodological Reflections About Gaining Meaningful Access', *Qualitative Research*, 20(6): 927–944.

Kaufmann, Mareile, Bonde-Thylstrup, Nanna, Burgess, J. Peter and Rudinow-Sætnan, Ann (2020) 'Data Criticality', *STS Encounters*, 11(1): 227–254.

Kaufmann, Mareile, Leese, Matthias (2021) 'Information in-formation: Algorithmic Policing and the Life of Data', in: Aleš Završnik and Vasja Badalič (eds) *Automating Crime Prevention, Surveillance, and Military*, Cham: Springer, pp 69–83.

Kirschenbaum, Matthew (2007) *Mechanisms: New Media and Forensic Imagination*, Cambridge, MA: MIT Press.

Kitchin, Rob (2016) 'Thinking Critically About and Researching Algorithms', *Information, Communication & Society*, 20(1): 14–29.

Kitchin, Rob (2021) *Data Lives. How Data Are Made and Shape Our World*, Bristol: Bristol University Press.

Kowal, Emma (2013) 'Orphan DNA: Indigenous Samples, Ethical Biovalue and Postcolonial Science', *Social Studies of Science*, 43(4): 577–597.

Kranzberg, Melvin (1986) 'Technology and History: Kranzberg's Laws', *Technology and Culture*, 27(3): 544–560.

Krasmann, Susanne (2019) 'Secrecy and the Force of Truth: Countering Post-truth Regimes', *Cultural Studies*, 33(4): 690–710.

Kubitschko, Sebastian (2015) 'The Role of Hackers in Countering Surveillance and Promoting Democracy', *Media and Communication*, 3(2): 77–87.

Küchler, Susanne (2008) 'Technological Materiality: Beyond the Dualist Paradigm', *Theory, Culture and Society*, 25(1): 101–120.

Landauer, Rolf (1961) 'Irreversibility and Heat Generation in the Computing Process', *IBM Journal of Research and Development*, 5(3): 183–191.

Landauer, Rolf (1999) 'Information is a Physical Entity', *Physica A*, 263(1–4): 63–67.

Lash, Scott (2006) 'Life (Vitalism)', *Theory, Culture & Society*, 23(2–3): 323–349.

Lash, Scott (2007) 'Power of Hegemony: Cultural Studies in Mutation', *Theory, Culture & Society*, 24(3): 55–78.

Latour, Bruno (1987) *Science in Action: How to Follow Scientists and Engineers through Society*, Milton Keynes: Open University Press.

Latour, Bruno (1990) 'Drawing Things Together', in: Lynch, Michael, Woolgar, Steeve (eds) *Representation in Scientific Practice*, Cambridge, MA: MIT Press, pp 19–68.

Latour, Bruno (2005) *Reassembling the Social: An Introduction to Actor-Network-Theory*, Oxford: Clarendon.

Law, John, Singleton, Vicky (2005) 'Object Lessons', *Organization*, 12(3): 331–355.

Lee, Raymond M., Fielding, Nigel G., Blank, Grant (2008) 'The Internet as a Research Medium: An Editorial Introduction to the Sage Handbook of Online Research Methods', in: Fielding, Nigel G., Lee, Raymond M., Blank, Grant (eds) *The Sage Handbook of Online Research Methods*, Los Angeles, CA: Sage, pp 3–20.

Leese, Matthias (2014) 'The New Profiling: Algorithms, Black Boxes, and the Failure of Anti-discriminatory Safeguards in the European Union', *Security Dialogue*, 45(5): 494–511.

Leonelli, Sabina (2016) *Data-Centric Biology: A Philosophical Study*, Chicago, IL: University of Chicago Press.

Lewandowski, Judith L. (2003) 'Stepping Off the Sidewalk: An Examination of the Data Collection Techniques of Websites Visited by Children', *Journal of School Violence*, 2(1): 19–63.

Lupton, Deborah (2015) 'Lively Data, Social Fitness and Biovalue: The Intersections of Health Self-Tracking and Social Media', *SSRN Electronic Journal*, http://dx.doi.org/10.2139/ssrn.2666324 (online only).

Lupton, Deborah (2016a) *The Quantified Self*, Cambridge: Polity.

Lupton, Deborah (2016b) 'Digital Companion Species and Eating Data: Implications for Theorising Digital Data-human Assemblages', *Big Data and Society*, 3(1): https://doi.org/10.1177/2053951715619947 (online only).

Lupton, Deborah (2018) 'How Do Data Come to Matter? Living and Becoming with Personal Data', *Big Data & Society*, 5(2): https://doi.org/10.1177/2053951718786314 (online only).

Lupton, Deborah (2020) *Data Selves*, Cambridge: Polity.

MacCormack, Patricia (2004) 'Parabolic Philosophies: Analogue and Affect', *Theory, Culture & Society*, 21(6): 179–187.

Maggiolino, Mariateresa (2019) 'EU Trade Secrets Law and Algorithmic Transparency', *Bocconi Legal Studies Research Paper No. 3363178*, https://ssrn.com/abstract=3363178 or http://dx.doi.org/10.2139/ssrn.3363178 (online only).

Magnet, Shoshana A., (2011) *When Biometrics Fail: Gender, Race, and the Technology of Identity*, Durham, NC: Duke University Press.

Manjoo, Farhad (2017) 'Tech's Frightful Five: They've Got Us', *New York Times*, https://www.nytimes.com/2017/05/10/technology/techs-frightful-five-theyve-got-us.html (Accessed 5 June 2018).

Mann, Monique, Devitt, S. Kate, Daly, Angela (2018) 'What Is (in) Good Data? Good Data', *Amsterdam: Institute of Network Cultures Theory on Demand Series*. https://ssrn.com/abstract=3297103 (online only).

Mannov, Adrienne, Oberborbeck Andersen, Astrid, Hojer Bruun, Maja (2020) 'Cryptic Commonalities. Working Athwart Cryptography, Mathematics and Anthropology', *STS Encounters*, 11(1): 27–58.

Manovich, Lev (2001) *The Language of New Media*, Cambridge, MA: MIT Press.

Marx, Gary, Steeves, Valerie (2010) 'From the Beginning: Children as Subjects and Agents of Surveillance', *Surveillance & Society*, 7(3/4): 192–230.

Massumi, Brian (2002) *Parables for the Virtual: Movement, Affect, Sensation*, Durham: Duke University Press.

Maxigas (2017) 'Hackers Against Technology: Critique and Recuperation in Technological Cycles', *Social Studies of Science*, 47(6): 841–860.

Mbembe, Achille (2003) 'Necropolitics. Translated by Libby Meintjes', *Public Culture*, 15(1): 11–40.

McGoey, Linsey (2012) 'The Logic of Strategic Ignorance', *The British Journal of Sociology*, 63(3): 533–576.

Mejias, Ulises Ali (2013) *Off the Network*, Minneapolis, MN: University of Minnesota Press.

Merleau-Ponty, Maurice (1964) 'Eye and Mind', trans. Carleton Dallery, in: Edie, James M. (ed) *The Primacy of Perception, and Other Essays on Phenomenological Psychology, the Philosophy of Art, History and Politics*, Evanston, IL: Northwestern University Press, pp 159–190.

Merleau-Ponty, Maurice (2003) *Nature: Course Notes from the Collège de France. Compiled and with notes by Dominique Séglard*, trans. Robert Vallier, Evanston, IL: Northwestern University Press.

Microsoft (nd) *FATE: Fairness, Accountability, Transparency, and Ethics in AI*, https://www.microsoft.com/en-us/research/theme/fate/ (Accessed 7 April 2021).

Mol, Annemarie (2008) 'I Eat an Apple. On Theorizing Subjectivities', *Subjectivity*, 22: 28–37.

Morgan, Colleen Leah (2012) *Emancipatory Digital Archaeology*. PhD Dissertation, University of California, http://www.academia.edu/2997 156/Emancipatory_Digital_Archaeology (Accessed 27 March 2023).

Naji, Myriem, Douny, Laurence (2009) 'Editorial', *Journal of Material Culture*, 14(4): 411–32.

Monahan, Torin (2018) 'Ways of Being Seen: Surveillance Art and the Interpellation of Viewing Subjects', *Cultural Studies*, 32(4): 560–581.

Monea, Alexander, Edwards, Paul N (2016) 'An Archive for the Future: Paul N. Edwards on Technology, Historiography, Self, and World', *International Journal of Communication*, 10: Feature, 3174–3185.

Montfort, Nick, Baudoin, Patsy, Bell, John, Bogost, Ian (2012) *10 PRINT CHR$(205.5+RND(1): GOTO 10*, Cambridge, MA: MIT Press.

Moore, Taylor R (2017) *Trade Secrets and Algorithms as Barriers to Social Justice*, Center for Democracy & Technology, https://cdt.org/wp-content/uplo ads/2017/08/2017-07-31-Trade-Secret-Algorithms-as-Barriers-to-Soc ial-Justice.pdf (Accessed 24 November 2022).

Morozov, Evegny (2017) 'So you want to switch off digitally? I'm afraid that will cost you …', *The Guardian*, https://www.theguardian.com/commentisf ree/2017/feb/19/right-to-disconnect-digital-gig-economy-evgeny-moro zov (Accessed 15 April 2019).

New Scientist (2018) 'Taming the Big Tech Beasts', *New Scientist*, 237(3164): 5.

Nissenbaum, Helen (2004) 'Hackers and the Ontology of Cyberspace', *New Media & Society*, 6(2): 195–217.

Palantir (nd) *www.palantir.com* (Accessed 7 April 2021).

Palmer, Charles C. (2001) 'Ethical hacking', *IBM Systems Journal*, 40(3): 769–780.

Pariser, Eli (2011) *The Filter Bubble: What the Internet is Hiding from You*, New York: Penguin Press.

Paul, George (2009) *Foundations of Digital Evidence*, Washington, DC: American Bar Association.

Perry, Walter L., McInnis, Brian, Price, Carter C., Smith, Susan C., Hollywood, John S. (2013) *Predictive Policing: The Role of Crime Forecasting in Law Enforcement Operations*, Santa Monica, CA: RAND Corporation.

Philipps, Dave (2021) 'Modern Crime-Solving Methods vs. the Mystery of World War II Deaths', *The New York Times*, https://www.nytimes.com/2021/04/06/us/soldiers-death-dna-identification.html?referringSource=articleShare (Accessed 7 April 2021).

Porter, Gina, Kate Hampshire, Alister Munthali and Elsbeth Robson (2011) 'Mobility, Surveillance and Control of Children and Young People in the Everyday: Perspectives from sub-Saharan Africa', *Surveillance & Society*, 9(1/2): 114–131.

Powell, Alison (2016) 'Hacking in the Public Interest: Authority, Legitimacy, Means, and Ends', *New Media & Society*, 18(4): 600–616.

Preciado, Beatriz (2014) *Manifesto Contra-sexual*, Helsinki: n-1 Publications.

Predpol (nd) https://www.predpol.com (Accessed 7 April 2021).

Publicdelivery.org (2021) *Nick Cave's Soundsuit sculptures – Everything You Need to Know*, https://publicdelivery.org/nick-cave-soundsuits/ (Accessed 4 November 2021).

Rahm, Erhard, Hai Do, Hong (2000) 'Data Cleaning: Problems and Current Approaches', *IEEE Data Engineering Bulletin*, 23(4): 3–13.

Raley, Rita (2013) 'Dataveillance and Counterveilance', in: Gitelman, Lisa (ed) *'Raw Data' is an Oxymoron*, Cambridge, MA: MIT Press, pp 121–145.

Ramsay, Stephen, Rockwell, Geoffrey (2012) 'Developing Things: Notes toward an Epistemology of Building in the Digital Humanities', in: Gold, Matthew K. (ed) *Debates in the Digital Humanities*, Minneapolis, MN: University of Minnesota Press, pp 75–84.

Ratto, Matt (2011) 'Critical Making: Conceptual and Material Studies in Technology and Social Life', *The Information Society: An International Journal*, 27(4): 252–260.

Raynes-Goldie, Kate, Matthew Allen (2014) 'Gaming Privacy: A Canadian Case Study of a Co-Created Privacy Literacy Game for Children', *Surveillance & Society*, 12(3): 414–426.

Resch, Gabby, Southwick, Dan, Record, Isaac, Ratto, Matt (2017) 'Thinking as Handwork: Critical Making with Humanistic Concerns', in: Sayers, Jentery (ed) *Making Things and Drawing Boundaries. Experiments in the Digital Humanities*, Minneapolis, MN: University of Minnesota Press, pp 149–161.

Ribes, David (2019) 'Materiality Methodology, and Some Tricks of the Trade in the Study of Data and Specimens', in: Vertesi, Janet, Ribes, David (eds) *digitalSTS: A Field Guide for Science and Technology Studies*, Princeton, NJ: Princeton University Press, pp 17–41.

Richterich, Annika, Wenz, Karin (2017) 'Introduction: Making and Hacking', *Digital Culture and Society*, 3(1): 5–21.

Ritzer, George (2014) Prosumption: Evolution, revolution, or eternal return of the same? *Journal of Consumer Culture*, 14(1): 3–24. https://doi.org/10.1177/1469540513509641

Roberts, Alasdair (2006) *Blacked Out: Government Secrecy in the Information Age*, Cambridge: Cambridge University Press.

Rooney, Tonya (2010) 'Trusting Children: How Do Surveillance Technologies Alter a Child's Experience of Trust, Risk and Responsibility?', *Surveillance & Society*, 7(3/4): 344–355.

Rosenheim, Shawn (1997) *The Cryptographic Imagination: Secret Writing from Edgar Poe to the Internet*, Baltimore, MD: Johns Hopkins University Press.

Rubinstein, Ira S (2013) 'Big Data: The End of Privacy or a New Beginning?' *International Data Privacy Law*, 3(2): 74–87.

Ruppert, Evelyne, Law, John, Savage, Mike (2013) 'Reassembling Social Science Methods: The Challenge of Digital Devices', *Theory, Culture and Society*, 30(4): 22–46.

Sandvik, Kristin Bergtora (2020) 'Wearables for Something Good: Aid, Dataveillance and the Production of Children's Digital Bodies', *Information, Communication & Society*, 23(14): 2014–2029.

Savage, Mike (2013) 'The "Social Life of Methods": A Critical Introduction', *Theory, Culture and Society*, 30(4): 3–21.

Saugmann, Rune, Möller, Frank, Bellmer, Rasmus (2020) 'Seeing like a Surveillance Agency? Sensor Realism as Aesthetic Critique of Visual Data Governance', *Information, Communication & Society*, 23(14): 1996–2013.

Schneider, Tim (2020) 'How a Mysterious Figure Known Only as 'American Artist' Is Exposing Hidden Histories of Social Control in Surveillance and Policing', *Artnet News*, https://news.artnet.com/art-world/american-artist-interview-policing-1888235 (Accessed 27 May 2021).

Schwarz, Elke (2016) 'Prescription Drones: On the Techno-biopolitical Regimes of Contemporary "Ethical Killing"', *Security Dialogue*, 47(1): 59–75.

Seyfert, Robert (2012) 'Beyond Personal Feelings and Collective Emotions: Toward a Theory of Social Affect', *Theory, Culture & Society*, 29(6): 27–46.

Sicart, Miguel (2014) *Play Matters*, Cambridge, MA: MIT Press.

Sheehey, Bonnie (2019) 'Algorithmic Paranoia: The Temporal Governmentality of Predictive Policing', *Ethics and Information Technology*, 21(1): 49–58.

Simmel, Georg (1906) 'The Sociology of Secrecy and Secret Societies', *American Journal of Sociology*, 11(4): 441–498.

Skinner, David, Wienroth, Matthias (2019) 'Was This an Ending? The Destruction of Samples and Deletion of Records from the UK Police National DNA Database', *The British Journal for the History of Science Themes*, 4: 99–121.

Singh, Rianka (2020) 'Resistance in a Minor Key: Care, Survival and Convening on the Margins', *First Monday*, 25(5), https://firstmonday.org/ojs/index.php/fm/article/view/10631 (online only).

Smart, Carol (2011) 'Families, Secrets and Memories', *Sociology*, 45(4): 539–553.

Smith, P., Buechler, G. (1975) 'A Branching Algorithm for Discriminating and Tracking Multiple Objects', *IEEE Transactions on Automatic Control*, 20(1): 101–104.

Söderberg, Johan (2017) 'Inquiring Hacking as Politics: A New Departure in Hacker Studies?', *Science, Technology, & Human Values*, 42(5): 969–980.

Söderberg, Johan, Delfanti, Alessandro (2015) 'Hacking Hacked! The Life Cycles of Digital Innovation', *Science, Technology, & Human Values*, 40(5): 793–798.

Sparrman, Anna, Lindgren, Anne-Li (2010) 'Visual Documentation as a Normalizing Practice: A New Discourse of Visibility in Preschool', *Surveillance & Society*, 7(3/4): 248–261.

Squire, Vicky (2013). 'Attuning to Mess', in: Salter, Mark, Mutlu, Can (eds) *Research Methods in Critical Security Studies. An Introduction*, Routledge: London, 37–41.

Srikant, Ramakrishnan, Agrawal, Rakesh (1995) *Mining Generalized Association Rules. Research Report*, New York: IBM Research Division.

SSL Nagbot (2016) 'Feminist Hacking/Making: Exploring New Gender Horizons of Possibility', *Journal of Peer Production*, 8, at http://peerproduction.net/issues/issue-8-feminism-and-unhacking-2/feminist-hackingmaking-exploring-new-gender-horizons-of-possibility/ (online only, accessed 16 April 2019).

Stagoff-Belfort, Aaron (2020) 'The Lessons of Chicago's Disastrous "Crime Prediction" Experiment', *Filter*, https://filtermag.org/chicago-crime-prediction/ (Accessed 18 March 2021).

Star, Susan L., Griesemer, James R. (1989) 'Institutional Ecology, "Translations" and Boundary Objects: Amateurs and Professionals in Berkeley's Museum of Vertebrate Zoology, 1907–39', *Social Study of Science*, 19(3): 387–420.

Star, Susan L., Ruhleder, Karen (1996) 'Steps Toward an Ecology of Infrastructure: Design and Access for Large Information Spaces', *Information Systems Research*, 7(1): 111–134.

Steeves, Valerie, Jones, Owain (2010) 'Editorial: Surveillance and Children', *Surveillance & Society*, 7(3/4): 187–191.

Steiner, Christopher (2012) *Automate This: How Algorithms Took Over Our Markets, Our Jobs. And the World*, New York: Portfolio.

Steinmetz, Kevin, Gerber, Jurg (2015) '"It doesn't have to be this way": Hacker Perspectives on Privacy', *Social Justice*, 41(3): 29–51.

Steyerl, Hito (2013) 'Too Much World: Is the Internet Dead?', *e-flux #49*, https://www.e-flux.com/journal/49/60004/too-much-world-is-the-internet-dead/ (online only, accessed 23 November 2022).

Steyerl, Hito (2014) 'Zach Blas', *ArtReview*, https://artreview.com/features/2014_futuregreats_zach_blas/ (Accessed 23 November 2022).

Suchman, Lucy (2000) 'Practice-Based Design of Information Systems: Notes from the Hyperdeveloped World', *The Information Society*, 18(2): 139–144.

Suchman, Lucy (2002) 'Located Accountabilities in Technology Production', *Scandinavian Journal of Information Systems*, 14(2): 91–105.

Syvertsen, Trine (2020) *Digital Detox: The Politics of Disconnecting*, Bingley: Emerald Group Publishing.

Szalai, Georg (2015) 'Google Chairman Eric Schmidt: "The Internet Will Disappear"', *The Hollywood Reporter*, https://www.hollywoodreporter.com/business/digital/google-chairman-eric-schmidt-internet-765989/ (Accessed 28 May 2021).

TAILS (nd) https://tails.boum.org (Accessed 11 May 2020).

The Hammond Times (1957) 'Work With New Electronic "Brains" Opens Field For Army Math Experts', *The Hammond Times*, 10 November 1957, p 65, https://www.newspapers.com/clip/50687334/the-times/ (Accessed 24 November 2022).

The New York Times (2017) 'From Chelsea Manning's DNA Springs an Art Show. Written by Sophie Haigney', *The New York Times*, https://www.nytimes.com/2017/06/30/arts/design/chelsea-manning-dna-art-show-lower-manhattan.html (Accessed 3 June 2021).

Thompson, Charis (2005) *Good Science: The Ethical Choreography of Stem Cell Research*, Cambridge, MA: MIT Press.

Thompson Klein, Julie (2017) 'The Boundary Work of Making in Digital Humanities', in: Sayers, Jentery (ed) *Making Things and Drawing Boundaries. Experiments in the Digital Humanities*, Minneapolis, MN: University of Minnesota Press, pp 21–31.

Thrift, Nigel (2005) *Knowing Capitalism*, London: Sage.

Thylstrup, Nanna B. (2019) 'Data Out of Place: Toxic Traces and the Politics of Recycling', *Big Data & Society*, 6(2), https://doi.org/10.1177%2F2053951719875479 (online only).

Thylstrup, Nanna B., Agostinho, Daniela, Ring, Annie, D'Ignazio, Catherine, Veel, Kristin (2021) *Uncertain Archives: Critical Keywords for Big Data*, Cambridge, MA: MIT Press.

TOR (nd) https://www.torproject.org (Accessed 11 May 2020).

Townsley, Michael, Homel, Ross, Chaseling, Janet (2003) 'Infectious Burglaries: A Test of the Near Repeat Hypothesis', *British Journal of Criminology*, 43(3): 615–633.

Tucek, Aaron (2019) 'Constraining Big Brother: The Legal Deficiencies Surrounding Chicago's Use of the Strategic Subject List', *University of Chicago Legal Forum*, 2018(1) Article 18: 427.

US Joint Inquiry (2003) *Report of the Joint Inquiry unto the terrorist attacks if September 2011, 2001*, Washington, DC: House Permanent Select Committee on Intelligence (HPSCI) and the Senate Select Committee on Intelligence (SSCI).

Van Brakel, Rosamunde, De Hert, Paul (2011) 'Policing, Surveillance and Law in a Pre-crime Society: Understanding the Consequences of Technology Based Strategies', *Journal of Police Studies*, 20(3): 163–192.

Van den Eynden, Veerle (2014) 'The Research Data Life Cycle', in: Corti, Louise, Van den Eynden, Veerle, Bishop, Libby, Woollard, Matthew (eds) *Managing and Sharing Research Data*, Los Angeles, CA: Sage, pp 17–23.

Verhoeven, Deb (2016) 'Opening Keynote: Identifying the Point of it All: Towards a Model of "Digital Infrapuncture"', Presentation, University of Oxford, https://debverhoeven.com/opening-keynote-identifying-the-point-of-it-all-towards-a-model-of-digital-infrapuncture/ (Accessed 24 June 2021).

Vermeir, Koen, Dániel Margócsy (2012) 'States of Secrecy: An Introduction', *The British Journal for the History of Science*, 45(2): 153–164.

Vertesi, Janet (2015) *Seeing Like a Rover: How Robots, Teams, and Images Craft Knowledge of Mars*, Chicago, IL: University of Chicago Press.

Vertesi, Janet (2019) 'Introduction: Infrastructure', in: Vertesi, Janet, Ribes, David (eds) *digitalSTS: A Field Guide for Science and Technology Studies*, Princeton, NJ: Princeton University Press, pp 263–265.

Walker–Rettberg, Jill (2018) '3.14 live med foredrag av Jill Walker Rettberg', *Universitetet i Bergen*, https://www.uib.no/machinevision/120304/314-live-med-foredrag-av-jill-walker-rettberg (Accessed 3 June 2021).

Walsh, James (2010) 'From Border Control to Border Care: The Political and Ethical Potential of Surveillance', *Surveillance & Society*, 8(2): 113–130.

Warren, Carol, Laslett, Barbara (1977) 'Privacy and Secrecy: A Conceptual Comparison', *Journal of Social Issues*, 33(3): 43–51.

Westcott, Nicholas (2009) 'Digital Diplomacy: The Impact of the Internet on International Relations', *OII Working Paper No. 16*, https://papers.ssrn.com/sol3/papers.cfm?abstract_id=1326476 (online only).

Wintle, Claire (2016) 'Decolonizing the Smithsonian: Museums as Microcosms of Political Encounter', *The American Historical Review*, 121(5): 1492–1520.

Yoo, Christopher S., Blanchette, Jean-Francois (2015) *Regulating the Cloud: Policy for Computing Infrastructure*, Cambridge, MA: MIT Press.

Zarzycki, Andrzej (2018) 'Mods, Hacks, Makers: Crowdsourced Culture and Environment', in: Lee, Ji-Hyun (ed) *Computational Studies on Cultural Variation and Heredity*, KAIST Research Series, Singapore: Springer, pp 73–82.

Zer-Aviv, Mushon (2021) 'Obfuscation', in: Thylstrup, Nanna Bonde, Agostinho, Daniela, Ring, Annie, D'Ignacio, Catheirne, Veel, Kristin (eds) *Uncertain Archives: Critical Keywords for Big Data*, Cambridge, MA: MIT Press, 359–368.

Zuboff, Shoshana (2019) *The Age of Surveillance Capitalism: The Fight for a Human Future at the New Frontier of Power*, London: Profile Books.

Index

References to figures appear in *italic* type.